THE DEVELOPMENT OF THE EGO: IMPLICATIONS FOR PERSONALITY THEORY, PSYCHOPATHOLOGY, AND THE PSYCHOTHERAPEUTIC PROCESS

THE DEVELOPMENT OF THE EGO:
IMPLICATIONS FOR PERSONALITY THEORY, PSYCHOPATHOLOGY, AND THE PSYCHOTHERAPEUTIC PROCESS

Stanley I. Greenspan, M.D.

INTERNATIONAL UNIVERSITIES PRESS, INC.
Madison   Connecticut

Library of Congress Cataloging-in-Publication Data

Greenspan, Stanley I.
  The development of the ego : implications for personality theory, psychopathology, and the psychotherapeutic process / Stanley I. Greenspan.
      p.   cm.
  Includes bibliographies and indexes.
  ISBN 0-8236-1230-9
  1. Ego (Psychology)   2. Psychology, Pathological.
  3. Developmental psychology.   I. Title.
  [DNLM: 1. Ego.   2. Models, Psychological.   3. Personality
Development.   WM 460.5.E3 G815d]
  RC455.4.E35G74   1989
  154.2'2—dc20
  DNLM/DLC
  for Library of Congress   89-2237
                                                              CIP

Manufactured in the United States of America

CONTENTS

Introduction

Central to all areas of clinical practice is an understanding of the development of the basic ego functions. Yet, general personality and clinical theory have not yet formulated a systematic integrated model of the stages in early ego development. This book will attempt to fill this gap by describing the developmental stages of the ego, beginning in early infancy, from the perspectives of tasks and challenges, internal self and object representations, and ego mechanisms and functions. The model will be based on the author's clinical experience and observational studies with both healthy and disturbed infants and children, as well as insights from clinical work with adults.

In the history of psychoanalysis, dynamic psychiatry, and clinical practice, the ego as a construct is confused with terms such as object relations, self, identity, personality, character, and coping. The construct, of the ego, designates the mental functions that perceive, organize, elaborate, differentiate, integrate, and transform experience. Experience, in this context, includes drive-affect derivatives, various levels of internal self and object organizations, and interpersonal relationships, as well as interactions with the relatively impersonal object world.

As the aspect of the mind that abstracts and categorizes experience, the ego through its functions organizes the various qualities, attributed to mental phenomena such as self and object representations, a sense of self, and identity. Understanding how the ego develops is central to comprehending both healthy (adaptive organization of experience) and psychopathological (deficits, constrictions, or conflictually derived encapsulations in the organization of experience) functioning. The processes of diagnosis, prevention, and treatment also depend on understanding the variations, change, and growth in ego functioning.

A lack of clarity regarding early ego development has led to lively debates. In the area of clinical practice, for example, the self psychologists, who build on the work of Heinz Kohut (1971) and emphasize empathy, and the classicists, who build on the work of Freud and stress conflict, argue the critical factors in early ego development. On an even broader scope, differences between practitioners in Europe and in the United States on early relationship patterns (and derivative practices and theories) divide how much of the world views clinical phenomena. Many schools of short-term psychotherapy, couples therapy, and family therapy evolve from different models of early ego development. Those models of family therapy, for example, that derive from theoretical assumptions on the central role of projection and projective identification are in stark contrast with those that derive from either altering the real family patterns and/or altering the states of mind and perceptions held by family members.

Not only clinical practice but developmental studies have led to debates on early ego development. Freud's early notions of drives as the basis of ego structure have been replaced by emphasis on the direct formation of the ego and object relationships. Nevertheless, debates continue between these different perspectives.

Recent empirical research with normal babies has enlivened this debate. On the one hand there are the traditional views suggested by Mahler, Pine, and Bergman (1975) of an early autistic and symbiotic phase in the development of the ego and by Bowlby (1952) and Spitz (1965) of infants' responses to stress. Challenging this are some empirical researchers (e.g., Stern [1985, 1988]) who characterize the early stages of infancy as being dominated by differentiated self-object representational systems.

Both the traditional and empirically derived views have important assets and limitations.

The traditional views, from observations of infants under different circumstances of emotional stress, characterize selected aspects of in depth psychological experience. Understandably, however these views do not incorporate findings regarding individual differences in sensory-affective and cognitive reactivity and processing from recent observational and experiential studies. Some of the empirically derived views of how early experience is organized usefully highlight the different ways the infant comprehends his world. But they fail to distinguish in-depth emotional experience from other types of experiences. They focus on impersonal cognition or aspects of affect under structured experimental conditions. The infant's ability to make cognitive discriminations are mistakenly assumed to characterize the infant's way of organizing in-depth psychological experience. The clinical challenges that would reveal the ego's operations under stress (the ego's true contour) are not taken into account.

With different clinical and developmental views stemming from a lack of understanding of early ego development, it is essential to formulate a systematic integrated perspective on the stages in the growth of the ego. The model presented in this work will postulate six stages in the development of the ego, based on both in-depth clinical and "normative" observations and studies of infants and young children and their families. These stages will be examined from the point of view of the development of the infant's underlying physical capacities (e.g., sensory-affect reactivity and processing, motor tone, and motor planning); sequence of early relationship patterns; and progressive levels in the child's ability to organize experience. It

will be seen how, from the infant's capacity to organize experience, areas of experience become organized, symbolized, and
differentiated in terms of drive-affect dispositions, defenses,
internal self- and object-representational patterns, and emerging intrapsychic structures. This work will present a comprehensive theory which looks simultaneously at the biological
(physical) and the interactive (relationship) underpinnings of
the ego, as well as the stages that the ego uses to organize itself,
namely, its own experience.

This model will also postulate the developmental pathways
by which biology and experience express themselves in various
psychopathologies. It will provide a model both for future
research and further theory building. It will, for example,
suggest a needed reexamination of a number of the core
concepts in dynamic thinking, including identification, repression defense, and drives. Most importantly, however, this work
will discuss applications to clinical practice; it will consider the
classic psychoanalytic situation with both children and adults; it
will also consider short-term psychotherapy and therapy involving couples, families, and groups. Futhermore, it will
evolve a model of preventive therapeutic work with both
children and adults which takes advantage of the ego's own
tendencies toward growth, conflict resolution, and new levels of
integration.

Chapter 1

The Stages of Ego Development

BACKGROUND

In an attempt to understand early development, my colleagues and I undertook a clinical descriptive intervention study of multirisk infants and families as well as normal infants and families (Greenspan, 1981; Greenspan, Wieder, Lieberman, Nover, Lourie, and Robinson, 1987). The study of each family began prenatally with the anticipated birth of a new infant. Because there were already severe emotional disturbances in the older children in the family, we expected there would be a high likelihood of a range of psychopathologies in the newborn infants. Infants and families with expected adaptive patterns were also observed for comparison. In order to understand the patterns that we expected to emerge, a broad theoretical perspective was formulated that would accommodate both the disturbed and adaptive, cognitive, and depth

The first part of this chapter (covering the 0–18 months was originally published in the *Journal of the American Psychoanalytic Association*, 1988, (Supplement): 3–55.

The different sections such as Homeostasis elaborates our earlier description of sensory and thematic-affective functioning (Greenspan and Porges, 1984).

1

psychological affective domains (i.e., a "developmental structuralist" model based on an integration of psychoanalytic and
Piagetian developmental psychology [Greenspan, 1979, 1981]).
This chapter will present an overview of the developmental
structuralist model, the clinical patterns and insights that
emerged, from this study and related in-depth work with
slightly older children and formulate a model of the early
stages in the development of the ego.

The clinical interest in early ego development and psychopathology in infancy and early childhood is based on an
impressive foundation. Perhaps most widely known are Spitz's
report (1946) on anaclitic depressions in institutionally reared
infants, and Bowlby's monograph, *Maternal Care and Mental
Health* (1952), describing the now well-known "syndromes" of
disturbed functioning in infancy. Child psychoanalysts' interest
in disturbances in infants, as indicated by the work of Bernfeld
(1929), Winnicott (1931), A. Freud and Burlingham, (1945,
1965), and Anna Freud (1965), as well as the work of Erik
Erikson (1959), amplified the complexity or multidimensional
nature of early problems. Important for current approaches
was the work relating individual differences in infants (constitutional and maturational patterns) to tendencies for psychopathology highlighted by the reports of Sybille Escalona and
Lois Murphy and their colleagues (Escalona, 1968; Murphy,
1974) and Cravioto and DeLicardie (1973).

Several existing developmental frameworks have provided
enormous understanding of individual lines of development in
infancy and early childhood; for example, Sigmund Freud
(1905), Erikson (1959), Piaget (1962), Spitz and Cobliner
(1965), Anna Freud, (1965), Kohut (1971), Kernberg (1975),
and Mahler, Pine, and Bergman (1975). In addition, there has
been a great deal of empirical research generating useful
developmental constructs; for example, Sander (1962), Emde,
Gaensbauer, and Harmon (1976), and Sroufe (1979). These
foundations, together with the rapidly growing body of clinical
experience with infants and their families (Fraiberg, 1979;
Provence, 1983; Provence and Naylon, 1983), provided direc-

tion for a much-needed integrated approach encompassing the multiple lines of development in the context of adaptive and disordered functioning.

There was the need for a truly integrated developmental theory reconciling our knowledge of development based on "emotional experience." This includes the presumed internalization and differentiation of experience based on human relationships, cognition, and emerging empirical research on neurophysiological, behavioral, and social development of infants and young children.

In order to meet this challenge, we developed an approach that focuses on the organizational level of personality along multiple dimensions and on mediating processes or "structures."

There are two assumptions that relate to this approach. One is that the capacity to organize experience is present very early in life and progresses to higher levels as the individual matures. The phase-specific higher levels in this context imply an ability to organize in stable patterns an ever-widening and complex range of experience. For example, it is now well documented that the infant is capable at birth or shortly thereafter, of organizing experience in an adaptive fashion. He or she can respond to pleasure and displeasure (Lipsitt, 1966); change behavior as a function of its consequences (Gewirtz, 1965, 1969); and form intimate bonds and make visual discriminations (Klaus and Kennell, 1976; Meltzoff and Moore, 1977). Cycles and rhythms, such as sleep–wake and alertness states can be organized (Sander, 1962), the infant evidences a variety of affects or affect proclivities (Tomkins, 1963; Ekman, 1972; Izard, 1978), and demonstrates organized social responses in conjunction with increasing neurophysiologic organization (Emde et al., 1976). It is interesting to note that this empirically documented view of the infant is, in a general sense, consistent with Freud's early hypotheses (1900, 1905, 1911) and Hartmann's postulation (1939) of an early undifferentiated organizational matrix. That the organization of experience broadens during the early months of life to reflect increases in the capacity to experience and tolerate a range of stimuli, including responding in social interactions in stable and personal configurations, is also consistent with recent empirical data (Sander, 1962; Escalona, 1968; Brazelton, Koslowski and Main, 1974; Sroufe, Waters, and Matas, 1974; Stern, 1974a,b; Emde et al., 1976; Murphy and Moriarty, 1976). There are a number of indications that increasingly complex patterns continue to emerge as the infant develops. Between seven and twelve months complex emotional responses such as surprise (Charlesworth, 1969) and affiliation, wariness, and fear (Bowlby, 1969; Ainsworth, Bell, and Stayton, 1974; Sroufe and Waters, 1977), have been observed. Exploration and "refueling" patterns (Mahler et al., 1975), and behavior suggesting functional understanding of objects (Werner and Kaplan, 1963) have been observed in the middle to latter part of the second year of life, along with the eventual emergence of symbolic capacities (Bell, 1970; Piaget, 1962; Gouin-Decarie, 1965).

The interplay between age-appropriate experience and maturation of the central nervous system (CNS) ultimately determines the characteristics of this organizational capacity at each phase. The active and experiencing child uses his maturational capacities to engage the world in every-changing and more complex ways.

The organizational level of experience may be delineated along a number of parameters, including age or phase appropriateness, range and depth (i.e., animate and inanimate, full range of affects and themes), stability (i.e., response to stress), and personal uniqueness.

In addition to a characteristic organizational level, a second assumption is that for each phase of development there are also certain characteristic types of experience (e.g., interests or wishes, fears, and curiosities) that play themselves out, so to speak, within this organizational structure. Here one looks at the specific drive–affect derivatives, including emotional and behavioral patterns, or later, thoughts, concerns, inclinations, wishes, fears, and so forth. The type of experience is, in a sense, the drama the youngster is experiencing, whereas the organizational level might be viewed metaphorically as the stage upon which this drama is being played out. To carry this metaphor a step further, it is possible to imagine some stages that are large and stable and can therefore support a complex and intense drama. In comparison, other stages may be narrow or small, able only to contain a very restricted drama. Still other stages may have cracks in them and may crumble easily under the pressure of an intense, rich, and varied drama.

According to the developmental–structuralist approach, at each phase of development there are certain characteristics that define the experiential organizational capacity, that is, the stability and contour of the stage. At the same time, there are certain age-expectable dramas, themes characterized by their complexity, richness, depth, and content.

The developmental–structuralist approach is unique in an important respect. In focusing on levels and organizations of experience, it alerts the clinician to look not only for what the infant or toddler is evidencing (e.g., psychopathology) but for what he or she is not evidencing. For example, the eight-month-old who is calm, alert, and enjoyable, but who has no capacity for discrimination or reciprocal social interchanges, may be of vastly more concern than an irritable, negativistic, food-refusing, night-awakening eight-month-old with age-appropriate capacities for differentiation and reciprocal social interchanges. In other words, each stage of development may be characterized according to "expected" organizational characteristics.

SENSORY PATHWAYS, AFFECT PROCLIVITIES, EVOLVING THEMATIC ORGANIZATIONS, DISTURBANCES OF, AND STAGES IN, EGO DEVELOPMENT

As indicated above, the developmental structuralist approach focuses attention on the way in which the infant and young child organize experience. Two ways of considering how the infant organizes experience are along the interrelated dimensions of sensory and affective–thematic experience. These two dimensions and their clinical implications for a theory of the disturbances in ego development and stages in ego development will be described for each of the developmental structuralist organizational levels.

The following framework will be used. First, there will be a brief overview of the stage specific characteristics of object relations and ego functions. Then there will be a description of the sensory-affective and thematic-affective foundations of the ego. A description of stage-specific ego deficits, distortions, and constrictions will follow. Finally, there will be a statement regarding the stage specific characteristics and functions of the ego.

HOMEOSTASIS (SELF-REGULATION AND INTEREST IN THE WORLD, 0–3 MONTHS)

During this stage, one may postulate a self– object relationship characterized by a somatic preintentional world self–object. Ego organization, differentiation, and integration are characterized by a lack of differentiation between the physical world, self, and object worlds. Ego functions include global reactivity, sensory–affective processing, and regulation, or sensory hyper- hyporeactivity and disregulation.

The Sensory Organization. The infants' first task in the developmental structuralist sequence is simultaneously to take an interest in the world and regulate himself. In order to compare the ability of certain infants to simultaneously regulate and take an interest in the world with those who cannot, it has been clinically useful to examine each sensory pathway individually as well as the range of sensory modalities available for phase-specific challenges.

Each sensory pathway may be (1) hyperarousable (e.g., the baby who overreacts to normal levels of sound, touch, or brightness); (2) hypoarousable (e.g., the baby who hears and sees but evidences no behavioral or observable affective response to routine sights and sounds—often described as the "floppy" baby with poor muscle tone who is unresponsive and seemingly looks inward); (3) or neither hypo- nor hyperarousable but having a subtle type of early processing disorder (hypo- or hyperarousable babies may also have a processing difficulty). A processing disorder may presumably involve perception, modulation, and processing of the stimulus and/or integration of the stimulus with other sensory experiences (cross-sensory integration), with stored experience (action patterns or representations), or with motor proclivities. Although more immature in form, processing difficulties in infants may not be wholly dissimilar from the types of perceptual–motor or auditory–verbal processing problems we see in older children. In this context, the capacity of babies to habituate to and process the various inanimate sights and sounds may apply to the entire experiential realm of the child, including the affective-laden, interpersonal realm. It is important to note that the differences in sensory reactivity and processing were noted many years ago and continue to be discussed in the occupational therapy literature (Ayres, 1964).

If an individual sensory pathway is not functioning optimally, then the range of sensory experience available to the infant is limited. This limitation, in part, determines the options or strategies the infant can employ and the type of sensory experience that will be organized. Some babies can employ the full range of sensory capacities. At the stage of homeostasis, for example, one can observe that such babies look at mother's face or an interesting object and follow it. When this baby is upset, the opportunity to look at mother helps the baby become calm and happy (i.e., a calm smile). Similarly, a soothing voice, a gentle touch, rhythmic rocking, or a shift in position (offering vestibular and proprioceptive stimulation) can also help such a baby to relax, organize, and self-regulate. Also there are babies who only functionally employ one or two sensory modalities. We have observed babies who brighten up, alert, and calm to visual experiences, but who are either relatively unresponsive, become hyperexcitable, or appear to become "confused" with auditory stimuli. (A two-month-old baby may be operationally defined as confused when instead of looking toward a normal high-pitched maternal voice and alerting he makes some random motor movements—suggesting that the stimulus has been taken in—looks past the object repeatedly, and continues his random movements.) Other babies appear to use vision and hearing to self-regulate and take an interest in the world but have a more difficult time with touch and movement. They often become irritable even with gentle stroking and are calm only when held horizontally (they become hyperaroused when held upright). Still other babies calm down only when rocked to their own heart rate, respiratory rate, or mother's heart rate. Studies of the role of vestibular and proprioceptive pathways in psychopathology in infancy are very important areas for future research.

As babies use a range of sensory pathways, they also integrate experiences across the senses (Spelke and Owsley, 1979; Lewis and Horowitz, 1977). Yet, there are babies who are able to use each sensory pathway but have difficulty, for example, integrating vision and hearing. They can alert to a sound or a visual cue but are not able to turn and look at a stimulus that offers visual and auditory information at the same time. Instead, they appear confused and may even have active gaze aversion or go into a pattern of extensor rigidity and avoidance.

As higher levels of sensory integration are considered, one may also consider the difference between perception as a general construct and sensory-specific perceptions. In this discussion, the focus will be on individual sensory pathways with the understanding that as sensory and affective information is processed, it can be considered in terms of sensory-specific perceptions and more integrated perceptions.

The sensory pathways are usually observed in the context of sensorimotor patterns. Turning toward the stimulus or brightening and alerting involve motor "outputs." There are babies who have difficulties in the way they integrate their sensory experience with motor output. The most obvious case is a baby with cerebral palsy. At a subtle level, it is possible to observe compromises in such basic abilities as self-consoling or nuzzling in the corner of mother's neck or relaxing to rhythmic rocking. Escalona's classic descriptions (1968) of babies with multiple sensory hypersensitivities therefore require further study in the context of a broader approach to assessing subtle difficulties in each sensory pathway, as well as associated master patterns.

Thematic Affective Organization. At this first stage the affective–thematic organizations can support the phase-specific task which in turn can organize discrete affective–thematic inclinations into more integrated organizations. For example, the baby who wants to calm down is, at the same time, learning the means for obtaining dependency and comfort. The baby who wants to be interested in the world can, with a certain posture or glance, often let his primary caregiver know he is ready for interesting visual, auditory, and tactile sensations.

In the first stages, there are babies who cannot organize their affective–thematic proclivities in terms of the phase-specific tasks. In addition to maladaptive caregiver patterns and infant–caregiver interactions (Greenspan, 1981), babies who are uncomfortable with dependency, either because of specific sensory hypersensitivities or higher-level integrating problems, often evidence a severe compromise on the regulatory part of this equation. Babies with a tendency toward hyper- or hypoa-rousal may not be able to organize the affective– thematic domains of joy, pleasure, and exploration. Instead, they may evidence apathy and withdrawal or a total disregard for certain sensory realms while overfocusing on others (e.g., babies who stare at an inanimate object while ignoring the human world).

Excessive irritability, hypersensitivities, tendencies toward withdrawal, apathy, and gaze aversion illustrate some of the dramatic, maladaptive patterns in this first stage of development. If there are maladaptive environmental accommodations, these early patterns may form the basis for later disorders, including avoidance of the human world, and de-

fects in such basic personality functions as perception, integration, regulation, and motility.

Ego Deficits, Distortions, and Constrictions. What are the
implications of the faulty formation of these capacities in adult
and child psychiatric conditions? These are basic regulatory
capacities, including the ability to process stimulus input and
organize it (without shutting down, becoming hyperactive, or
hyperreactive). In many conditions this capacity is not well
established. For example, the child with severe attentional
difficulties cannot process information well, and those who are
most seriously affected may clinically look withdrawn, retarded,
or both. Some children who have only mild attentional difficulties, which are labeled attentional deficit disorders, actually
have more problems in one sensory mode than in another.
Some children are more distracted by sounds, others by visual
stimuli, while still others have tactile defensiveness, a pattern
which is not described well in the psychiatric literature. In many
clinical populations, there are individuals who are hyperreactive to light touch. Sensory processing difficulties are also seen
in child and adult schizophrenic populations who have been
studied experimentally. Separating and studying each processing capacity in terms of the sensory pathway involved, in
relation to both impersonal and affective stimuli (i.e., the
auditory, tactile, vestibular, olfactory, and proprioceptive systems, etc.) is an important research area. We are starting such
studies with infants and also hope to study the same phenomenon in adult and child psychiatric populations.

Sensory processing difficulties may also involve problems
in making discriminations. In addition to a sensory system
being hypo- of hyperarousable, we have observed infants in the
first few months of life who, although not at these extremes,
seem unable to tune in to the environment. When mother talks
to them, instead of decoding her rhythmic sound and brightening up (as most infants do), they almost look confused.
Clinically, we have observed that this is present in some
children with regard to one sensory pathway, but not another.
For example, an infant with intact hearing, unable to focus on

rhythmic sound, may be able to focus on facial gesturing. When an infant looks confused in reaction to vocal stimuli, we may coach a mother to slow down, to talk very distinctly, not to introduce too much novelty too quickly (most infants love novelty), and to use lots of animated facial expressions, movements (to encourage the use of vision), and tactile sensations. Often this infant will begin to become alert, brighten up, and become engaged.

It is instructive to consider what happened to deaf children before they were diagnosed early in infancy. By two years, many often looked very withdrawn (some were diagnosed as autistic) and were functionally retarded as well. The early diagnosis of deafness led to the introduction of sensory input through the intact modes—visual, tactile, olfactory. With these compensatory experiences, deaf children developed well both cognitively and emotionally. In other words, it may be that critical ego functions follow a certain required sequence of experiential inputs.

These experiential inputs, however, can be made available in many different ways, especially with regard to sensory pathways. In the theory we have developed from our observations of infants and young children, there is a sequence of psychological stages from interest in the world to forming a human attachment, to cause-and-effect interactions, to engaging in complex organized behavioral and affective patterns, to constructing and differentiating representations; yet, no single sensory pathway appears critical. For example, auditory input is not required to construct symbols. Symbols can be constructed from visual and tactile input.

What may have happened with many, partially or fully, deaf babies, however, was that their mothers did not know their infants could not hear. A concerned mother would understandably become anxious if she was not getting a brightening response for her new infant. She may have then talked even more, even louder, and even faster. Becoming discouraged, she may have become so anxious that she rigidly and repetitively tried the same pattern. Other sensory modes were not experimented with. The mother in this example is overwhelming the nonfunctioning auditory mode, not trying other modes, and her infant becomes more and more confused. It is not surprising in this context that in some of the old descriptions, very withdrawn and avoidant children were not in severely disturbed families but often in professionally successful families with obsessive–compulsive patterns. Infants with hypersensitivities or discrimination difficulties may do worse with an anxious, intrusive, overwhelming stimulus world. On the other hand, the youngster who is hyporeactive, who needs to be revved up, may do very well with a highly energetic caregiver. The luck of the draw or fit is always a factor. By profiling individual sensory processing differences and motor and affect patterns in infancy, however, it may become possible through counseling to improve the flexibility or intuitive patterns of the caregiver. How well the "informed" environment can find a unique way to provide the stage-specific experiences even for the infants with significant maturational differences (i.e., on a biological basis) will be the focus of future research and is certainly, at this time, an open question. My clinical hunch is that we have not yet found the limits of human adaptability.

In future research, we will be exploring a few explicit hypotheses to be described in Chapter 2, emerging from our clinical observations regarding the role of specific sensory processing difficulties, coupled with specific pathogenic environments in the genesis of disorders of thought and affect.

Implications for a Theory of Ego Development. During homeostasis, regulation and a multisensory interest in the world are the infant's two major goals. As indicated, clinically we observe a range of patterns of sensory arousal and reactivity as well as sensory (motor) discrimination and integration in clinical and normal groups of infants and their families, including hyperarousal and hypoarousal (both extreme apathy and hypotonicity). And one observes these patterns in reaction to both animate and inanimate stimuli. For the most part the infant is using what may be considered "prewired," rather than learned approaches to his world. In addition to the well-known primitive reflexes, the sensory and sensorimotor abilities referred to earlier allow the infant to cuddle, follow his caregiver's voice and face, and copy selected facial expressions, including tongue protrusion. The child will show preferences for different vocal patterns (e.g., mother's), and show visual preferences for objects that have been explored orally (cross-sensory integration), and so forth. Yet even though these and other behaviors can come under operant control (e.g., respond to reinforcements), there is no reason to assume that these basic abilities are not part of the functional capacities many infants are born with.

It may be postulated, therefore, that there are adapted sensorimotor patterns that are part of the "autonomous" ego functions present shortly after birth. It is then useful to consider how these capacities (e.g., the autonomous ego functions of perception and discrimination) are used to construct an emerging organization of an experiential world, including drive derivatives, early affects, and emerging organizations of self and object(s). It would be a logical error to assume that these seemingly innate capacities are themselves a product of early interactional learning or structure building, even though secondarily they are influenced by experiences.

One cannot yet postulate differentiated self–object experiential organizations. This is because the infant's main goals appear to be involved in a type of sensory awakening and interest and regulation without evidence of clear intentional object seeking or self-initiated differentiated affective interactions. In our observations of both at-risk and normal infants, it was observed that they responded to the overall stimulus qualities of the environments, especially human handling. Likewise, there is little evidence for a notion that the infant is impervious to his emotional surroundings. In fact, in our studies of multirisk families (Greenspan et al., 1987) the quality of self-regulation, attention, and sensory–affective interest in the world in the first month to two of life was influenced to a great degree by the physical and emotional qualities of the infant–caregiver patterns (i.e., soothing and interesting caregiving patterns rather than hyper- or hypostimulating ones).

But this does not mean that those who, like Mahler et al. (1975), suggest a qualitative difference in this early stage (i.e., the autistic phase) may not have an important insight. Even though mother's voice can be discriminated from other sounds, this does not mean there is a caregiver–physical world (sound of a car) differentiation in terms of abstracting and organizing types of experiences according to general characteristics. In other words, one must distinguish what the infant is capable of (e.g., complex discriminations) from how the infant is functionally involved in phase specific tasks and goals. For example, the three-year-old with separation anxiety associated with fear of loss of the affective object may have excellent capacities for conserving his impersonal objects. A six-year-old may be capable of advanced logic in math or science and lag considerably in the logic of reality testing and confuse fantasy and reality. A cognitive capacity may or may not be used for organizing in-depth emotional experience. Our clinical observations would suggest that early in life the capacities the infant uses to organize in-depth emotional experience lag behind the capacities he uses to process relatively impersonal experience or affective experience lacking in psychological depth.

One must not simply look at the infant's capacities, but at how he organizes around age-specific critical psychological tasks. Because these tasks involve complex spontaneous and, at times, highly challenging or even stressful interactions with emotionally important caregivers, and because the infant cannot control the behavior of the caregiver, his pattern of in-depth psychological growth is different from his pattern of cognitive growth. It must be described in its own right and not "assumed" or generalized from his functioning in other domains. Just as a passing cocktail conversation with an adult may not reveal the turmoil and boundary diffusion of his inner emotional life, the infant's inner life cannot be assumed from only selected aspects of his behavior.

In terms of the tasks of this stage, regulation and interest in the world, both animate and inanimate experiences are used by the infant to further his aims. As both types of experience help the infant calm, regulate, and attend to and process sensory information, one could argue that, in terms of phase specific tasks, there is a physical-human world sensory unity at this time.

Therefore, one may consider a preintentional stage of object relatedness (i.e., prewired patterns gradually come under interactive control) and a stage in the organization of experience where the sense of self and object are not yet organized as distinct entities. At this stage, the experience of "self" and "other" is closely intertwined and unlikely to be yet separate from other sensory experiences involving the physical world. It is worth repeating that differential infant responses do not necessarily mean differentiated internal experiences, because responses or behaviors can simply be constitutional, reflexive (like to heat or cold), and/or conditioned responses according to respondent (Pavlovian) or operant learning.

Therefore, the concept of an experiential organization of a *world object,* including what later will become a self–other–physical world, may prove useful. This state of ego organization may be considered to be characterized by two central tendencies: to experience sensory and affective information through each sensory (motor) channel, and to form patterns of regulation. Furthermore, these tendencies may be further characterized by the level of sensory pathway arousal (i.e., sensory hyper- and hypoarousal) in each sensory (motor) pathway and by emerging sensory (motor) discrimination and integration capacities. Under optimal conditions, the early sensory and affective processing, discrimination, and integration capacities, the early functions of the ego, are being used for the gradual organization of experience. Under unfavorable conditions these early ego functions evidence undifferentiated sensory hyperarousal, undifferentiated sensory hypoarousal, and lack of discrimination and integration in all or any of the sensory–affective (motor) pathways. Therefore the early stage of global undifferentiated self–object worlds may remain or progress to higher levels of organization, depending on innate maturational patterns and early experiences as together they influence each sensory–affective (motor) pathway in terms of arousal, discrimination, and integration.

In addition, as early drive–affect organizations are now being harnessed and integrated by the emerging ego functions of sensory–affect (motor) processing, differentiation, and integration, it is useful to consider drive–affect development from the perspective of the ego. From this perspective, the concept of the oral phase may be considered more broadly as part of a system of "sensory–affective" pleasure which involves all the sensory–affective (motor) pathways of which the mouth is certainly dominant (in terms of tactile, deep pressure, temperature, pain, and motor, especially smooth muscle, patterns. The mouth's dominance is due to the highly developed nature of its sensory–affective and motor pathways. From the perspective of the ego, however, drive–affect derivatives are elaborated throughout the "sensory surface" of the body.

ATTACHMENT (2–7 MONTHS)

During this stage, one may postulate a self–object relationship characterized by an intentional part self–object. Ego organization, differentiation, and integration are characterized by a relative lack of differentiation of self and object. There is, however, differentiation of the physical world and human object world. Ego functions include part-object seeking, drive–affect elaboration, or drive–affect dampening or liability, object withdrawal, rejection, or avoidance.

The Sensory Organization. The second stage involves forming a special emotional interest in the primary caregiver(s). From the perspective of sensory pathways, one can observe babies who are adaptively able to employ all their senses under the orchestration of highly pleasurable affect in relation to the primary caregiver(s). The baby with a beautiful smile, looking at and listening to mother, experiencing her gentle touch and rhythmic movement, and responding to her voice with synchronous mouth and arm and leg movements, is perhaps the most vivid example. Clinically, however, we observe babies who are not able to employ their senses to form an affective relationship with the human world. The most extreme case is where a baby actively avoids sensory and, therefore, affective contact with the human world. Human sounds, touch, and even scents are avoided either with chronic gaze aversion, recoiling, flat affect, or random or nonsynchronous patterns of brightening and alerting. We also observe babies who use one or another sensory pathway in the context of a pleasurable relationship with the human world but cannot orchestrate the full range and depth of sensory experience. The baby who already listens to mother's voice with a smile but gaze averts and looks pained at the sight of her face is such an example.

Thematic Affective Organization. The task of attachment organizes a number of discrete affective proclivities—comfort, dependency, pleasure, and joy, as well as assertiveness and curiosity—in the context of an intense, affective caregiver–infant relationship. In the adaptive baby, protest and anger are organized along with the expected positive affects as part of his emotional interest in the primary caregiver. A healthy four-month-old can, as part of his repertoire, become negativistic, but then also quickly return to mother's beautiful smiles, loving glances, and comforting.

On the other hand, babies can already have major limitations in certain affect proclivities. Rather than evidencing joy, enthusiasm, or pleasure with their caregivers, they may instead evidence a flat affect. Similarly, rather than evidencing assertive, curious, protesting, or angry behavior in relationship to their primary caregiver, they may only look very compliant and give shallow smiles. In addition to being constricted in their affective range, babies may also evidence a limitation in their organizational stability. An example is a baby who, after hearing a loud noise, cannot return to his earlier interests in the primary caregiver. Where environmental circumstances are unfavorable or for other reasons development continues to be disordered, early attachment difficulties may occur. If these are severe enough, they may form the basis for an ongoing defect in the baby's capacity to form affective human relationships and to form the basic personality structures and functions that depend on the internal organization of human experience.

Ego Deficits, Distortions, and Constrictions. As indicated, if the early experience of the world is aversive, the affective interest in the human world may be compromised. A total failure of the attachment process is seen in autistic patterns, in certain types of withdrawn and regressed schizophrenics, and intermittently, in children who are diagnosed as having pervasive developmental disturbances.

We also see shallow attachments. There is some involvement with the human world, but it is without positive affect or emotional depth. We see a compromise in the depth of human connectedness in some of the narcissistic character disorders, illustrating a subtle deficit in the range of emotion incorporated into an attachment pattern. A severe lack of regard for human relationships is seen in what used to be called the chronic psychopathic personality disorder (now the sociopathic or antisocial personality disturbance). Although some individuals are involved in sociopathic behavior because of neurotic conflicts or anxiety (i.e., acting out), in the primary sociopathic disturbances, there is a failure to see the human world as human. Human beings are seen as concrete objects, only as a means to concrete gratifications. It would be interesting to study hardened repeat offenders with histories of violent crimes against other individuals (i.e., showing a total disregard of other humans as human) and observe whether in addition to the reports on neurologic problems and early abuse one could document a failure of early attachments. Perhaps a higher than average percentage would have had multiple foster care placements, disturbed and withdrawn parents, or unusual constitutional tendencies, which interfered with the formation of warm relationships.

Implications for a Theory of Ego Development. This stage (attachment), characterized by clear affective pleasurable inclinations toward the human world, also evidences enormous variation; infants who are apathetic, or mechanical, may prefer the physical world. They may be passively compliant not joyful, and/or active avoiders of their caregivers' gaze and vocalizations. They may be indiscriminating or, past the age of eight months, unselective or even promiscuous in their object ties. In this stage, under optimal circumstances, all the senses and the motor system become coordinated toward the aim of pleasurable interaction with a caregiver. Not only pleasure, but distress and curiosity also are beginning to emerge in a more organized fashion.

The pleasurable preference for the human world suggests interactive object seeking. Apathy in reaction to caregiver withdrawal, preference for the physical world, and chronic active aversion in clinically disturbed populations also suggest emerging organized object-related patterns, be it in the maladaptive direction.

Yet, there is no evidence of the infant's ability to abstract all the features of the object in terms of an organization of the whole-object. Infants seek the voice, smiling mouth, twinkly eyes, or rhythmic movements alone or in some combinations, but not yet as a whole. In addition, the tendency toward global withdrawal, rejection, or avoidance suggests global undifferentiated reaction patterns as compared to differentiated patterns where the influence of a "me" on a "you" is occurring. The four-month-old does not evidence the repertoire of the eight-month-old in "wooing" a caregiver into a pleasurable interaction. The four-month-old under optimal conditions evidences synchronous interactive patterns, smiling and vocalizing in rhythm with the caregiver. When under clinical distress he evidences global reactivity; in comparison, the eight-month-old can explore alternative ways of having an impact on his caregiver. This suggests that not until this next stage is there a full behavioral (prerepresentational) comprehension of cause and effect or part self–object differentiation. Representational/comprehension does not occur until late in the second year of life.

Most likely, during this stage the infant progresses from the earlier stage of a self–other–world object (where both human and not-human worlds are not yet distinct, and the human self and nonself are not distinct) to a stage of intentional undifferentiated human self–object organization. There is the sense of synchrony and connectedness to a human object which suggests the infant's experiential organization differentiates the human object from physical objects. But even at a behavioral level there is not yet evidence of a self–object differentiation. In this sense the concept of symbiosis (Mahler et al., 1975) is not at odds with the clinical observation of a lack of self–object differentiation.

The functioning of the ego at this stage is characterized by intentional object seeking, differentiated organizations of experience (physical from human but not-human, self from human object), and global patterns of reactivity to the human object. These patterns of reactivity include seeking pleasure, protest, withdrawal, rejection (with a preference for the physical world which is based on what appears to be a clear discrimination), hyperaffectivity (diffuse discharge of affects), and active avoidance.

To the degree that later self and object organization are undifferentiated, aspects of experience may combine or seemingly organize in different ways. This is due to a lack of structure formation, and it is perhaps a precursor to condensations, displacements, and projective and incorporative–introjective mechanisms. Projection, incorporation, and introjection in a differentiated sense, where distinct images are transferred across boundaries, are not yet in evidence. We therefore see a progression from a stage of undifferentiated world self–object to an undifferentiated human self–object.

SOMATOPSYCHOLOGICAL DIFFERENTIATION (PURPOSEFUL COMMUNICATION, 3–10 MONTHS)

During this stage, one may postulate a self–object relationship characterized by a differentiated behavioral part self–object. Ego organization, differentiation, and integration are characterized by a differentiation of aspects (part) of self and object in terms of drive–affect patterns and behavior. Ego functions include part self–object differentiated interactions in initiation of, and reciprocal response in, a range of drive–affect domains (e.g., pleasure, dependency, assertiveness, and aggression), means–ends relationship between drive–affect patterns, and part self–object patterns. Ego functions may include undifferentiated self–object interactions, selective drive–affect intensification and inhibition, constrictions of range of intrapsychic experience and regression to states of withdrawal, avoidance, or rejection (with preference for the physical world), or object concretization.

Sensory Organization. Building on a solid attachment, the task is now to develop the capacity for cause-and-effect, or means–end type communications. Here, we observe even more profoundly the differential use of the senses. Some babies do not possess the capacity to orchestrate their sensory experiences in an interactive cause-and-effect pattern. A look and a smile on the mother's part do not lead to a consequential look, smile, vocalization, or gross motor movement on baby's part. This baby may perceive the sensory experiences mother is making available but seems unable to organize these experiences, and either looks past mother or evidences random motor patterns. We also observe babies who can operate in a cause-and-effect manner in one sensory pathway but not another. For example, when presented with an object, they may clearly look at the object in a purposeful way and then examine it. However, when presented with an interesting auditory stimulus, instead of responding vocally or reaching toward the person or the object, the infant behaves chaotically with increased motor activity and discharge-type behavior, such as banging and flailing. Similarly, with tactile experience, some babies, instead of touching mother's hand when she is stroking their abdomen begin evidencing random motor responses that appear unrelated to the gentle stimulus. We observe even more profoundly the differential use of the senses as infants are now also learning to "process" information in each sensory mode and between modes in terms of seeing relations between elements in a pattern. For example, some babies learn that a sound leads to a sound or a look to a look. Other infants do not possess the capacity to orchestrate their sensory experiences. The implications for later learning problems of certain sensory pathways not becoming incorporated into a cause-and-effect level of behavioral organization are intriguing to consider (e.g., the differences between children with auditory–verbal abstracting and sequencing problems and those with visual–spatial problems). In organizing cause-and-effect type communications, a compromise in a sensory pathway not only limits the strategies available for tackling this new challenge but may restrict the sensory modalities that become organized at this new development level. Motor differences, such as high or low tone or lags will also obviously influence the infant's ability to signal his wishes. In organizing cause-and-effect type communications, therefore, a compromise in a sensory or motor pathway not only limits the strategies available for tackling this new challenge, but may restrict the sensory and motor modalities that become organized at this new developmental level and, as will be discussed, the associated drive affect patterns as well.

As babies learn to orchestrate their senses in the context of cause-and-effect type interactions, we observe an interesting clinical phenomenon—in relationship to what has been described in the early neurological literature as "proximal" and "distal" modes. At this time, we may begin seeing a shift toward distal rather than proximal modes of communication. Proximal modes of communication may be thought of as direct physical contact, such as holding, rocking, touching, and so forth. Distal modes may be thought of as involving communication that occurs through vision, auditory cuing, and affect signaling. The distal modes can obviously occur across space, whereas the *proximal* modes require, as the word implies, physical closeness. The crawling eight-month-old can remain in emotional communication with his primary caregiver through various reciprocal glances, vocalizations, and affect gestures. Some babies, however, seem to rely on proximal modes for a sense of security. Early limitations in negotiating space will be seen later on to affect the capacity to construct internal representations.

Thematic–Affective Organization. At this stage the full range of affective–thematic proclivities, evident in the attachment phase, become organized in the context of cause-and-effect (means–end) interchanges. The baby joyfully smiles or reaches out in response to a motor movement or affective signal, such as a funny look from the mother, in a reciprocal exchange. Where the caregiver does not respond to the baby's signal, such as returning a smile or a glance, we have observed that the baby's affective–thematic inclinations may not evidence this differentiated organization. Instead they may remain either synchronous, as in the attachment phase, or shift from synchrony to a more random quality, where they appear almost hypomanic, evidencing many affect proclivities in quick succession. The expected range may be present but not subordinated into a cause-and-effect interchange.

There are also many babies who, because of a lack of reciprocal responses from their caregiver, seemingly, evidence affective dampening or flatness and a hint of despondency or sadness. This may occur even after the baby has shown a joyfulness and an adaptive attachment. In some cases at least, it seems as though when not offered the phase specific "experiential nutriments" (the cause-and-effect interactions he is now capable of), but only the earlier forms of relatedness, the baby begins a pattern of withdrawal and affective flattening. It is as though he needs to be met at his own level to maintain his affective–thematic range. Most interesting are the subtle cases where the baby can reciprocate certain affects and themes, such as pleasure and dependency, but not others, such as assertiveness, curiosity, and protest. Depending on the baby's own maturational tendencies and the specificity of the consequences in the caregiving environment, one can imagine how this uneven development occurs. For example, caregivers who are uncomfortable with dependency and closeness may not afford opportunities for purposeful reciprocal interactions in this domain but may, on the other hand, be quite "causal" in less intimate domains of assertion and protest.

The baby's own affective–thematic "sending power," and

the degree of differential consequences he is able to elicit, may have important implications for how he differentiates his own internal affective—thematic life (as well as how he organizes these dimensions at the representational or symbolic level later on).

Ego Deficits, Distortions, and Constrictions. As indicated, early in the stage of somatopsychological differentiation, an infant seems capable of almost the full range of human emotional expressions. This capability now sets the stage for more differentiated patterns of ego deficits, distortions, and constrictions. If one divides the emotional terrain into its parts, one can see the full range of emotions. In terms of dependency, the eight-month-old can make overtures to be cuddled or held. He shows pleasure with beatific smiles and love of touching (if he does not have a tactile sensitivity). He is already playing with his own genitals in a pleasurable manner and is experiencing gratification through sucking (and also putting everything in sight in his mouth, using his mouth as an organ of exploration). Unquestionably, there is also curiosity and assertiveness. The eight-month-old is already reaching, exploring, and banging objects, learning about having impact, and about cause and effect. There is also anger and protest. Try to take away the favorite food from an eight-month-old who does not want to give it up. Or he may throw his food on the floor in a deliberate, intentional manner and look at you as if to say, "What are you gonna do now?" There is protest, even defiance (e.g., biting and banging). These infants may prefer biting, or sometimes butting, as an expression of anger because at eight months they have better motor control of their mouths, heads, and necks than of their arms and hands.

Although empathy and consistent love will emerge later, one sees a range of emotional inclinations or affective–thematic proclivities at this age. What determines whether these affective inclinations develop and become differentiated from each other or remain undifferentiated, so that eventually pleasure, dependency, and aggression cannot be experienced as separate from one another? During the 4- to 8-month phase, the differential reciprocal signaling of the caregiver tells the child that pleasure is different from pain, that hunger for food is different from hunger to be picked up, that assertiveness is different from aggressiveness, and so forth. If each of the infant's feelings and expressions receives a different empathetic and overt response from the caregiver, the child experiences each of his own inclinations. Hilda Bruch (1973) anticipated what we now observe directly when she suggested that in some of the primary eating disturbances the dyadic signal system was not well formed because caregivers were rigid and unresponsive to the child's communications. For example, the child never learned to distinguish basic physical hunger from other sensations, such as dependency needs.

Therefore, during this stage, the affect system is differentiated to the degree to which the caregiving environment subtly reads the baby's emotional signals. Some infants do not experience reciprocity at all; others experience selective limitations. Cause-and-effect feedback in one or another thematic or emotional area is missing. No family will be equally sensitive and responsive in all areas. Some families are conflicted around dependency, and others around aggression. Thus, there will be more anxiety in some areas than in others, and children will receive different feedback for different emotional areas. Although this is, in part, what makes people different, when a whole area like dependency, pleasure, or exploration does not receive reciprocal, purposeful cause-and-effect feedback, early presymbolic (prerepresentational) differentiations may be limited.

It is also useful to think of this stage of development as a first step in reality testing. At this time, prerepresentational causality is established. The child is learning that reaching out, smiling, vocalizing, pleasurable affect, and aggressive affect all have their consequences. Causality is the sense of one's own behavior and emotions as having consequences. Cause-and-effect experiences teach a child that the world is a lawful place. When cause-and-effect behavioral patterns do not occur, the most fundamental aspect of the sense of causality may be compromised. Later in development, ideas or representations are also organized according to the cause-and-effect patterns. It may prove interesting to separate psychotic patients who have a failure of reality testing at the level of behavioral causality (4–8 months) from those who have a failure of reality testing at the later representational level (the two to four-year level of representational causality). For example, some psychotic individuals tend to think and talk crazy (they can be hallucinating, delusional, and have thought disorders), but they behave realistically. When I was a resident in psychiatry, I was very impressed with a lady who traveled from downtown New York in a totally delusional state and wound up in the Columbia Presbyterian emergency room. She didn't know how she got there. Behaviorally, she was very purposeful, even though her thinking was disorganized. There are also individuals who talk in an organized way, but at the behavioral level, they seem to operate in a crazy way. Perhaps severe psychotic sociopathic patients may have this type of pattern, suggesting a failure at the earlier level. Hence, it may prove useful to consider two levels of reality testing and related disorders.

Therefore, at the stage of somatopsychological differentiation, the fundamental deficit is in reality testing and basic causality. There are also subtle deficits which may be part of a lack of differentiation along a particular emotional–thematic proclivity. In various character disturbances and borderline conditions, we observe patients who are undifferentiated when it comes to aggression but not dependency, or vice versa. Certain areas of internal life remain relatively undifferentiated; yet in other areas, differentiation and reality testing are very good. This uneven pattern is part of many definitions of borderline syndromes.

In summary, a variety of symptoms may be seen in relationship to disorders of somatopsychological differentiation. They include developmental delays in sensorimotor functioning, apathy, intense chronic fear, clinging, lack of explorativeness and curiosity, lack of emotional reactions to significant caregivers, biting, chronic crying and irritability, and difficulties with sleeping and eating. Additional symptoms may be evident if, secondary to the lack of forming differentiated patterns, there are compromises in the infant–primary caregiver relationship (e.g., the infant becomes frustrated and irritable as his new capacities for contingent interactions are ignored or misread). If the basic comforting and soothing functions that support the baby's sense of security begin to falter, we may then see compromises in attachment and homeostatic patterns leading to physiologic disorders and interferences in already achieved rhythms and cycles such as sleep and hunger. Where disorders of differentiation are severe and are not reversed during later development, they may set the foundation for later disorders. These disorders may include primary personality (ego) defects in reality testing, the organization and perception of communication and thought, the perception and regulation of affects, and the integration of affects, action, and thought.

Implications for a Theory of Ego Development. In this phase characterized by cause and effect type interactions, one observes the infant take initiative and participate in reciprocal (rather than synchronous) interchanges. These occur across a range of sensorimotor pathways and affective patterns. The range of maladaptive options available to the infant is suggested by the following: the tendency to constrict or never develop the full range of potential affective–thematic patterns (e.g., only initiate dependency–reaching out, but not assertiveness or aggression or vica versa) or more worrisome, the tendency to never enter into cause-and-effect signaling (e.g., fragmented nonpurposeful activity) and/or become chaotic, indifferent, rejecting or withdrawn. Clinically we have observed infants initiate and reach out repeatedly to a depressed caregiver, sometimes succeeding in communicating their interest and love. Other times we have observed infants selectively reject or angrily poke a caregiver who has been away or is preoccupied (e.g., an infant refuses to look at mother, but is eager to look and smile at father or grandmother).

The intentionality of the infant in both adaptive (reaching

out, protesting, etc.) and maladaptive (rejecting) modes suggests at least a behavioral comprehension of a "self" influencing an "other." It also suggests self–object differentiation at the behavioral level. Behavioral level in this context means the organization of behavioral patterns or tendencies rather than the later organization of symbols. Only late in the second year does a child begin to have the ability to create mental representations, through higher-level abstractions. At this time, however, the "I" is likely an "I" of behavior ("If I do this it causes that") rather than the "I" of a mental representation ("if I feel or think or *am* a certain way, it will have this or that impact"). The capacity to construct mental representations will allow the growing child to organize and even rearrange different elements of the "self" or "other" into mental images. Because there is behavioral cause and effect or differentiated interaction, one can think of a behavioral or prerepresentational type of reality testing.

There is no evidence yet for the child having the ability to abstract all aspects of the "self" or "other." Experiences are still in fragmented pieces. Temporal and spatial continuity, while rapidly developing, are not yet fully established. The "I" is a physical and behavioral "I"; an "I" that can make things happen in the behavior pattern of the "other." The "I" and the "other" is not yet an "I" or "other" which represents or organizes all the aspects of the self or other, however, so it is possible to consider this stage as characterized by somatic and behavioral part self–object differentiation. The ego is characterized now by a capacity to differentiate aspects of experience in both the impersonal and drive–affect domains. It is worth emphasizing the point again that only at this stage are differentiated internal relationships possible. But even at this stage, there is likely to be differentiated part-object schemes of behavior, not whole-objects in a representational form. This view differs from other interpretations of infant behavior which is based on normative samples of infants in experimental situations.

In this context, a brief digression on the limitations of generalizing from certain experimental approaches may prove useful. There is a tendency to overgeneralize from selected focused experimental findings to psychodynamic domains. For example, Stern (1985, 1988) argues that the infant's ability to make discriminations of visual designs or sounds means that his ego structure is differentiated. Furthermore, he says that the existence of cognitive memory means there are, in early infancy, drive-affect-object based internal mental representations, and that all experience is the same for an infant or child (i.e., cognitive, emotional, including sexual, aggressive, traumatic, pathogenic, etc.). Stern feels this is because infants form a mental image not on any single event but on the average of many similar events. This last notion challenges the centrality of certain types of organizing fantasies and early experiences related to phase specific drive-affect and object relationship patterns. This challenge however is based on only a very narrow area of perceptual research and, therefore, highlights the danger of overgeneralizing from narrow experimental to psychodynamic domains. The research involved a visual preference task. A small number of presumed normal infants in a limited age range (i.e., ten months old) were presented with different inanimate visual configurations. In showing the expected preference for the novel configuration, the children tended to average together the features of the visual configuration they were familiar with in order to determine the novel one. Here, an interesting finding on visual perception in ten-month-old infants is taken out of context and, without appropriate research proving its generalizability, is applied broadly to all aspects of experience including drive-affect patterns at all ages. One cannot, without explicit research, assume that the way the brain functions in something as specific as preference behavior at ten months of age is the same as the way the brain functions generally in other domains. In fact, both with children functioning well and especially with children with special needs, there are often important differences in the way they process information in one modality in comparison to another (e.g., receptive language versus visual-spatial).

In general, the tendency to overgeneralize from narrow

experimental findings to psychodynamic domains tends to ignore three facts. One, there is a difference between what an infant is capable of and what is functionally part of his age-expected ego operations. For example, as indicated earlier a twenty-month-old can conserve the image of inanimate objects but still have great difficulty in conserving the image of his libidinal objects under emotional pressure (object constancy). A six-year-old may be great at the logic of numbers and science and lag in the logic of reality testing, confusing fantasy and reality. Two, the types of dynamic experience that constitute in-depth psychology are quite different from the types of experience that constitute impersonal cognition, and in all likelihood have a different organizational time table (Greenspan, 1979). Three, each infant organizes experience differently in the context of his or her own individual differences and stage of ego organization. There are even differences in terms of sensory-affective pathways. Some infants and children organize visual-spatial information in a more differentiated manner than auditory-verbal information. Therefore, one cannot generalize across different modalities, developmental stages, and groups of infants unless there is explicit experimental evidence proving the generalizations. But even more important is the need for reports of work on clinical populations of infants and young children to reveal through the comparison of distorted and adaptive patterns the underlying functions and mechanisms of the ego.

To return to the earlier discussion, it is also possible to consider that organized behavioral aspects of "self" and "other" may under stress undergo dedifferentiation; hence, during this stage one may speculatively wonder about projective or incorporative tendencies in regard to behavioral patterns and accompanying drive–affect dispositions. When the presumably angry infant actively rejects the caregiver (e.g., a ten-month-old refusing to look at mommy after she has been away for a while), one may wonder about the tendency to incorporate the behavior of the "other" as part of one's own strategy. With the very angry, insecure infant, who for no obvious reason is exceedingly fearful of novel situations or persons, one may wonder about the expected cautiousness regarding strangers, due to improved cognitive discrimination, being intensified via projective mechanisms. Interestingly, abused infants evidence fear much earlier than nonabused infants, suggesting that in certain affective–thematic domains precocious differentiation may serve a protective purpose. Now that differentiated islands of behavioral experience can be organized (part-objects), various configurations, including dynamically relevant part-object drive–affect dispositions are possible.

STAGE OF BEHAVIORAL ORGANIZATION, INITIATIVE, AND INTERNALIZATION (9–18 MONTHS); A COMPLEX SENSE OF SELF

During this stage, one may postulate a self–object relationship characterized by a functional (conceptual) integrated and differentiated self–object. Ego organization, differentiation, and integration are characterized by an integration of drive–affect behavioral patterns into relatively "whole" functional self–objects. Ego functions include organized whole self–object interactions (in a functional behavioral sense). These functions are characterized by interactive chains, mobility in space (i.e., distal communication modes), functional (conceptual) abstractions of self–object properties, and integration of drive–affect polarities (e.g., shift from splitting to greater integration). Alternatively, ego functions may be characterized by self–object fragmentation, self–object proximal urgency, preconceptual concretization, or polarization (e.g., negative, aggressive, dependent or avoidant, self–object pattern), and/or regressive states. The latter may include withdrawal, avoidance, rejection, somatic dedifferentiation, and object concretization.

Sensory Organization. This stage involves a baby's ability to sequence together many cause-and-effect units into a chain or an organized behavioral pattern (e.g., the fourteen-month-old who can take mother's hand, walk her to the refrigerator, bang on the door, and, when the door is opened, point to the desired food). Wish and intention are organized under a complex behavioral pattern. This organized behavioral pattern can be viewed as a task that involves coordinated and orchestrated use of the senses. Here the toddler who is capable of using vision and hearing to perceive various vocal and facial gestures, postural cues, and complex affect signals is able to extract relevant information from his objects and organize this information at new levels of cognitive and affective integration. A toddler who is not able to incorporate certain sensory experiences as part of his early cognitive and affective abstracting abilities (Werner and Kaplan, 1963) may evidence a very early restriction in how his senses process information.

Balanced reliance on proximal and distal modes becomes even more important during this phase of development. The mobile toddler enjoying his freedom in space presumably can feel secure through his distal communication modes. It is interesting in this context to examine traditional notions of separation anxiety and the conflicts that some toddlers have over separation and individuation (Mahler et al., 1975). With the use of the distal modes, the toddler can have his cake and eat it too. It he can bring the caregiving object with him through the use of distal contact with her, he does not have to tolerate a great deal of insecurity. He can "refuel" distally and use proximal contact when necessary. The youngster who has difficulty in using his distal modes to remain in contact with the primary caregiver may need more proximal contact. This difficulty often occurs because of the insecurity generated by an ambivalent primary caregiver, but the limitations of his own sensory organization may also be an important factor.

Thematic–Affective Organization. The piecing together of many smaller cause-and-effect units of experience involves a range of types of experience, such as pleasure, assertiveness, curiosity, and dependency, into an organized chain. For instance, it is not unlikely for a healthy toddler to start with a dependent tone of cuddling and kissing his parents, shift to a pleasurable, giggly interchange with them, and then get off their laps and invite them to engage in an assertive chase game where he runs to a room that is off-limits, such as the living room. When the parents say "no, you can't go in there," protest and negativism may emerge. Under optimal circumstances, the interaction may come to a relative closure with the toddler back in the playroom, sitting on his parent's lap, pleasurably exploring pictures in his favorite book. Here the child has gone full circle, suggesting that he has connected the many affective–thematic areas.

Around eighteen months, as children begin to abstract the meaning of objects, their understanding of the functions of the telephone or brush may have its counterpart in their experiencing the caregiver as a "functional" being invested with many affective–thematic proclivities. Between twelve and eighteen months, while children are able to integrate many behavioral units, they do not seem to be able to integrate intense emotions. For the moment at least, they lose sight of the fact that this is the same person they love and experience pleasure with. By eighteen to twenty-four months, the sense of split-off fury seems, at least in clinical observations, to be modified at some level by an awareness of love and dependency.

Ego Deficits, Distortions, and Constrictions. As indicated, as the child moves closer to eighteen months, the ability emerges to gradually relate to the object world in a more functional way and to see objects according to their functional properties. Werner and Kaplan (1963) describe how babies can take a comb or toy telephone and use it purposefully. This is not yet imaginary play guided by mental representations or ideas; it is semirealistic play with an understanding of the functional use of the object. Children can also understand the emotional proclivities of their parents in a functional sense. They sense either nurturing, warm, supportive patterns or undermining, controlling, intrusive patterns. One little girl was able to see her mother as a teasing, envious person, although she did not understand what her mother was saying. She would pull away whenever her mother verbally teased her.

As indicated above, we have also observed that toddlers shift from an early stage (12–13 months), akin to ego splitting in adults, to a stage of greater integration of different self-object organizations by eighteen to nineteen months. When I am involved in therapeutic play with a twelve to thirteen-month-old and that child becomes angry, it feels as though if he had a gun at that moment, he could shoot me. It feels much like it does with the borderline adult patient, although connections between stages of childhood and adult pathology are never so simple as a direct expression of a behavior or function from one age to another (it is more often an early capacity that is not established, or vulnerably established, that influences subsequent stages in terms of organization, flexibility, or context). When you are the bad object, there is no simultaneous connection with you as the object of security and comfort. For that moment, you are all bad. It feels frightening and vicious. By the time a toddler is eighteen months old, you may feel his anger, but you also sense that he sees you as an object of security, love, and dependency. You feel more like you would with a neurotic adult. There is anger, but the backdrop of security and relatedness is still there.

Thus, during the stage of behavioral organization, initiative, and internalization, we observe a progression from a type of ego splitting or part-object relatedness to a more cohesive sense of the functional, emotional proclivities of the object. Presumably, this integration is also occurring in the sense of self. Just as toddlers are sensing their parents as loving, or undermining, or both, they are also abstracting their own patterns of feelings and behaviors. They no longer see themselves as islands of discrete behaviors or feelings, aggressive one moment and pleasurable the next. They are abstracting a pattern. These are higher-level abstractions of feelings and behaviors, but still prerepresentational patterns of the object and the self.

One way to think of the second year of life is as involving the development of a conceptual attitude toward the world. In the first year of life, what might be called a somatic attitude is in evidence because events are experienced somatically and physiologically and through sensorimotor and affect patterns.

In the second year, the youngster abstracts larger patterns. Concept building occurs. The child understands the world in terms of its functions and can communicate and abstract across space (i.e., the distal modes). The ability to abstract time, organized in terms of the creation of representational memory organizations of the self and object, will only come next in the representational phase of development.

As part of the toddler's emerging conceptual capacities, he also communicates more and more effectively by using gestures. Gestural communications involves facial expressions of affect (e.g., happy, sad, angry, etc.), motor movements, (e.g., clenching fists, reaching out to be hugged), body postures (e.g., turning away or toward another person), vocal patterns (including sound sequence, tone, and rhythm), and so forth. Gestural communication, which begins in the first year of life, now reaches a crescendo and, one could hypothesize, creates a critical foundation for representational communication.

The importance of this level of communication cannot be overestimated. Consider the critical information which is conveyed presymbolically; for example, safety versus danger, acceptance versus rejection, concern versus indifference, respect versus humiliation, support for a person's uniqueness versus undermining and controlling patterns. The most basic emotional messages of life needed for survival (e.g., danger versus safety) and for a sense of security (e.g., acceptance versus rejection) are communicated presymbolically through the gestural system. In fact, we tend to trust this system more than the representational one. If someone says, "I am a nice person," but acts in a menacing fashion, we tend to trust what we perceive in terms of their gestures over the meaning of their words.

This gestural level, which we have in common with other members of the animal kingdom, is surprisingly well mastered by eighteen to twenty-four months of age. Toddlers can make their own intentions known and are learning to comprehend the intentions of others.

When this system is not mastered and children progress to higher representational levels, they seem to try to use higher representational modes to master what for others have become automatic tasks. Rather than listening to the teacher's instructions on how to match the "ah" sound to the letter A, they might be working very hard to figure out what she intended with her stern look: "Is she dangerous?" "Will she hurt me?" Many severely disturbed adults evidence this same pattern of preoccupation with figuring out basic intentions. Deficits in this system of gestural interaction as a contributor to various types of psychopathology will be an area of future research.

The potential value of this line of research was highlighted recently, when working with a group of children who had difficulties controlling their impulses, I noticed a subtle deficit in gestural communication. This was a group of bright, focused (not hyper) children who would suddenly poke another child or an adult. Both these children and their parents showed very little affect variation in their facial expressions, looking like good poker players (poker-faced). Perhaps, the lack of gestural variation removes the early warning system, so to speak. So the children don't learn to modulate their behavior because there is no graded gestural feedback, only all or nothing punishments, much like the all or nothing quality of their own behavior. In addition, the ability to gesture provides a form of feedback. Our gestures, in part, help us define our feelings (e.g., muscle tension and anger). Gestures also are a form of expression of feelings (it could be viewed as a very early form of sublimation as well as a safe form of affective discharge). The intricate posturing and signaling so characteristic of *safe* negotiations among both animals and people seemed to be missing in these families. It is not uncommon to see this type of impulsivity in children who are distractible, overly active, and/or have information processing problems. In fact, the maturational lags of these children often make successful negotiation of the gestural level quite difficult. It was surprising to see the "poker faces" in a group of maturationally advanced children and their families. For these children, it appeared that the lack of gestural communication was predominantly related to psycho-social issues and a failure of early learning.

The gestural system, therefore, appears to play an essential role in broadening the communications capacity of the child. As he abstracts his own and others intentions, he is more and more able to relate in terms of larger patterns. Both he and his objects are taking on a more integrated (at a functional behavioral level) quality.

Problems in the early integration of the functional self relate to syndromes where there is ego splitting, or a lack of cohesive sense of self, or a lack of an ability to abstract the range of emotional properties of self and others. The tendency to remain concrete rather than to develop conceptual and, eventually, a representational self–object organization is also related to limitations at this stage of development. Many adult patients, for example, talk of themselves in terms of discrete behavioral patterns (e.g., "I pushed her; she bit; I went out drinking."). Life is a series of interrelated but somewhat discrete behaviors. There is no sense of, "she is a frustrating person; therefore, I get upset," or "I go out drinking because I can't tolerate the pain and anguish of her frustrating me," or "she's a sweet person who loves me, but I get scared of the closeness, and therefore I can't handle it and I go out and drink."

Often we inadvertently supply the missing representational level in therapy. The patient says, "I hit her." We say, "You must have felt angry." In fact, the patient's problem is that he does not have the capacity for representational labeling of affect states. He only feels the tendency to hit and not the feeling of anger in a representational mode. For many with severe character disorders and borderline conditions, life is a series of discrete behavior patterns. In normal development, as early as eighteen to nineteen months, a more conceptual attitude toward the world is developed. But many patients do not develop this capacity in the emotional spheres of their life. They possess it intellectually; they can do math and other abstract impersonal problems, but when it comes to emotions, they are not able to operate at the eighteen to nineteen-month level. Or they may operate at different developmental levels with different emotions, for example, pleasure and dependency at one level, assertion and anger at another (depending on their caregiving environment).

Therefore, two extremes were observed. At one extreme, the capacity for organizing behavior, emotions, and a conceptual stance toward the world is not formed at all. We see fragmented images of the self and the object world. These individuals can relate to others, but they are at the mercy of moment-to-moment feelings. There is no integration of discrete experiences. It is not surprising that borderline patients have affect storms and keep shifting their behavioral and emotional inclinations. Their part-self and object images are not tied together; they have not made it to the eighteen-month level where they have a sense of themselves and their significant others as operating individuals. Their part-selves are fueled by unconnected drive–affect proclivities.

This is an especially interesting stage of development because most of the severe character and borderline conditions (which are probably the most frequent conditions we treat today) have important normative parallels in the second year of life.

We also see in the second year of life the emergence of an internal signaling system. Affect, as a signal, seems to develop both as part of a more general conceptual attitude toward the world and as an outgrowth of the gestured communications. By eighteen to nineteen months, we see a toddler who, when he does not get what he wants, is not necessarily driven to temper tantrums or other driven behavioral patterns. There is now a capacity to pause and make a judgment regarding what to do. The toddler can consider alternative behavioral patterns. Most eighteen to nineteen-month-olds, for example, may pester mother, pull at her leg, and so forth, but with one look from mom, they can go back to their play area and wait for a while longer. Or, a toddler will want to do something, and you will look at him and make the gesture, "no, no, no." He may stop in his tracks, challenge you, stop again, and so forth. The signal function is in the process of being developed. To be sure, many toddlers may not use this new capacity at all or may not yet have it.

Nemiah (1977) has suggested that in certain psychosomatic conditions, such as drug abuse and impulse disorders, there is the lack of a signal affect capacity. Hence, there is a lack of the transitional capacity to elevate dysphoric affect into a conceptual, and subsequently a representational, signal.

It is interesting to consider what helps the child develop a signal function. One component is the capacity to shift from proximal modes to distal modes of relating. An infant relates to the adult world with proximal modes, through being held and being touched. These modes are proximal in the sense that the infant is using his skin, a sense of pressure, and so forth. By four to eight months, one begins seeing the distal modes come into use; vision and hearing are used in reciprocal signaling, and infants stay in touch by vision and hearing with direct touch. By twelve to eighteen months, the toddler, although across the room, can stay connected to mother or father through these distal modes. Vocalizations, visual signals, and affect gestures (a grin or smile) are used to remain in emotional contact. The refueling that Mahler et al. (1975) discuss occurs not only through proximal modes (coming back and hugging mother), but through the distal modes. The youngster, while playing, looks, sees mother's alert attentiveness, and feels reassured. Studies by Sorce and Emde (1981) on social referencing show that children are more exploratively confident when their mother is looking at them and taking an interest in their play, compared to when she is reading a newspaper in the same room. A child can explore, have the freedom of space, and still feel connected. He relates across space, but he cannot yet relate across time. He does not possess the ideational or representational mode.

A child may not establish this distal communication capacity because a parent is overanxious, overprotective, or overly symbiotic. Or the child may not have optimal use of the distal modes because of a unique maturational pattern. Consider, for example, the child discussed earlier who has an auditory processing problem; he may not be able to decode mother's "that's a good boy." Or he may have a visual–spatial organizing limitation and have difficulty reading facial gestures or interpersonal distance. He may need to rely more on the proximal modes. He may have to be held to feel secure.

The use of distal modes may be an important key in the transition to the development of the ideational or representational mode. With the ideational or representational mode, one has mobility not only across space but across time because one can create ideas (one can conjure up the object). As Mahler et al. (1975) suggest, one feels security through the fantasy of the object.

As adults, there is a balance between proximal modes (to be held and cuddled, in close tactile and physical contact with our loved ones) and distal modes (we enjoy warmth and security through the nodding and gesturing of a close friend in a good conversation, or even a new acquaintance at a cocktail party). Adults who cannot receive experience through the distal modes often feel deprived and isolated. They often resort to proximal modes. This makes adult life very difficult. As far as I know, this deficit has not been looked at as a significant part of borderline disturbances and severe character disorders in which there is an inordinate sense of isolation, emptiness, and loneliness. The transition to distal and then to ideational modes, therefore, creates flexibility. One can carry with one the love object, first over space and eventually over time. One sees a failure at this stage in deficits in the functional–conceptual self and object, and limitations in functional–conceptual self–object affective–thematic proclivities.

A special type of functional conceptual self-object limitation at this age may be evidenced in the lack of an emerging sense of gender. Normally an abstracted sense of being more masculine or feminine appears to be emerging. A lack of abstracting a sexual gender sense, however is in evidence at this time in children who become fragmented in an anxious interest with different sexually relevant body parts in isolation from an overall sense of gender.

In summary, a severe disorder at this phase affects the basic capacity for organizing behavior and affects. Most worrisome is the toddler who pulls away entirely from emotional relationships in the human world or remains fragmented as he develops his affective–thematic proclivities. A less severe disorder at this stage will be reflected in the narrowness of the child's range of experience organized, as seen in extreme character rigidities (e.g., the child who never asserts himself or is always negative, or has difficulties with affiliative behavior, or cannot use imitation in the service of temporary gratification and delay). As such children are tied to concrete and immediate states of need fulfillment, they may never form the intermediary warning and delay capacities that complex internal affects are used for. They often will tend to see people only as fulfilling their hunger for physical touch or candy, cake, or other concrete satisfactions.

Symptomatic problems at the stage of behavioral organization are chronic temper tantrums, inability to initiate even some self-control, lack of motor or emotional coordination, extreme chronic negativism, sleep disturbance, hyperirritability, withdrawal, delayed language development, and relationships characterized by chronic aggressive behavior. In addition, if basic attachments and comforting functions are secondarily disrupted, one may see attachment and homeostatic disorders.

Implication for a Theory of Ego Development. The new capacities for behavioral organization, affective integration, and behavioral sense of self and object in functional terms (a conceptual stand toward the world) characterizes this stage of ego development. Now there is what may be thought of as a conceptual self–object relationship because different self behaviors and object behaviors are not only differentiated from each other (as in the earlier stage), but are now viewed as part of a whole. Teasing behavior, jokes, anticipation of emotional reactions, and awareness of how to get others to evidence different emotional proclivities all point to this new conceptual affective ability. But even more important is how the toddler uses his ability to organize in all dimensions of life. This is

illustrated by his tendency, under stress, to organize his negativism, or become sophisticated in his clinging dependency,
develop intricate aggressive patterns, or exploit or manipulate
peers and adults in new interpersonal patterns. In worrisome
situations one also observes the toddler regress from organized
behavioral patterns to highly fragmented patterns, or become
withdrawn or rejecting. Here complex adaptive and maladaptive patterns as well as regressive potential suggests the emerging whole-object patterns. The ego now has new capacities; it
can integrate behavioral and emotional differences or opposites
(begin to deal with ambivalence). As indicated previously, early
in this phase (12–14 months) ego splitting or lack of integration
is characteristic, but by seventeen to eighteen months more
integrated patterns are possible. The ego abstracts the properties of experiences of the self with others along functional lines
rather than stimulus topography. Daddy is not just big or fat or
wearing a brown shirt, but is warm or aggressive or supportive
or fun. Just as the toy telephone is used to call people, not
simply as a piece of wood to bang, "daddy" or "mommy" as well
as "self" are functional interactive beings. Functional grouping
of behavioral experience permits greater awareness, anticipation, and planning. It facilitates the gestural level and the
automatic negotiation of basic emotional themes such as safety
and acceptance. The ego can now organize experience in terms
of functional expectancies. This capacity of the ego also facili-
ties integrated functional identifications. Instead of simply
copying a behavior, a child can copy or identify with a functional interpersonal pattern. These functional patterns can also
be projected or incorporated. Now not simply an isolated
behavior (e.g., hitting) but a "behavioral attitude" (e.g., being
controlling) can be projected or incorporated. Perhaps most
defenses exist on a hierarchy related to stages in the functioning of the ego.

     As has been indicated, organization of experience at this
stage occurs through experiencing oneself in relationship to
significant others. Reciprocal patterns allow one to experience
an emotional partnership where elements of self and other are

continually abstracted from a variety of contexts. I believe the tendency to learn through identifications, often considered a primary way of learning, is secondary to learning through reciprocity. The innate tendency to copy (a likely preceptual–perceptual motor tendency) can become encouraged as part of feeling admired for one's ability to be like another, or may be used defensively. Identifications motivated by defensiveness, anger, or disphoria probably occur in an "undigested manner." Metaphorically the child says: "I will copy what I do not like to better be able to defeat you at your own game." Hence rejection leads to rejection or abuse to abuse. But this is the child's way of reciprocating or trying to protect himself and get even. In other words, it is part of a reciprocal pattern.

The degree to which the ego experiences conflicts or deficits at this stage is also important to consider. Where the ability to functionally organize self and object behavior patterns is not achieved, or where it is achieved in certain thematic–affective realms but not others (e.g., dependency but not aggression), a deficit or constriction may occur. Dysphoric affects may also be mobilized as a product of a "no win" situation where two behavioral tendencies are in opposition to each other (e.g., hitting behavior and being punished, or independent behavior and a feeling of isolation, or assertive curious behavior and realistic anticipation of being under-mined and humilated). Because by sixteen to eighteen months of age "anticipation" is clearly possible, the potential for conflict is clearly in evidence as toddlers search for ways to meet competing needs. For example, they may use avoidance, aggression, or behavioral compromise formations. It would appear that a type of "behavioral pattern" conflict is a feature of ego functioning.

During this stage ego structure formation is undergoing rapid progress. Both deficits of experience and conflicts between behavioral–affective tendencies will likely undermine structure formation. One therefore does not need to postulate either deficit models or conflict models of the mind. Rather, the two tendencies can be seen to be working together.

For example, Kohut (1971) would suggest that lack of parental empathy leads the toddler to experience a deficit in terms of his self-esteem regulation (an early affective self-object pattern). Kernberg (1975) would suggest that the unadmiring, overcontrolling, or intrusive caregiver creates a condition where the toddler experiences rage and conflict and then resorts to primitive splitting defenses in order to cope with this situation. It is suggested here that based on clinical work with, and observations of, toddlers that both tendencies are operative. A lack of empathy and intrusive overcontrol leads to painful humiliation, rage, and fear of object loss as well as deficits in self–object experiences and the formation of structures regulating self-esteem. For example, the eighteen-month-old experiencing rage and fear, without therapy, usually resorts to passive compliance, indifferent impulsivity, and avoidance. This regressive way of dealing with conflict during this phase leads to a structural deficit because the ability to abstract affective polarities is not learned. Likewise, a lack of empathic admiration and availability seems to leave the toddler feeling too uncertain about his objects to experiment with his behavioral and affective polarities. Reconstructive work with older children and adults must deal with both the reality of the early object relationship and the rage, humiliation, fear, and conflict, and the primitive strategies employed at the time and subsequently repeated. At this age, conflict, therefore, leads to deficits, and deficits (e.g., a lack of capacity to abstract behavioral polarities and deal with ambivalence) create the increased probability of unresolvable conflicts. Which comes first becomes a chicken or egg question because appropriate structure is necessary to resolve conflict and conflicts at an early ago often lead to structural deficits.

This stage of ego development is characterized by many new capacities and is transitional to the next stages, where mental representations and differentiated self–object representational structures are possible.

REPRESENTATIONAL CAPACITY (18–30 MONTHS)

During this stage, one may postulate a self–object relationship characterized by a representational self–object. Ego organization, differentiation, and integration are characterized by an elevation of functional behavioral self–object patterns to multisensory drive–affect invested symbols of intrapersonal and interactive experience (mental representations). Ego functions include representational self-objects characterized by mobility in time and space (e.g., creation of object representation in the absence of object); drive–affect elaboration (themes ranging from dependency and pleasure to assertiveness and aggression now elaborated in symbolic form as evidenced in pretend play and functional language). There is gradual stabilizing of drive–affect patterns (self–object representations survive intensification of drive–affect dispositions). Or there is behavioral concretization (lack of representation), representational constriction (only one emotional theme at a time), drive–affect liability, regressive states, including withdrawal, avoidance, rejection, and behavioral dedifferentiation, and object concretization.

Sensory Organization. As a toddler shifts from organizing behavioral patterns to the ability to abstract the functional meaning of objects, and then to the ability to construct mental representations of human and inanimate objects, we observe the establishment of the "representational" capacity. A mental representation is multisensory and it involves the construction of objects from the perspective of *all* the objects' properties (including levels of meaning abstracted from experiences with the object). Therefore, the range of senses and sensorimotor patterns the youngster employs in relationship to his objects is critical, for the object is at once an auditory, visual, tactile, olfactory, vestibular, proprioceptive object, and an object that is involved in various affective and social interchanges. Where the range, depth, and integration of sensory experiences are limited, the very construction of the object will obviously be limited in either its sensory range and depth or affective investment and meaning. Therefore, in such a situation, important limitations in the child's early representational world may result.

Thematic–Affective Organization. As the child learns to construct his own multisensory, affective–thematic image of his experiential world, he organizes affective–thematic patterns at a level of meanings. This new level of organization can be thought of as operating in two ways. The youngster with a representational capacity now has the tool to interpret and label feelings rather than simply act them out. A verbal two and one-half-year-old can evidence this interpretive process by saying "me mad," or "me happy." Pretend play is, perhaps, an even more reliable indicator than language of the child's ability to interpret and label. Pretend play is an especially important indicator because many children have language delays. For example, a child soon provides a picture of his representational world as he plays out dramas of dependency (two dolls feeding or hugging each other); of excitement and curiosity (one doll looking under the dress of another); or of assertiveness (searching for monsters).

The representational capacity also provides a higher-level organization with which to integrate affective–thematic domains. Therefore, we observe new experiences as the child develops from two to five years of age. These include empathy, consistent love (object constancy, a love for self and others that is stable over time and survives separations and affect storms such as anger [Mahler et al. 1975]), and later on the ability to experience loss, sadness, and guilt.

Because of the complexities of representational elaboration, the conceptualization of this stage may be aided by subdividing the representational capacity into three levels or subcategories. The first level is the descriptive use of the representational mode (the child labels pictures and describes objects). The second level is the limited interactive use of the representational mode (the child elaborates one or two episodes of thematic–affective interactions, such as statements of "give me candy," "me hungry," or a play scene with two dolls feeding, fighting, or nuzzling). The third level is elaboration of representational, affective–thematic interactions. Often by the age of two and one-half or three, the child sequences a number of representational units into a drama—the doll eats, goes to sleep, awakens, goes to school, spanks the teacher, comes home and has a tea party, begins looking under the dress of another doll, becomes overexcited, is comforted by mommy, and then goes back to sleep. Initially, the elements in the complex drama may not be logically connected. Over time, along with representational differentiation, the causal–logical infrastructure of the child's representational world emerges in his pretend play and use of language. Over time, the child's thematic elaboration can be observed to include a range of themes, including dependency, pleasure, assertiveness, curiosity, aggression, self-limit-setting, and eventually empathy and love.

Ego Deficits, Distortions, and Constrictions. If, for any reason, the child is not getting practice in the interpersonal emotional use of language and pretend play (i.e., elevating these proclivities to the ideational plane); we often see the beginnings of a deficit or constriction in representational capacity. Deficits or constrictions may occur because mother or father becomes anxious in using ideas in emotionally relevant contexts. For example, they may be afraid of emotional fantasy, in general, or in specific thematic–affective areas such as separation or rejection, aggression, or assertiveness. Many adults are more frightened or conflicted by the representation of a theme such as sexuality or aggression than the behaving or acting out of the same theme. Parental anxiety often leads to overcontrolling, undermining, hyperstimulating, withdrawn, or concrete behavioral patterns (i.e., let's not talk or play; I will feed you). In addition, because of unique constitutional–maturational patterns or early experiences, the child may become overly excited and thus afraid of his own use of ideas and new feelings (e.g., sexual themes in the play). As a result, he may regress to concrete prerepresentational patterns. If the parent cannot help the child return to the ideational level (i.e., the child is beating the ground and cannot reorganize and get back into the play), the child does not practice affective–thematic proclivities at the ideational mode, and remains at the behavioral action pattern mode (acting out).

The ideational mode allows for trial action patterns in thought (to contemplate and choose among alternatives). One can reason with ideas better than with actual behaviors. Therefore, one has an enormous deficit if a sensation, or series of sensations, that are distinctly human do not have access to the ideational plane. Parents often ask about aggression ("Should I take away aggressive toys?"). If parents ignore elevating aggression to the representational plane, they are leaving aggression to the behavioral discharge mode. As children go from the conceptual mode to being able to label affects, they learn to talk about feelings. Adaptive four-year-olds can label most of the basic feelings and begin to deal with them in their pretend play.

In summary, disorders in this phase include children who remain concrete and never learn to use the representational mode (e.g., only fragments of play or language). Impulsive or withdrawn behavior often accompanies such a limitation. The child's relationship patterns are also usually fragmented.

At a somewhat less severe level, we see children who have developed a representational capacity in both the inanimate and animate spheres but show severe limitations or regressions with even minor stress in certain areas of human experience. For example, they may be able to use symbolic modes only around negativism, dominance, and aggression and consequently look solemn, stubborn, and angry, showing little range of representational elaboration in the pleasurable or intimate domain. When frustrated or angry some children may quickly regress to behavioral modes.

Implications for a Theory of Ego Development. This stage of ego organization is characterized by the capacity to elevate experiences to the representational level. Current experience can be organized into multisensory-affective "images" and these images are mobile in time and space (e.g., children imagine images of objects in the absence of the object). The representational system can also construct multisensory images of sensations or patterns from within the organism which may have

occurred in the past. These earlier patterns of somatic sensation and simple and complex chains of behavior and interaction
will now be "interpreted" via representation. How well formed,
accurate, or distorted these representations of earlier prerepresentational experience will be will depend on the character
of the early patterns, their repetition in the present, the
abstracting ability of the ego, and the emerging dynamic
character of the ego; that is, its ability to represent some areas
of experience better than others.

As a feature of the ego's abstracting capacity one must also
consider the maturational capacities of the child. If, for example, a child evidences a lag in processing sensory information in
either the auditory–verbal, symbolic, or visual–spatial symbolic
pathways (e.g., can't sequence, and thereby abstract units of
experience), then the ability to abstract large patterns of
experience may be compromised. Therefore, organizing early
representations will obviously be more challenging to the child
with difficulty in perceptual sequencing. Since many children
evidence a range of individual differences in sequencing and
organizing information, this capacity, as it interacts with interpersonal experiences, must also be considered.

The ego at this stage evidences the adaptive capacity for
representational elaboration. It also evidences a range of maladaptive options, including a lack of representation where the
physical world can be represented but the drive–affect invested
interpersonal world is not represented. This global lack of
representational capacity is often associated with interpersonal
withdrawal and/or regressive behavioral and somatic discharge
patterns. Where there is support for representational elaboration in some areas but not others, or where certain child-
initiated themes lead to parental anxiety and/or parental
undermining behavior, one observes representational constrictions. One also observes in some instances that these constrictions can be accompanied by intense patterns of behavioral and
affective expression. These intense patterns may be in the same
or the opposite thematic–affective realm as the representational constriction. One may also observe a lack of representa-

tion of delineated self-object thematic patterns (e.g., only dependency with intrusive mother figures) rather than entire areas of emotion (such as dependency with everyone). This limited access to representational elaboration often stems from more circumscribed conflicts in parent-child interaction patterns (e.g., the parent only becomes intrusive or withdraws when the child behaves like the parent's sister) and sets the stage for neurotic conflicts and circumscribed character pathology. Patterns that remain outside of representational life are denied access to unconscious or conscious symbolic processes and are therefore more likely to seed the formation of unconscious neurotic configurations.

How children remain concrete (i.e., not develop a representational capacity) constrict the representation of certain drive-affect realms, form delineated limited areas of nonrepresentated access, and develop compensatory regressive behavioral and affective patterns, reveals the range of functioning available to the ego. The ego organizes current and past experience (behavioral and somatic) in representational configurations. Initially, these are descriptive. They quickly become functional and interactive. The physical, temporal, and spatial properties of experience are the initial organizers. Representational meanings are quickly learned, however. Each "representational" or interpersonal interaction creates a context for abstracting meanings. To the degree there is a less than optimal interactive experience available (the caregiver is concrete or ignores or distorts certain representational themes), we observe a series of ego operations which include:

1. Concretization of experience (access to representation is never achieved).
2. Behavioral–representational splitting (some areas gain access, but core areas remain at behavioral level).
3. Representational constriction (global dynamically relevant areas remain outside of the representational system).
4. Representational encapsulation—limited dynamically relevant areas remain in more concrete form.

5. Representational exaggeration or lability—domains of experience which are ignored or distorted become exaggerated and/or labile, their opposites become exaggerated and/or labile, or other "displaced" dynamically related thoughts, affects, or behaviors become exaggerated or labile.

During this stage, as self and object relationships are being organized at a representational level, they are not differentiated, even though the early prerepresentational behavioral and somatic organizations are differentiated. There is a paradox: Differentiation at an earlier level alongside emerging differentiation at the new higher level.

At this time we can postulate an undifferentiated representational self-object built on a foundation of somatic and behavioral differentiated self-objects. The behaving child is clearly intentional and behaviorally understands his actions have impact on others. Yet he is learning to give meanings to his behaviors and feelings and only beginning to learn about intentionality and consequences at the level of meanings. Thus awareness, in a symbolic sense, is expanding rapidly and is in evidence in the elaboration of pretend play and the functional use of language. Yet we are also observing how symbolic awareness or consciousness may be concretized, constricted, or incapsulated, or selectively exaggerated depending on the opportunities the child has to engage his new ability in appropriate interpersonal contexts.

From the perspective of the ego's capacity to organize unconscious phenomena, it is possible to consider the different levels of experience within which drive–affect dispositions express themselves: somatic sensations, behavioral patterns (including inhibition), and emerging mental representations. Early in development, somatic and behavioral patterns exist in various degrees of differentiation (e.g., along the lines of physical versus human, and human self versus nonself). Now the same is true for emerging mental representations.

In this context, it is perhaps useful to rethink concepts often used to understand the organization and dynamics of

organizing primitive experience, namely, projection, incorporation, condensation, displacement, and so forth. At each level
of organization—somatic sensation, behavioral patterns, and
emerging mental representation—the infant initially does not
differentiate experience sufficiently for one to postulate an
organized defense such as projection. As differentiation occurs,
however, self and object experiences gradually become
grouped along a number of dimensions, including: (1) physical
properties; (2) spatial relationships; (3) temporal relationship
(e.g., contingencies based on sequencing in time); (4) functional
properties (in the second year of life); and (5) emerging
meanings (18–24 months and on). At each level, somatic
behavioral, and representational, at a certain point experience
is sufficiently differentiated to consider the various ways in
which experiences can be reorganized to serve the defensive
and adaptive needs of the moment. In other words, it is proper
to postulate altering experiences only after some differentiation has occurred. This differentiation defines some boundaries for the experience. There is a difference between a lack of
differentiation and a dynamically motivated alteration of differentiated experience however primitive. In earlier sections,
we discussed ways in which these mechanisms operate at the
prerepresentational levels. At the representational level we can
again look at primitive defense mechanisms. What is put out,
projected, taken in, incorporated, or combined (condensation)
is a mental image that is acquiring meaning (and these images
are related to earlier somatic and behavioral organization). It is
appropriate now to also consider *displacement* as a defense
mechanism. One image can substitute for another as the ability
to construct images allows for greater representational mobility
in the intrapsychic world. Condensations will also certainly be
richer and more economic once mental representations acquire
meanings. Symbols of dynamic meaning provide the basis not
only for logical thought but new drive-affect organizations of
experience. As a higher level organization of experience (then
somatic or behavioral patterns) mental representations or symbols change the nature of defensive phenomena.

With the advent of mental representations, it is also now possible to consider the beginnings of sublimation. Traditionally sublimations have been considered to occur only later in development (i.e., late oedipal and latency periods) when sexual or aggressive drive derivatives are displaced and achieve the aim of subliminated gratification by integrating them with the factors of reality, superego constraints, and emerging ego ideal. These integrations are often associated with symbolic transformations. The very capacity to represent experience and therefore go beyond behavior discharge is an early form of sublimation, however. For example, an angry, hitting, biting, spitting, head-banging two-year-old can learn to put the behavior into pretend play and words. As this occurs and the "soldiers" are hitting each other, the tendency to directly aggress on the parent or younger siblings may diminish without a sense of inhibition, and with a sense of conscious satisfaction and gratification.

Often, at this stage of development, representational elaboration is associated with primary process thinking. Because behavioral and somatic differentiation is already occurring, and representational differentiation, as will be discussed shortly, occurs simultaneously with representational elaboration, it may prove best to rethink our notions of primary process thinking.

REPRESENTATIONAL DIFFERENTIATION (24–48 MONTHS)

During this stage one may postulate a self–object relationship characterized by a differentiated, integrated representational self-object. Ego organization, differentiation, and integration are characterized by an abstraction of self–object representations and drive–affect dispositions into a higher level representational organization, differentiated along dimensions of self–other, time, and space. Ego functions include representational differentiation characterized by:

1. Genetic (early somatic and behavioral patterns organized by emerging mental representations);

2. Dynamic integration, (current drive– affect proclivities organized by emerging mental representations);

3. Intermicrostructural integration (i.e., affect, impulse, and thought);

4. Structure formation (self–object representations abstracted into stable patterns performing ongoing ego functions of reality testing, impulse control, mood stabilization, etc.);

5. Self and object identity formation (i.e., a sense of self and object which begins to integrate past, current, and changing aspects of fantasy and reality); or

6. Representational fragmentation (either genetic, dynamic, or both);

7. Lack of, or unstable, basic structures (e.g., reality testing, impulse control, etc.);

8. Defective, polarized, or constricted (global or encapsulated) self–object identity formation.

The Sensory Organization. For the child to meet the challenges of organizing and differentiating his internal world according to "self" and "other," "inside" and "outside," dimensions of time and space and affective valence, he is, in part, dependent on the integrity of the sensory organization that underlies his experiential world. Now, even more than earlier, the capacity to process sensory information is critical, including sequencing auditory–verbal and visual—spatial patterns according to physical, temporal, and spatial qualities in the context of abstracting emerging cognitive and affective meanings. The child is now challenged to understand what he hears, sees, touches, and feels, not only in terms of ideas, but in terms of what is me and not-me; what is past, present, and future; what is close and far, and so forth. These learning tasks depend on the ability to sequence and categorize information. Therefore, if anywhere along the pathway of sensory processing there are difficulties, the subsequent ability to organize even impersonal information will likely be compromised. For example, if sounds are confused, words will not be easily understood.

If spatial references are confused, spatial configurations will not be easily negotiated. If short-term memory for either verbal or spatial symbols is vulnerable, information will be lost before it can be combined with, and compared to, other information (to abstract meanings). And if higher level auditory–verbal symbolic or visual–spatial symbolic abstracting capacities are less than age appropriate, the very capacity to categorize experience will be limited. When one considers that the challenge is now to process and organize not only impersonal, cognitive experiences, but highly emotional, interpersonal experiences (which keep moving, so to speak), this challenge to the sensory system is formidable. Furthermore, categories such as "me," "not me," "real," and "make-believe" are high-level constructs. Not surprisingly, learning difficulties often are first evidenced in emotional functioning.

Thematic–Affective Organization. In contrast to earlier views by Freud (1900) and Mahler et al. (1975), our clinical observations suggest that a parallel path of differentiation exists simultaneously with the onset of the representational capacity and its elaboration. The child appears to use his new representational capacity to simultaneously elaborate and differentiate experience. There does not appear to be a period of magical representational thinking followed by one of reality thinking. The child continually differentiates affective– thematic organizations along lines that pertain to self and other, inner–outer, time, space, and so forth. This differentiation is based on the child's capacity to experience the representational consequences of his representational elaborations with the emotionally relevant people in his world, usually parents, family, and friends. The parent who interacts with the child, using emotionally meaningful words and gestures, and engages in pretend in play in a contingent manner (offering, in other words, logical representational feedback) provides the child with consequences that help him differentiate his representational world. In this view, reality testing—the capacity to separate magical from realistic thought—appears to be a gradual process beginning with the onset of the representational capacity proper and stabilizing prior to the child's formal entry into school.

One observes the child's elaborate representational themes along two dimensions. In the horizontal dimension, the child broadens the range of his or her themes to eventually include a range of emotional domains or drive–affect realms, including closeness or dependency, pleasure and excitement, assertiveness, curiosity, aggression, self-limit-setting, the beginnings of empathy and consistent love. For example, not infrequently one observes repetitive pretend play of a feeding or hugging scene suggesting nurturance and dependency. Over time, however, the dramas the child may initiate (with parental interactive support) will expand to include scenes of separation (one doll going off on a trip and leaving the other behind), competition, assertiveness, aggression, injury, death, recovery (the doctor doll trying to fix the wounded soldier), and so forth. At the same time, the logical infrastructure of the child's pretend play and functional use of language becomes more complex and causally connected. The "He Man" doll is hurt by the "bad guys" and therefore "gets them." After the tea party, the little girl doll goes to the "potty" and then decides it is time to begin cooking dinner. In discussions, the three-and-a-half-year-old sounds more and more like a lawyer with "buts" and "becauses"—"I don't like that food because it looks yucky and will make me sick." There is, therefore, both thematic elaboration and differentiation. Even though the themes may be pretend and fantasmagoric, the structure of the drama becomes more and more logical. The rocketship to the land of "He-Man" uses N.A.S.A. rocket fuel.

As indicated, representational differentiation depends not only on a child being representationally engaged in thematic–affective areas but experiencing cause-and-effect feedback at the representational level. Parents have to be able not only to engage but also to interpret experiences correctly. The parents who react to play with a gun as aggression one day, as sexuality another day, and as dependency on a third day, or who keep shifting meanings within the same thematic play session, will confuse the child. This child may not develop meanings with a reality orientation. Parents who confuse their own feelings with the child's feelings, or cannot set limits, may also compromise the formation of a reality orientation.

Ego Deficits, Distortions, and Constrictions. The child needs to learn how to shift gears between the make-believe and the real world. Ordinarily, we see this occur gradually between the ages of two and four. As part of this process, we see more planning in children's play, as Piaget (1962) highlighted (e.g., going upstairs to get just the right cup for the tea party). What happens if there are failures of development during this stage? Earlier it was suggested that if representational elaboration is not occurring, the child is left with a preideational or prerepresentational, somatic, and behavioral orientation. If there are limitations in representational differentiation (confused meanings), a child's self and object differentiation at the representational level may be compromised. It is interesting to consider those people who can engage others warmly (have mastered attachment) and organize their behavior, but who have "crazy" thoughts. They often cannot separate their own thoughts from someone else's. They may have organized delusions, but are extremely warm and can relate to others (they are not autistic or schizoid).

On the other hand, one may also see constrictions; that is, people who cannot represent or differentiate aggression or sexuality and are left only with the behavioral–action mode, or who are confused about their own and others' ideas or feelings in these thematic areas (but not other thematic areas). Constrictions at this stage may be associated with relatively more differentiated and internalized conflicts (i.e., between opposing differentiated tendencies in relation to relative degrees of undifferentiation).

It is also interesting to discuss psychosexual trends at this stage. The phallic trend is clearly present beginning at age two to three. Kids love to build towers, pretend to be Superman, and undress, to show off their bodies. I have not seen an equal preoccupation with the anal concerns (eliminative or retentive patterns). Therefore, I wonder if the anal body interest is elaborated as much in the representational sphere as is the phallic one.

It may be useful to consider the oral, anal, and phallic stages of psychosexual inclinations in terms of observable thematic–affective inclinations. I suspect there may be a sensory, tactile, or oral mode early in life. In the second year of life, muscle control may predominate (better gross and fine motor coordination, including anal control by the end of the second year). Then, by two and one-half years, one sees the phallic inclinations as part of the ever-increasing body control and investment in the body and its parts (which begins at seventeen to eighteen months). The phallic inclinations become part of an emerging more differentiated sense of childhood sexuality as the interest in the genitals becomes integrated with the overall emerging sense of the body as part of an internal bodily representation. In summary, even though there is fascination with feces, I have not observed the representational derivatives of anal body interest in normal children to the same degree as phallic derivatives. On the other hand, where development is not progressing optimally, either exaggerated phallic trends or excessive anal preoccupation is not uncommon.

To return to the earlier discussion, inclinations that do not have access to the representational mode and its differentiation, even in mild degrees, are perhaps sowing the seeds for severe character pathology and/or neurotic conflicts. What is often referred to as magical thinking is more probable where representational elaboration and differentiation have not fully occurred. Later on, in the triangular oedipal and latency phases of development, earlier patterns obviously are reenacted and reworked.

In summary, it is useful to clinically observe and assess the representational capacity along the two simultaneous dimensions of representational elaboration and representational differentiation. Clinically one observes defects and constrictions in both domains. These are evidence by the child who:

1. remains concrete and never learns to use the representational mode to elaborate "inner sensations" to the level of meanings;
2. is severely constricted and is only able to represent a few of the affective–thematic domains characteristic of human functioning;
3. evidences the full range of representational affective–thematic life but remains undifferentiated along the dimensions of ideas or thoughts (thought disorder), affective proclivities (mood disturbances), self and object organizations (reality testing and "self" and "other" boundary disturbances), intentionality (impulse disorders), sense of time and space (disorders of learning, concentration, and planning);
4. in order to differentiate avoids affective–thematic realms that are potentially disruptive (character disorders).

Contributing to these limitations is the caregiver who cannot engage representationally in all domains because he or she is fearful of certain affective–thematic realms and therefore withdraws or becomes disorganized. Another is the caregiver who engages in all realms but has difficulty operating at a representational contingent level. The child's own limitations from earlier maturationally based processing problems and psychosexual difficulties also contribute to representational disorders.

Implications for a Theory of Ego Development. Parallel with its capacity to create and elaborate mental representations, as ego development progresses it abstracts representational units into groupings leading to representational differentiation. These groupings occur along a number of dimensions including physical, spatial, and temporal aspects of experience. Self representations are differentiated from the other, nonself, or object representations along all the relevant dimensions. But most importantly, these groupings also occur along the lines of affective *meanings*. Now, drive–affect colored self–object pat-

terns coalesce into representational organizations according to
the characteristics of the drive–affect dispositions as they both
define and are defined by early relationship patterns.

As one observes both healthy and disturbed children, it
appears that experience can now be categorized, and each
category of experience can undergo, depending on the appropriateness and adaptiveness of environmental–representational feedback, relative degrees of differentiation. As indicated earlier, the areas of pleasure, dependency, assertion,
curiosity, anger, self-limit-setting, love, and empathy may be
seen as a way to categorize experience (e.g., separation anxiety
would be a feature of dependency). Therefore, drive–affect
derivatives are now organized by the ego according to the
principles of representational differentiation. As realms of
experience are defined and differentiated, each affective–
thematic domain becomes a basis for further interaction and
more refined meanings.

Thus, self–object patterns at this stage of ego development
are characterized by differentiated elaborated self–object representations. The range and stability of these organizations,
however, may vary considerably. Differentiated self–object representations may encompass a broad range of themes or be
narrow and constricted. To the degree there are areas where
interpersonal feedback is lacking or has been distorted, self–
object representations may remain unelaborated, undifferentiated, or may undergo dedifferentiation.

The primary ego functions now develop from the ego's
ability to abstract patterns along dimensions of self and object
meanings, affective tendencies, and the dimensions of time,
space, and causality. These include reality testing (a representational me separate from a representational other); impulse
control (a representational me impacting on, and eliciting
consequences from, a representational other); mood stabilization (a representational me and other becomes organized along
a dominant mood as affects are abstracted into larger affective
patterns); focused attention and a capacity for planning (a

representational me causes events to occur in a temporal context); and a more integrated body self–object representation (the parts of me and object are abstracted in spatial contexts).

During this stage, ambivalence can be dealt with in a new way and an integrated representational self can be organized, or one may observe a lack of integration. Different self–object representational units may exist, depending on interpersonal factors or maturational factors, at various degrees of differentiation. The sexual self–object, assertive self– object, dependent self–object, and so on, may each achieve its own relative degree of differentiation. As indicated earlier, sensory processing difficulties may undermine differentiation in auditory–verbal or visual–spatial modes. Or a lack of representational feedback or distorted or illogical feedback in certain realms of experience will tend to leave those areas of representational life relatively undifferentiated.

As is well known, anxiety and conflict now tend to play a new role, but perhaps earlier than previously thought. With growing representational capacity anxiety can be interpreted via the emerging representational system. Conflicts between self–object representations can occur in terms of an "internal debate" at the level of ideas (e.g., the good me and you versus the angry evil me and you). Conflicts between self–object representations and external expectations can also occur (the "greedy" me and the "strict" limiting other). Therefore, while anxiety and internal conflict have been thought to be dominant only in the late oedipal and postoedipal phases (because of the necessity of internalized prohibitions, i.e., superego formation), our clinical observations of young children suggest that representational differentiation alone may be a sufficient condition.

What operations are now available to the ego to deal with anxiety and conflict? The ego now has new approaches in addition to the primitive mechanisms described earlier.

Observations of both normal and disturbed young children suggest that the approaches available to the ego include:

1. Global lack of differentiation (reality and the object ties that provide reality feedback are too disruptive or "scary").

2. Selective dedifferentiation (blurring of boundaries and changing meanings, as with "my anger won't make mother leave because we are the same person").

3. Thought–drive–affect dedifferentiations ("I can think anything, but I won't have feelings so I won't be scared").

4. Thought–behavior (impulse) dedifferentiation ("If I do it, it's not me. Only when I think and plan it is it me").

5. Selective constrictions of drive–affect–thematic realms (areas such as anger or sexual curiosity are avoided and may remain relatively undifferentiated, often due to being associated with disorganizing interactive experience such as withdrawal, overstimulation, etc.).

6. Affect, behavioral, or thought intensification ("If I exaggerate it or its opposite, it can't scare me").

7. Differentiated representational distortions (changing meanings along lines of drive–affect dispositions—"I am supergirl, the strongest." But basic reality testing is maintained—e.g., "It is only pretend.").

8. Encapsulated distortions (dynamically based conflict driven, highly selective shifts of meanings; e.g., "I am the cause of mother's anger").

9. Transforming differentiational linkages. This is an early form of rationalization. As the child's capacity to connect representational units is forming, he or she can elaborate. ("I like mommy because she is home all the time and am mad at daddy because he travels a lot".) These logical links can undergo subtle shifts to change meanings for defensive purposes. ("I like daddy to travel a lot because he brings me presents. I am mad at mommy," etc.)

10. Compromises in representational integration and representational identity. The integration of somatic, be-

havioral, (and representational self–object organizations) and associated drive–affect proclivities are not
fully maintained, as evidenced by the irritable-looking
three-year-old who "feels fine" or the hitting three-
year-old who "loves everyone."

In summary, we have considered in this section how the
ego grows in its ability to organize experience. Somatic and
behavioral experience is now abstracted to a higher plane, that
of representation. In addition, somatic and behavioral patterns
are interpreted or labeled. Most importantly, new experience is
now organized and elaborated in representational modes.
Representational elaboration and differentiation creates the
basis for internal life to be symbolized and categorized along
dimensions of self and nonself, affective meanings, time, and
space. The categorization of experience in turn becomes the
basis for basic ego functions, new relationship patterns, relatively more differentiated and internalized conflicts, higher
level defenses, and psycho-sexual advances.

It should be emphasized that in this work, only the early
stages of the ego are described. Ego functions progress to make
possible triangular patterns and higher-level transformations
of meanings, including the development of new structures such
as the superego and ego ideal (i.e. new representational capacities are constructed). The levels in ego development characterizing latency, adolescence, and adulthood will not be
discussed in this work. Following is a summary outline of the
stages in early ego development (see table 1.1).

TABLE 1.1
Stages of Ego Development

Self-Object Relationship	Ego Organization, Differentiation & Integration	Ego Functions
Homeostasis—0–3 Months		
Somatic preintentional world self-object	Lack of differentiation between physical world, self, and object worlds	Global reactivity, sensory-affective processing and regulation or sensory hyper- or hyporeactivity and disregulation
Attachment—2–7 Months		
Intentional part self-object.	Relative lack of differentiation of self and object. Differentiation of physical world and human object world	Part-object seeking, drive-affect elaboration or drive-affect dampening or liability, object withdrawal, rejection, or avoidance
Somatopsychological Differentiation—3–10 Months		
Differentiated behavioral part self-object	Differentiation of aspects (part) of self and object in terms of drive-affect patterns and behavior	Part self-object differentiated interactions in initiation of, and reciprocal response to, a range of drive-affect domains (e.g. pleasure, dependency, assertiveness, aggression), means-ends relationship between drive-affect patterns and part-object or self-object patterns or undifferentiated self-object interactions, selective drive-affect intensification and inhibition, constrictions of range of intrapsychic experience and regression to stages of withdrawal, avoidance, or rejection (with preference for physical world), object concretization

TABLE 1.1 (*continued*)

Self-Object Relationship	Ego Organization, Differentiation & Integration	Ego Functions
Behavioral Organization—Emergence of a Complex Self, 10–18 Months		
Functional (conceptual) integrated & differentiated self-object	Integration of drive-affect behavioral patterns into relative "whole" functional self-objects	Organized whole (in a functional behavioral sense), self-object interactions characterized by interactive chains, mobility in space (i.e. distal communication modes), functional (conceptual), abstractions of self-object properties, integration of drive-affect polarities (e.g., shift from splitting to greater integration)
		or
		Self-object fragmentation, self-object proximal urgency, preconceptual concretization, polarization (e.g., negative, aggressive, dependent, or avoidant, self-object pattern, regressive state, including withdrawal, avoidance, rejection, somatic dedifferentiation, object concretization)
Representational Capacity and Elaboration—1½–3 Years		
Representational self-object Elaboration 1½–3 yrs.	Elevation of functional behavioral self-object patterns to multisensory drive-affect invested symbols of intrapersonal and interactive experience (mental representations). Interactive experience (mental representations)	Representational self-objects characterized by mobility in time and space; e.g., creation of object representation in absence of object drive-affect elaboration (themes ranging from dependency and pleasure to assertiveness and aggression now elaborated in symbolic form evidenced in pretend play and functional language), gradual drive affect stability (self-object representations slowly survive intensification of drive-affect dispositions)
		or
		Behavioral concretization (lack of representation), representational constriction (only one or another emotional theme), drive-affect liability, regressive states including withdrawal avoidance, rejection, and behavioral dedifferentiation and object concretization

TABLE 1.1 (*continued*)

Self-Object Relationship	Ego Organization, Differentiation & Integration	Ego Functions
Representational Differentiation—2–4 Years		
Differentiated, integrated representational self-object	Abstraction of self-object representations and drive-affect dispositions into higher level representational organization. Differentiated along dimensions of self-other, time, and space	Representational differentiation characterized by genetic (early somatic and behavioral patterns organized by emerging mental representations) and dynamic integration, (current drive-affect proclivities organized by emerging mental representations) intermicrostructural integration (i.e., affect, impulse, and thought). Basic structure formation (self-object representations abstracted into *stable* patterns performing ongoing ego functions of reality testing, impulse control, mood stabilization, etc.) Self and object identity formation (i.e., a sense of self and object which begins to integrate past, current and changing aspects of fantasy and reality) or Representational fragmentation (either genetic, dynamic, or both). Lack of, or unstable basic structures (e.g., reality testing, impulse control, etc.) defective, polarized or constricted (global or encapsulated) self-object identity formation

Chapter 2

Biological and Environmental Specificity in the Psychopathological Developmental Process and the Selection and Construction of Ego Defenses

In this chapter the relationship between individually different patterns of sensory–affective processing and specific environmental (experiential) patterns will be considered. A series of hypotheses and research strategies will be suggested which may prove helpful in studying how biology and experience interact in highly specific ways in the formation of psychopathology and the construction of defensive structures.

Freud's prediction that we would one day find biological roots or concomitants to aspects of drive and ego functioning, including defenses, was part of his goal for psychoanalysis to integrate the role of biology and experience into a complete and integrated model of human behavior. Observations and

An altered version of this chapter was originally published in the *Journal of the Amer. Psychoanl. Assn.* 37:27–59.

in-depth case studies of both normal and disturbed infants (Greenspan, 1981; Greenspan and Porges, 1984; Greenspan, Wieder, Lieberman, Nover, Lourie, and Robinson, 1987) in keeping with Freud's goal, have led to developmentally based hypotheses about how individually different biological patterns and experiential family patterns may come together to foster either psychopathology or adaptation. It should be emphasized, however, that these hypotheses, while based on observations and case studies, are not based on experimental data. They are of potential value, therefore, only to the degree that they frame questions about how biology and experience interact in a newer, more specific, and/or researchable manner than has been done before. In the following sections these hypotheses will be considered in relationship to severe and moderate disorders of thought and affect and in relationship to specific defenses.

HYPOTHESES REGARDING DISTURBANCES OF THOUGHT AND AFFECT

In working with at-risk infants and their families, an early observation of our staff, consistent with earlier observations by Escalona (1968), Fish, Shapiro, Halpern, and Weil (1965), Weil, (1970), Fish and Hagin (1973), was that infants had a range of individual differences in dealing with experiences via different sensory channels, beginning in the earliest months of life. For example, some infants, when presented with high-pitched maternal voice patterns, seemed to overreact. Their bodies became stiff, they turned their heads away from rather than toward the stimulus, and their faces took on a look of panic. It was as though what for most infants would be a pleasurable stimulus (one which they would turn toward, brighten up, and alert to) was, for a certain group of infants, highly aversive. Other infants showed similar patterns with visual stimuli, including bright lights. At a more subtle level, we noticed that some infants were not hyperreactive to auditory information, but had difficulty recognizing a vocal pattern. When mother would talk to them in what sounded like rhythmic, high-pitched maternal vocalizations (which the majority of babies would alter and brighten to), a group of babies would look confused and would look past their mothers rather than orienting to their voices. Other babies could orient to vocalizations but had trouble orienting and alerting to the presentation of various facial expressions. It was as though visual–spatial experiences were not processed easily. We also noted that reactivity and processing of information was relatively independent of each other. We also noticed that the early environment could accentuate or ameliorate these individual constitutional, maturational differences. In some families, where the infant seemed to have difficulty organizing auditory experience, caregivers responded with anxiety and talked to the baby very rapidly, overwhelming the system that was having the most difficulty. Their infants often withdrew from the human environment. On the other hand, there were rare caregivers who intuitively slowed down their vocalizations and experimented with pitch and rhythm. They talked, for example, in low-pitched voices and repeated themselves, offering less novelty to the infant who was slow to process auditory information. They also appealed to the infant's visual, tactile, and other senses as a way to communicate information. These infants seemed to do better. They would form an attachment, learn cause-and-effect signaling, organize complex patterns of emotion and behavior, and eventually construct symbols to guide emotions and behavior.

In addition to visual and auditory differences we also noted, as described in chapter 1, differences in tactile sensitivity, sensitivity to movement in space, reactions to odors, reactions to feedback from movement and differences in motor tone, motor planning and attention, and alertness. Many of these differences were found in different types of infants such as tactile sensitivity and difficulty in processing sound or tactile sensitivity, increased motor tone and visual spacial processing difficulty.

These observations regarding individual differences in the

infants and the environmental patterns, led to hypotheses regarding the relationship between early sensory and affective experiences and specific processing difficulties, and the developmental sequence leading to thought disorders, on the one hand, and affective disorders, on the other. While there was overlap between a number of sensory and motor patterns, the auditory and visual spacial pathways seemed specific for different types of disorders.

Thought disorders, it is hypothesized, stem from two concomitant circumstances: a difficulty in processing auditory–vocal–verbal information combined with an environment that tends to operate by confusing the meanings of communications. In this hypothesis the infant at risk for a thought disorder evidences difficulty processing auditory–vocal–verbal information, beginning early in life with difficulty in abstracting the sequence of certain sounds. Most infants, for example, quickly become familiar with their mother's and father's vocal rhythms. They often alert and brighten in expectation of the next sound in the sequence. Some infants cannot decode these early rhythmic patterns and look confused in response to a simple vocal pattern. Most importantly, affect, which will further challenge a vulnerable sensory processing system is conveyed through auditory–vocal–verbal sensory channels. The auditory-vocal channels are important for the gestural level of affective communication discussed earlier and for the successful negotiation of the basic emotional themes of this level (e.g., safety, security, acceptance). We have observed in a number of cases that in such situations there is early compromises in distinguishing and communicating basic affective meanings.

It is further hypothesized that the environment which will bring out this underlying constitutional–maturational deficit early in life overwhelms the vulnerable sensory pathway (in this case, the auditory–vocal–verbal one). In subsequent developmental stages the "high-risk" environment for disorders of thought tends to confuse the meaning of affective communications. For example, in infancy this high-risk environment would tend to speed up rather than slow down vocalizations and increase the variation and novelty so rapidly that the infant would have trouble becoming familiar with any one pattern. In the second and third years of life, this same high-risk environment would keep overwhelming the youngster's auditory–vocal–verbal–symbolic ability in other ways, namely, through confusing gestures and meanings. A number of years ago, investigators such as Jackson (1960), Lidz (1973), and Wynne, Matthysse, and Cromwell (1978) discussed schizophrenogenic families and their confusing patterns of communication, but they did not focus equally on the type of child who was vulnerable to such patterns or who might even inadvertently cause the family to accentuate them. Family members can become so anxious with an infant who is not processing their verbal or gestural cues that, in trying harder, they become more overwhelming and confusing. At the gestural and then symbolic or representational level, this may lead to confusion between what are the parent's feelings or ideas and the child's at a time when a representational sense of self and other is in potential formation. One day the child's aggression is aggression; the next day it is love; or one day it is "my feeling" and the next day it is "your feeling." In such circumstances, even a competent child's ability to appropriately label and organize experience along the dimensions of self and nonself, and in terms of different thematic and affective proclivities (i.e., being able to identify dependency, pleasure, aggression, assertion, curiosity, love, etc.) may be compromised. The paradigmatic high-risk environment for a child with an auditory sequencing problem, therefore, is one that further compounds the child's constitutional–maturational difficulty in abstracting affective meanings. The result is impairments at three levels: somatic–sensory, gestural, and representational–interpretative.

It is not surprising that such a child, as an infant, may turn away from the human world, confused by auditory and auditory–vocal–affect signals. Compromises may follow in presymbolic reciprocal cause-and-effect interaction patterns, the ability to organize affect and behavior, and the formation of a functional (conceptual) self (also prerepresentational). If, subsequently, the representational interpretive system is not able to organize these earlier fragmented developmental patterns, the combination of sensory–affective sequencing and representational limitations may result in a variety of deficits in organizing behavior, affect, and thinking.

CLINICAL EXAMPLE

Michael was the product of a seemingly normal pregnancy and delivery; a thin, but otherwise healthy, twenty-two-inch, six-pound, eight-ounce infant. He appeared very competent because of his extraordinary visual interest in the world. He focused on mother's face and brightened to her smiles, even in the first few days. Motorically and physically, he seemed to be progressing. In response to vocalizations, however, he seemed to look blank and confused. Hearing examinations were unremarkable. His visual interest and ability to focus on his mother's and father's smiles, and on inanimate objects, seemed so extraordinary that there was little attention paid to the fact that he was not equally responsive to vocal patterns. In fact, during one of the early assessments, if the examiner tried to gain his attention while he was looking at a bright object by talking to him from the side, his attention to the sound of her voice would only be fleeting, and he would return to his visual interests. If the examiner caught his attention and started making animated facial expressions, however, his interest in the examiner would persist. It seemed clear that he was using vision to an extraordinary degree to understand his world.

His parents were well-intentioned, motivated, successful professionals who were also extremely anxious and controlling. They had little tolerance for anything other than "following the rules." They took great interest in his precocious development, in terms of his ability to examine objects and see how they worked. Frequently, they claimed they had a "brilliant young child."

In the first months of life, mother dealt with his unresponsiveness to her vocalizations by focusing completely on his visual interest in objects. She would try to get him to do exactly what she wanted. She ignored the fact that he had little emotional range, only evidencing shallow smiles now and then, and that she was not getting feedback for her own vocal emotional communications.

This family moved away, but fortunately moved back into the area before his fifth birthday. When we saw him at age five, he was a tall, thin, healthy-looking child, who scored extremely well on all the intelligence tests. On the clinical examination, however, he related all too quickly with the clinician, putting his arm on the clinician's arm within the first few minutes. He talked clearly, quickly, and spontaneously about school, his parents, and his activities of the day, in a rambling, free-associative style. While he seemed quite sophisticated for a five-year-old, there was little logic or coherence to his stream of interesting anecdotes. Each one, however, did have a certain internal consistency.

As the interviewer empathized with his verbal abilities and interest in describing his day, he confided to the interviewer that he actually had "more exciting experiences." He then went on to talk about his relationship with "underwater creatures" and his "extraordinary powers," in that he can talk to people through his thoughts without speaking. As his ongoing delusional system emerged, he insisted that this material be confidential. If his parents knew about it, they would think he was "crazy." He did not have friends, felt "different" from the other kids, and related more to his teacher and inanimate objects in the schoolroom than to other children.

The initial impression of this child was that his emerging delusions and intrusion of primary processing thinking would be correctable with intensive psychotherapeutic work. This view was supported by his considerable strengths, including his capacity to relate to the interviewer, organize his behavior and aspects of his thoughts, his brightness, interest in talking about his experiences, and, most importantly, his sense of perspective ("I'm different," "My parents would think I'm crazy"). The organization of his representational world was not fully differ-

entiated, according to real–unreal or self–other, even though
he had an extraordinary capacity for representational elaboration.

In this case, we were impressed with the fact that an early
circumscribed difficulty in auditory affective processing preceded a later difficulty in the organization of thought and affect
along self–other dimensions. That the environment accentuated rather than ameliorated the early vulnerability was also of
special interest.

In contrast to the high-risk environment for this
constitutional–maturational vulnerability, consider the intuitively gifted environment. This environment helps the child
organize early experience by using the intact sensory pathways
(e.g., vision, touch, smell, proprioception, etc.). It does not
overwhelm the auditory–vocal processing capacities. It, instead
provides individually tailored, age-appropriate experiences for
developing early regulation and interest in the world, a satis-
factory attachment, reciprocal cause-and-effect interactions,
and organized functional, behavioral, and affective patterns. It
accomplishes this by offering and engaging in experience
through the well-functioning sensory pathways. It also intuitively remediates the auditory system by slowing down and
offering extra repetition rather than excessive novelty (in
essence, it keeps the child at a particular stimulus configuration
until the child seems to understand it). Later, at the gestural
and representational levels, the family is empathic to the child's
meanings, communicates clearly in each thematic affective area
(dependency, pleasure, assertion, curiosity, setting one's own
limits, etc.), facilitates the child's differentiating feelings and
thought of the self and nonself, and sets effective limits. It
provides practice, so to speak, in helping the child develop the
representational ability that may be especially helpful in interpreting sensations from within, sensations that may be confusing because of the early difficulties in processing auditory
information. In the optimal case, the environment ameliorates
the early sensory decoding difficulty, strengthens sensory processing in other modes, and supports a representational inter-

pretive system that can use higher level abstractions to make sense, even out of a "somatic underbelly" which tends to send up confusing sensations.

AFFECTIVE DISTURBANCES

It is hypothesized that whereas "thought disorders" emanate from an underlying constitutional–maturational vulnerability in auditory–vocal–verbal processing, affective disorders emanate from an underlying constitutional–maturational vulnerability in visual–spatial processing and integration which has as a feature of its pattern a vulnerability in affective and behavioral regulation.

Visual–spatial processing ability in infancy, it is further hypothesized, is related more to the perception of the intensity of affect than its meaning. Affective meanings in this model are communicated predominately through the auditory–vocal–verbal channel, whereas intensity of affect is communicated more through the visual–spatial pathway. In other words, one understands whether someone is happy or sad through the sequencing of vocal patterns, but one understands the intensity of affect through how one organizes what one sees in space. There is emerging evidence for part of this hypothesis from work with six- to eight-month olds. The auditory–vocal pathway seems more essential for identifying sad and happy affects than does the visual pathway (Caron and Caron, 1982). Documenting that the visual–spatial pathway is used for the perception of affect intensity requires further research.

Just as a child learns to sequence various auditory–vocal signals and construct a pattern to maintain these in relationship to one another and examine them, the child also learns to sequence and organize visual–spatial experiences in order to make sense of the visual–spatial world. For example, one of the earliest experiences of a newborn infant is to recognize the configuration of the human face and to compare one visual configuration with another. This involves spatial relationships between the mouth, nose, eyes, the differences between a smile and a frown, and so forth (Caron and Caron, 1982).

The capacity for abstracting visual features of the inanimate and animate world is present quite early in the first year of life. By the second and third years, children are able to experiment in space by constructing various simple visual–spatial configurations (e.g., towers, a line of blocks to represent a train, simple closures such as a fenced-in area for the animals), and by the fourth and fifth years, children can construct complex interrelated spatial configurations (e.g., houses which are connected by bridges, drawings of houses with rooms, windows, and interconnecting doors). In other words, children organize spatial relationships much as they organize auditory–vocal–verbal symbols. Some children develop more rapidly in one sphere and others more rapidly in the other.

Visual–spatial capacities, however, may be fundamental for both abstracting intensity and other high-level order pattern abstractions, and in this context, the visual–spatial domain is different in some respects from the auditory–vocal–verbal domain. The visual–spatial domain is a continuous rather than discrete space (e.g., number sequences or various spaces under a changing line representing intervals are on a continuous dimension). Auditory–verbal space, in contrast, tends to be discrete or segmented (e.g., each word has its meaning). Verbal symbols can form classes, but the words and classes are usually still relatively discrete rather than part of continuous categories. In part because of their continuous properties, spatial configurations lend themselves both to abstracting the dimension of intensity, which is also a continuous dimension (as compared to the dimension of meaning which is segmental), and other higher order abstractions or patterns, as in mathematics. It may be that the visual–spatial mode is necessary for constructing higher order organizations of the self and nonself and that without this capacity, the sense of self and other, by necessity, is more concrete and potentially more fragmented.

Consider a hypothetical infant who has difficulty in abstracting the properties of his physical space and finds it difficult to regulate his state, motor behavior, and affect patterns. Although many babies may be labile in the first few weeks or even months of life, our prototypical infant does not evidence increasing regulation and organization. Instead of looking into his caregiver's eyes and finding solace in her animated facial expression, he continues to rev up when overly excited. He looks left, right, up, and down, often past his caregiver. When looking at his caregiver's face, he is unable to abstract enough of a pattern in the caregiver to use it for self-comfort and self-organization. As he develops he is further unable to determine or organize into a pattern his caregiver's or his own affect and behavioral intensity because of his lag in abstracting interactional spatial–affective patterns. This is an example of an early constitutional–maturational pattern in which the ability to use the visual–spatial system to regulate and organize state, affect, and behavior is not well developed.

What is the prototypical high-risk environment for this type of constitutional–maturational vulnerability? Here the high-risk environment is not one of confused meanings,but one where there is a failure of empathy, regulation, and effective setting of limits. Consider the following developmental sequence. Assume this infant has formed an attachment, be it somewhat chaotic, as he experiences difficulty in calming down and controlling his own affect and motor discharge patterns. Also assume that as he progresses into the four- to eight-month phase, he learns cause-and-effect communications when not over-excited. There is a blurring of cause-and-effect patterns, however, when he is revved up. He easily becomes chaotic, and in a sense overwhelms any cause-and-effect interactions offered by the caregiver. In addition he has difficulty abstracting the spatial patterns he does engage in. In the second year, his parents have difficulty understanding the intensity of his affect and motor discharge tendencies. For example, when he cries, he does so inconsolably for a half-hour, and his parents are unsure whether to "ignore him," or "indulge him," and feel a mixture of anger, fear, and concern and also feel overwhelmed.

It is not an uncommon tendency, even for parents who feel confident with an easier child, to find it difficult to empathize with such a child's discomfort. There is often a tendency to become mechanical and even aloof. Competent parents who are organized along obsessive–compulsive lines may vacillate; one day they try to wait the child out and not spoil him, hoping the intense crying and discomfort will stop by itself. Another day, overwhelmed and exhausted, they try indulging him. This vacillation may be experienced by the toddler as a lack of empathy, and perhaps at times as a lack of feeling connected to his human environment.

Not infrequently, as with older children and adults, this sense of not being empathized with and feeling unconnected may lead the child to "rev up" even more. It is as though the toddler himself tries to generate the affect necessary to create a feeling of well-being. Initially, this hypomanic style is used partially in the service of reassurance. In a way, the child is saying to himself, "If they can't make me feel good, I'll try to create this good feeling all by myself." A type of denial is operating. The child's own revving up is to create a false sense of bliss and to ignore the lack of appropriate empathy. The deficit (limit-setting) with such a child, which is part of the empathic failure, is related to the expectable inconsistency one often sees when parents try to discipline a very difficult child. Furthermore, his difficulty in comprehending affective intensity and spatial–affective relationships (e.g., dependence and independence) further accentuates this pattern.

The child with a lag in visual–spatial abstracting ability is now in a situation of double indemnity, so to speak. He has difficulty abstracting, comprehending, and organizing affect intensity because of a visual–spatial processing lag. Yet he finds himself in an environment where the shifts in affect intensity are increasingly overwhelming his vulnerable capacity.

If the caregivers themselves have difficulty in modulating affect, the problems are compounded. They rapidly shift from states of extreme indulgence to withdrawal, and from concrete limit-setting to excessive permissiveness, all of which only further accentuate the child's basic difficulty in regulation.

Project this environment into the third and fourth years of life when the representational system is becoming formed. Assume that this child has enough adequate caregiving experiences to form symbolic and representational capacities. One may observe a developmental sequence where meanings are sharply demarcated but where interpretations of affect intensity are distorted. The child who already tends toward poor control of affect expression (i.e., every minor frustration is a major calamity) is now part of a family where distortions of affect intensity are present. His own difficulty is therefore intensified. The child may construct new affect states in order to feel connected and maintain a sense of well-being. At the representational level, the child is able to construct not only new complex feeling states, but to give meanings to these feelings. As a result, he may further distort his own and others' affect intensity.

The deficit is visual–spatial pattern abstraction may limit the child in another way that is consistent with what is observed in affective disorders. The deficit in higher order pattern recognition and organization will limit the formation of representational capacities. This limitation will occur in the organization of an affective self and object. Instead of organized, integrated self and object representations, there may be concrete islands of self and object representations governed by discrete affect states (e.g., the sad or depressed self, the hypomanic self, etc.), each one with little relational connection to the other. In this situation, the self is not fragmented at the level of meanings but in terms of affect proclivities. Clinically, one is impressed that adults with affective disorders are concrete in terms of understanding emotional patterns (their own and others), in spite of their brilliance in other spheres of endeavor.

The tendency of the self to be fragmented leaves the organization of a sense of self vulnerable to affect intensity and stress, especially the stresses of loss or over excitement. In this context it is interesting to consider the etiology of depressive symptoms. Perhaps they are not a direct response to loss or an underlying biological vulnerability which interacts with loss or other stresses. Perhaps depressive symptoms (or even manic symptoms) are secondary phenomena. The symptoms occur because of one internal loss of the self or object representation. Similar to anaclitic depression in a baby who losses its real object, the individual losses the internal representation of an object and then has secondary symptoms. Even when there are biological predispositions toward depression, in this model, the mediating process would be the inability to conserve the image of the internal self or object representation, or self-object representation based on a vulnerability in visual-spacial processing.

CLINICAL EXAMPLE

Molly was a robust,extremely alert, eight pound infant with good muscle tone, a voracious appetite, an unusual ability to "tune into" sounds, and according to her mother, a "willfulness you wouldn't believe." She was very difficult to console after crying for long periods of time and took little solace from looking at her mother's smiling face. Mother described a pattern where, "I could never get into rhythm with her"; "When I wanted to hug her, she wanted to pull away"; "When I was busy she would pull on my nose or poke her hand in my eye." By the time she was eight months old, her behavior was characterized by rapid fluctuations in mood, being upset, gleeful, calm, or fussy. When she was vocalizing or reaching, her behavior was more random than purposeful and lacked a sense of a synchronous fit. Interestingly, she seemed to decode sounds and even words very well. She listened carefully, and by fourteen months could follow simple instructions if they were associated with something she wanted, such as a certain food. For example, when her mother said, "Come into the kitchen for a cookie," she would come rapidly. She had a precocious mastery of simple words.

At the same time, however, she seemed to have difficulty in the visual–spatial domain. Making faces or using motor gestures rarely had impact, as though these were harder for her to decipher. Also she would become confused in new settings about how rooms were connected and frequently would wind up crying rather than being able to retrace her steps and find her mother. Her ability to organize space seemed to lag behind her considerable verbal abilities.

Her father tended to absent himself from the family through twelve-hour workdays, and mother, while very attentive, vacillated between states of depression and frenetic activity when she felt "hyper." With Molly she said, she could never tell "what she was feeling," and always felt "guilty I wasn't doing enough," so she never set limits. Molly by eighteen months was "running the house." There were limitations in both empathy and limit-setting.

After no contact, mother brought Molly in at age seven and a half for a clinical evaluation because of "rapid mood changes," demanding behavior, and problems with friends and with school. At this time Molly appeared to be a healthy, well-coordinated, articulate seven and a half-year-old who evidenced an extremely intense quality of relatedness. But she also evidenced a great deal of affect lability, was impulsive, often fragmented in her thinking (staying on each subject for only a few seconds), and deeply concerned with themes of loss, rejection, and humiliation. Dynamically she seemed to operate according to the principle: "I will hurt your feeling and reject you before you can hurt or reject me." A false sense of bravado permeated her words and behavior and only intensified her tendency toward fragmented feeling states, thought patterns, and behaviors. The impression was of primary difficulties in affective and behavioral regulation and organization, not unlike affective disorders in adults.

In contrast to the high-risk environment, consider what would be an optimal environment for this constitutionally and maturationally at-risk child. In infancy, the intuitively gifted caregiver uses soothing vocalizations (appealing to the infant's strength) to help calm the infant when he is excessively excited. He learns that affect and motor discharge can be regulated, particularly with the help of auditory–vocal and other sensory pathways and motor control (e.g., being held tightly and later by working with the child on motor exercises to provide a sense of regulation and organization in space).

The optimal environment balances a sense of empathy (the difficult task of feeling the distress of the out-of-control child when he is excessively excited) with the firm and consistent setting of limits. The latter is achieved by limiting disorganized motor activity in infancy and later on by providing an extraordinary affective holding environment and setting firm limits on impulses and excessive demandingness. Therefore, the toddler going out of control may be talked to, or engaged in one way or another, and held when necessary to help him regain control. Sometimes the limit-setting will demand extraordinary conviction and follow-through. Consistency, empathy, and limit-setting take the place of inconsistency, vacillation, and failures or empathy. A key issue is to always increase empathy and limit-setting together rather than the more common practice where one becomes polarized into only giving in or having power struggles. Later on, at the representational level, the same gifted environment places special emphasis on helping the youngster understand the intensity of feelings. Caregivers work with the child through this intact and highly developed auditory–vocal–verbal pathway to understand gradations of feeling intensity through a focus on the subtlety of meanings. For example, they help him describe, represent, verbalize, and play out degrees of feelings (e.g., very upset, a little upset, a tinge upset; pleased, happy, excited; a little sad, very sad; mixed feelings). Even though the sense of continuity of feeling based on the spatial dimension is relatively less developed, extra pretend play can be critical in facilitating this ability. Segmented verbal meanings are used in a novel way to communicate gradations of feeling.

The issue of delay is difficult for a child with an affect regulation problem. Here it might be reasoned that a visual–

spatial difficulty (being able to organize the world according to spatial configurations) is closely related to a difficulty in temporal sequencing (how the world works in time). The sense of time is probably more closely allied with a visual–spatial pathway than the auditory–vocal–verbal pathway because the time dimension can be more easily understood along a continuous space than it can with more discrete segmented auditory–symbolic–verbal abstractions. Interestingly, music may have elements of both continuous spatial and verbal meaning. Time and learning how to delay, however, can also be taught in the auditory–verbal mode through creating ordinal sequences (i.e., less than/more than types of perspectives). In addition, visual–spatial configurations can be practiced through interactions and games involving affect intensity, building, drawing, and coordinated motor patterns. While structured activities can be helpful, spontaneous pretend play and verbal–affective interactions often provide the best bases for learning the needed new representational abilities.

The overall goal is to help this type of at-risk child learn how to identify and respond to patterns (see the forest for the trees), because he tends to get overwhelmed by the moment-to-moment meanings. This is no easy task, because over focusing on the "big picture" will be experienced as a lack of empathy. Empathizing with a child's hurt at being rejected by a peer, for example, must come first. But eventually it is important to help that child see the larger pattern of acceptance and rejection that occurs as part of his peer relationships. Helping the child see the larger pattern, even when upset, strengthens the child's capacity to offset the primary vulnerability in visual-spacial processing and construct a stable, affectively integrated internal self-object representation. The symptoms of affective disturbance, be they sadness, low self-regard, and apathy, or agitation, euphoria, and speeded-up thinking, may, as indicated earlier, be a secondary reaction to the primary one involving spatial processing capacities. As internal representations are fragile (they lack the spatial and temporal stability), there is always a danger of loss and separation, not from an external object, but from the internal representation of one. Of course, real separations or other stresses (loss of self-esteem, anger, etc.) will also undermine a fragile internal structure. The reaction to this internal loss may be dysphoric affect and associated symptoms (depression or mania). In this view, the dysphoric affect is secondary to a primary disturbance in visual-spatial processing that undermines the capacity to construct a spatially and temporally stable and affectively integrated self and object representation. It is the loss of the internal representation that then leads to the familiar symptoms. It would be of interest to see if biological findings on affective disturbance could be more usefully organized in relationship to this hypothesized underlying perceptual difference than in relationship to specific symptoms. It is also of interest that cognitive behavioral therapy, certain forms of dynamic therapy, and biological treatments all do reasonably well with certain types of depressive symptoms. Perhaps, in one way or another the underlying capacity to process and abstract a stable, affectively internal self-object representation is supported in all these approaches.

THE MILDER FORMS OF THESE DISORDERS AND THE STRUCTURE OF SELECTED EGO DEFENSES: OBSESSIVE–COMPULSIVE, HYSTERICAL, AND PHOBIC PATTERNS

It is interesting to speculate on the milder forms of these disturbances. The milder form of an auditory–vocal–verbal–affective processing difficulty, it is hypothesized, would tend to be associated with the severe obsessive–compulsive character disorders. The milder form of the visual–spatial–affective difficulty would tend to be associated with the hysterical personality disorders. These character structures are prototypes for a variety of defenses and symptom patterns. As with the more severe disorders, these nonpsychotic disorders may also have prototypical environmental contributions in addition to underlying constitutional–maturational patterns.

The reasoning behind these hypotheses is as follows: The obsessive–compulsive who is functioning reasonably well uses isolation of affect as a major defense. The obsessive–compulsive experiences the content of his internal life. He can discuss almost any idea or feeling intellectually but simply does not experience the feelings. The isolation of affect is often related to the presenting complaints (e.g., marital problems where his wife complains that he has no feelings, or depression and having no sense of joy). In addition, the obsessive–compulsive often has extraordinary abstracting ability. The developmental sequence may be as follows: There is an auditory sequencing difficulty early in life, which either is not severe or is not accentuated by the environment (perhaps even ameliorated). In order to compensate for this mild auditory–vocal–verbal sequencing difficulty, the obsessive uses his relative strength in the visual–spatial area. He may be gifted in seeing or abstracting patterns, which is a visual–spatial challenge. He therefore constructs higher-level patterns of verbal symbols and operates in the abstract mode as a way of trying to figure out the simple emotional puzzles of life, which unfortunately for him are less than obvious. In spite of his abstracting ability, he has difficulty in sequencing the concrete aspect of auditory–vocal–verbal life. Because the sequencing of simple auditory signals is related to the detection of the meaning of affect, he has difficulty understanding basic meanings such as pleasure, dependency, warmth, and love (i.e., abstracting and labeling, though these affects are all experienced in a presymbolic way much earlier). Yet he can construct the higher order abstract categories and even philosophize about simple feelings that are not felt because his underlying vulnerability in auditory sequencing is part and parcel of his isolation of affect. Therefore, isolation of affect may be related to a lack of ability to decode simple affective meanings. The degree to which a person substitutes higher order abstractions related to his intact visual–spatial abstracting ability, as part of his compensation for the lag in the auditory–verbal area, is often related to specific conflict and anxieties, namely, those which challenge him to find internal representational solutions or compromises. These invariably call forth the specific tools one has for higher-level integrations and synthesis, and these tools are based on one's constitutional tendencies and early experiences. The absent-minded professor who is lost in abstract scholarly activities or the harried business executive who finds it difficult to deal with the emotional aspects of family life, are typical examples of this type of character structure.

Obsessive compulsive symptoms have also been discussed in a group of patients who respond selectively to a few relatively new antidepressants. From in-depth clinical work, these patients' ego structure, however, seem to resemble the affective disorder continuum more than the obsessive-compulsive, schzoid, thought disorder continuum. Shifting mood states, extreme sensitivity to interpersonal cues, and a tendency to become overwhelmed and preoccupied with fragmented self-object patterns, doing and undoing, rejections, anticipated failures, ominous forecasts or guilty feelings and not being able to see the forest for the trees (a visual spacial processing deficit) characterize some of these patients. The obsessive-compulsive symptoms in these patients are often driven by their labile moods and anxieties and do not appear to be related to isolation of affect.

The hysterical personality, in contrast to the obsessive, uses denial of content (i.e., repression) as a major defense. The hysteric has no difficulty discussing many different feelings with extreme intensity, but does have difficulty revealing the full content or pattern. Why he is so upset, excited, depressed, or aroused is never fully clear to the hysteric. He has pieces of the puzzle but never the whole puzzle. His overly dramatic, theatrical posture is not matched by the ability to abstract the patterns of content that would explain such ranges of feelings.

The hysteric's presenting complaints are often related to his inability to abstract the pattern of ideas related to his feelings. Such people often come in with depression, fear, anxiety, panic reactions, and the dilemma of feeling totally overwhelmed by feelings. Yet they have little idea of the basic pattern of issues or content that is troubling them, even though they provided detailed "blow by blow" accounts of their lives.

The hysteric, it is proposed, is on a continuum with the affective disorders. The basic deficit is in the visual–spatial organizing capacity (a deficit in abstracting patterns). These individuals may have extraordinary auditory–vocal–verbal sequencing abilities which allow them to experience the moment-to-moment meanings of affect (i.e., the feelings). In other words, there is a great awareness and decoding of the moment-to-moment emotional intent of themselves and others. What is lacking, however, is the ability to abstract these into higher order patterns (i.e., they cannot see the forest for the trees). They cannot organize spatially related abstractions and construct a sense of self that operates over time in various patterns with others. They are victims of the moment-to-moment meanings of their affective states.

Along these lines it is interesting to observe the hysteric's tendency to use body gesturing and posturing (i.e., motor patterns) for conveying affect. An area that is vulnerable, namely, the regulation of motor patterns and spatial gesturing, is used in an exaggerated way, much as the obsessive uses verbal abstracting to an excessive degree.

Phobic patterns are often also related to visual spatial sequencing differences. They may in addition, however, be related to difficulties in the regulation of the body in space. In addition to auditory and visual–spatial sequencing difficulties, the earlier discussions of the sensory basis of ego development also discussed hypo- and hypersensitivities to movement in space, postural insecurity, and motor planning difficulties (see chapter 1). To further consider Freud's goal of teasing out the biological constitutional contributions to the defenses of the ego, it is interesting to speculate about vulnerabilities in regulation of one's own body in space (the infant who craves or is overly scared of being held out and moved horizontally or vertically as part of robust play). These constitutional patterns may become intensified if with movement-fearful infant, the environment either avoids spatial movement or overwhelms him with movement, or with the movement-craving infant, the environment fails to teach self-control. It may be that this type of vulnerability is associated with a tendency toward phobic and counterphobic defenses, where displacement, projection, avoidance, or counterphobic behaviors are prominent. Defenses obviously involve complex psychological processes. These hypothesized physical contributions are suggested as only one aspect of this process. The physical and psychological processes may interact in the following manner. Phobic patterns are related to a vulnerability in integrating one's own body in space; that is, an increased likelihood of fragmentation or compartmentalization of "body space." This vulnerability has its roots in observable patterns in infancy (i.e., of hypo- or hyperreactivity to movement in space). On the one hand, the fact that the phobic creates meanings for physical spaces or objects and then avoids these spaces or objects is a sign of displacement and/or projection with avoidance. On the other hand the individual's organization of his physical world in space can be too easily fragmented and compartmentalized and thereby given ideosyncratic nonintegrated meanings. It was never well integrated in the first place. To the degree the ego organizes integrated, differentiated structures of self and object representations in time and space, it perhaps is resiliant to compartmentalization or fragmentation. To the degree the ego does not fully organize or differentiate a certain dimension of experience, perhaps there is a greater tendency to use that dimension of experience to deal with anxiety (i.e., for defensive purposes).

Therefore it may prove interesting to consider the basic proposition that differences in early sensory processing, integration, and differentiation, contribute, in highly specific ways, to characteristics of the ego and its tendency to employ certain defenses (when specific pathogenic environmental experiences are present). (1) auditory–verbal–affective vulnerabilities may be associated with disorders of thought and obsessive–compulsive patterns; (2) visual–spatial–affective vulnerabilities may be associated with disorders of affect regulation and hysterical patterns; and (3) spatial, motor movement (vestibular) vulnerabilities may be associated with phobic and/or counterphobic tendencies. These hypotheses are sufficiently specific and testable to lead to new research opportunities.

THE NATURAL HISTORY OF THE DISORDERS AND THEIR ONSET

If these hypotheses are correct, important questions remain: Why does the clinical onset of many thought and affective disturbances often not occur until later childhood, adolescence, or certain stages of adulthood? Shouldn't the clinical onset of these disorders always be gradual from early childhood?

To answer these important questions, one must consider three possible precipitants of the manifest version of these disturbances. The precipitants include cognitive changes, psychosocial challenges, and neuroanatomical and neurochemical shifts during the course of development. These precipitants are often interrelated. Cognitive shifts make possible new psychosocial challenges and are undoubtedly related to shifts in underlying brain structure and chemistry. Nevertheless, each may be considered independently.

Consider the example of the child with difficulty in sequencing auditory–vocal–verbal symbols. As he gets older, this child has trouble maintaining verbal–affective symbols in juxtaposition and examining the functional relationships between them. In general, the child with an auditory–verbal sequencing deficit has difficulty creating what might metaphorically be viewed as a lattice structure of his auditory–vocal–verbal organization of self and object representations. In addition, various self and object affect proclivities from dependency and pleasure up to assertiveness and aggression are also organized according to auditory–vocal–verbal symbols. Assume, however, that these aspects of the lattice structure are vulnerable because the child had difficulty sequencing and therefore creating the relational bridges that form the lattice. Assume also that the child is able to hold the lattice together, but just barely. The severity of the organizational deficit may be based on the severity of the early sequencing difficulty and the environmental accommodation to it.

In this hypothetical case he can make sense out of some relationship patterns with one or two friends, for example. But he continually becomes confused over the meaning of either his own or their emotional expressions. He is often not sure whether he has a feeling or someone else has the feeling, and whether people like him or hate him, admire him or pity him. This child progresses up the developmental ladder shakily. Then because of cognitive advances in midadolescence, he becomes capable of hypothetical deductive thinking. He not only tries to understand relationships in the present but also in terms of future probabilities. This cognitive advance is usually a great boon to most children, even though it does make them anxious to consider their own future.

But what does this advance do to a child who had a lattice structure that can barely hold onto and examine verbal–affective symbolic relationships in the present? The system may become overwhelmed. A metaphor would be a computer program that can do cross-sectional tasks, which suddenly is given future information. Either the information is ignored or the system becomes overloaded and breaks down. The attempts of adolescents to create superabstract systems in their delusions can be partly understood as an unsuccessful attempt to organize new information. As the barely held together relational structure of verbal symbols is overloaded, the former organization of self and nonself and organization of various affect proclivities may become fragmented. Islands of delusional thinking or even hallucinations are not a surprising result. Interestingly, tangential thinking, certain types of delusions and hallucinations, all involve deficits in the ability to organize auditory–verbal–affective information along the self–nonself, temporal, and spatial dimensions. Therefore, a cognitive advance can overwhelm the system.

From a psychosocial perspective, it is not infrequent that

breakdowns in ego functioning occur at the end of adolescence as teenagers attempt to separate from parents and become more independent. It is often thought that they are reworking earlier separation–individuation issues. It is not unreasonable to assume that a fragile representational organization of the self and nonself (in the verbal–affective domain), and related affective self–object proclivities, can be organized in the auditory–verbal–affective symbolic domain by the presence of a continually affirming object, even if that object is viewed ambivalently. The ability to hold onto the representation of the object, in the absence of the object, may not be well established because of the underlying auditory–verbal symbolic sequencing deficit. The latter makes the organization of the internal object representation as a series of interrelated verbal symbols (in terms of affective meaning), fragile. An impending or real separation undermines the opportunity for concrete holding on. The fact that one often sees ambivalence is not surprising. The underlying anxiety and sense of disillusion leads to fear, rage, a sense of being engulfed, and feelings of boundary diffusion between the self and object.

Biological shifts are poorly understood during the course of development, including exactly when different central nervous system (CNS) tracts complete their myelinization and when and how accompanying neurochemical changes occur. We do know, however, that different systems mature at different times in the course of life up into middle life (ages 40–45) and that they parallel some of the cognitive shifts in late adolescence and adulthood. For example, improvements in certain types of judgment and reasoning ability may be related to the myelinization of certain integrating tracts in midlife. It is possible to assume that CNS biological shifts create the opportunity for new cognitive and psychological experiences, including new affect proclivities, and higher levels of integration and synthesis. Such changes, although usually adaptive, may create new challenges in a person with a vulnerable foundation. The expected extra integrative challenge ironically overwhelms a vulnerable lattice structure. In this context, it will prove inter-

esting to map the cognitive, psychological–affective, and neuroanatomical and neurochemical shifts at each stage and age to
look for relationships that have propensities for types of mental
disorganizations.

The precipitants of affective disturbances may be similar to
those discussed for thought disorders. With affective disturbances, the system is vulnerable because of visual–spatial–affect
organizational deficits. Changes in affect intensity and regulation rather than the meaning of the affect can also be precipitated by new cognitive and psychosocial challenges, as well as
maturing biological systems.

RESEARCH AGENDA

A research strategy to investigate the foregoing hypotheses
would depend on having the technology to assess sensory
processing in the auditory–vocal–verbal–affective symbolic
area and the visual–spatial–affective area during infancy and
early childhood. Furthermore, approaches would be needed to
assess the caregiving environment from the perspective of
either accentuating or ameliorating the auditory–verbal and
visual–spatial organizational differences.

Therefore, the major challenge in testing these hypotheses
is the development of methods to assess affective–thematic and
sensory organizations in distinct clinical populations. There
have been studies of children with psychoses and severe atypical behavior (Hobson, 1986; Shapiro, Sherman, Calamari, and
Koch, 1987) but there have not been specific tools for teasing
out aspects of sensory–affective processing in each modality at
different ages of infancy. We have developed an approach to
the former, the Greenspan–Lieberman Observation System
(GLOS), a system of quantifying indicator behaviors representing clinically relevant features of the infant, caregiver, and their
interaction patterns at each developmental–structuralist organizational level. A description of the system (Greenspan and
Lieberman, 1980), a scoring manual (Poisson, Lieberman and
Greenspan, 1981), reliability studies (Poisson, Hofheimer,

Strauss, and Greenspan, 1983; Hofheimer, Lieberman, Strauss, and Greenspan, 1983), and rules of interpretation (Greenspan, 1983) are now available. Studies and reports of the psychometric properties of the GLOS instrument on approximately 500 dyads are in progress (Hofheimer, Strauss, Poisson, and Greenspan, 1981).

Although developing methods to assess the integrity and organization of infants' sensory processing capacities is obviously a difficult challenge, there are some promising approaches that merit brief comment. The reliance on the voluntary motor performance in relationship to a task which involves sensory discrimination, has limitations because in early infancy there is variability of motor development, which often may be independent of sensory processing abilities. Yet there are promising techniques emerging where the motor task from which sensory processing may be inferred is of minimal complexity, such as sucking behavior or visual preference behavior (Lipsitt, 1966; Caron and Caron, 1982).

Another output from which sensory processing capacities may be inferred involves using the autonomic nervous system as the output behavior and employing a time-series stimulus interrupt model (Campbell and Stanley, 1966). This means looking for deviations in physiological functioning as a way of noting the child's ability to process a particular experience. By using time-series models, such as Box and Jenkins's (1976) ARIMA models, it is possible to detect significant deviations from baseline activity for a given autonomic variable. This approach, suggested by Porges (Greenspan and Porges, 1984) involves using autoregression techniques to model the baseline, using the baseline model to forecast into the future when the stimulus is to be presented, and then setting up confidence intervals around the forecasted value to see if a deviation from the baseline due to the experimental stimulus is statistically significant. This method would lend itself to studying a stimulus challenge in each sensory system with any autonomic variable as an output. Such studies could range from the evaluation of whether an infant has detected and/or habituated to a stimulus, to studies of expectancy and discrimination (where the stimulus configurations presented become gradually more complex). In addition, the stimuli could involve affective animate as well as inanimate types.

In selecting an autonomic output variable, there may be an advantage to selecting one from the parasympathetic nervous system because of the shorter response latency and greater specificity of this system. In this regard, the measure developed by Porges (1983a, b), and Fox and Porges (1983) of heart-rate variability at the respiratory sensory pathway, would be useful to evaluate integration at the brainstem level. Here an extremely promising continuity model, where a component of peripheral physiological activity is presumably a reflection of CNS regulatory capacity, has been developed by Porges (1983b). Individual differences in rhythmic modulation of heart rate appear to be a sensitive index of vagal control of the heart (Porges, 1983a). In applied studies, variations in the rhythmic modulation of heart-applied studies, and variations in the rhythmic modulation of heart-rate, differentiate healthy infants from infants with a compromised nervous system (Porges, 1983a), and are related to the developmental course of cognitive processes (Fox and Porges, 1983). Adjunctive methods, such as brainstem potentials, could evaluate neural transmission of auditory stimuli (Despland and Galambos, 1980). In addition, the coupling between respiratory and heart-rate patterns may also have potential as an individual difference measure of an aspect of CNS integration (Porges, Bohrer, Keren, Cheung, Franks, and Drasgow, 1981). Studies of early processing limitations may also profitably include a search for biochemical correlates of specific sensory and affective thematic organizational limitations. We would expect that particular processing disorders may provide greater specificity for partitioning clinical syndromes than the symptom clusters often used in later childhood and adulthood. The latter may constitute global secondary or tertiary sequelae of a primary defect.

In order to apply and refine methods to detect early limitations in sensory and affective–thematic organizations, the initial selection of the clinical populations is quite important. Often in the study of developmental psychopathology, clinical populations are not selected on the basis of psychopathology, but on a global developmental risk factor for cognitive or neuromotor lags. We would suggest, therefore, that in the selection of initial subjects, an unmistakable psychopathology in infancy be present. For example, two groups that would qualify would be infants with two or more months of an extreme state, and affective lability with chronic panic reactions and clinging behavior, and infants with two or more months of social unresponsiveness including apathy, withdrawal, or avoidance. Potential target pathologies in children between two and four (e.g., withdrawn, autistic types of children and children characterized by panic reaction and unrelenting, clinging behavior) may be intriguing to study for similarities in sensory processing and thematic–affective organization deficits and limitations.

As the underlying mechanisms for processing animate and inanimate information are identified, it would be possible to study with greater specificity the traditional high-risk groups such as small-for-gestational-age babies, low birth weight babies, and offspring of schizophrenics and manic depressives. However, it would be critical in such studies to control for the relative adaptiveness of the caregivers, because the experiential milieu may have the potential to ameliorate or intensify the early disorders.

Animal studies, in which experience can be more readily manipulated, may also prove valuable to refine and test these hypotheses. Two types of experiments should receive high priority. In one type, experience would be manipulated so that one group of animals experienced confusing auditory signals, another group confusing visual signals, and other groups would serve as controls receiving experience as usual. The animals' ability to experience at each developmental phase in the context of expected physiological, social, or interactive behavior for that species would be studied. As it becomes appropriate to sacrifice the animals at various intervals, the neuroanatomical and neurochemical patterns could be studied in relationship to differences in the early sensory environment.

An interesting strategy with nonhuman primates would be to put a device into the animal's ear to distort auditory signals. The device should distort the sequencing of signals and create a random sequence, perhaps similar to that heard by infants who cannot decode or abstract sequences. It would be of great interest to study the effects of this one change in auditory reception on social behavior and the ability to organize experience. In a related experiment, the visual experience of nonhuman primates could be altered through sets of eyeglasses or contact lenses, which would distort visual–spatial experiences. One could then study the effect of this distortion on the regulation of affect intensity, behavior, and motor patterns. The hypothesis is that in the inability to observe the intensity of affective expression through gesturing and other means in peers and in adult animals would lead to a syndrome not unlike affective disorders.

In another series of experiments, nonhuman primates might be bred for genetic loading toward lability in response to separation (thought to be related to affective disorders). It has been hypothesized that this may be similar to a type of affective disorder. Measurements of sensory and affective processing in each sensory pathway and at the midbrain level could then be used to profile individual affect patterns.

In addition, if underlying differences in sensory processing patterns were identified in children at risk for thought and affective disorders, it would then be possible to consider clinical trial preventive–intervention research. Infants at high risk, both from the point of view of underlying constitutional–maturational patterns and environmental patterns for either thought or affective disorders, would receive systematic intervention. Randomly selected comparison groups would receive traditional care. Preventive interventions would be based on the following principles. The intact sensory pathways would be used to communicate appropriate information. Visual, tactile, olfactory, proprioceptive, and vestibular pathways may be used for infants with an auditory processing vulnerability; auditory, tactile, olfactory, and vestibular modes may be used for infants with a visual–spatial processing vulnerability. In addition, the impaired pathway would be slowly remediated through special counseling and instructions to parents or other caregivers, as well as through direct work with the infant. Repetition and slow exposure to the difficult-to-process stimulus configurations, and coupling the difficult-to-process sensory information with similar information using the intact pathways, would be the basis for enhancing the already vulnerable mode. Caregiver counseling would focus on optimizing the environmental conditions necessary for prevention and recovery. They would be helped to provide clear auditory–vocal–verbal– affective meanings in the auditory processing vulnerable group and improved empathy and limit setting in the visual–spatial processing vulnerable group. Family problems that undermined the environment's ability for focusing on intact pathways, working with vulnerable pathways, or providing clear affective meanings, empathy, and limit-setting (e.g., depression, character pathology, marital difficulties, etc.) would be worked with. The hypothesis is that there would be decreases in the incidence of severe psychiatric disturbances in the experimental intervention compared to traditional intervention groups. Furthermore, it would be hypothesized that the more extreme the initial risk, the more robust the effects of the intervention at outcome.

These explicit hypotheses, from a developmental perspective, offer a way of understanding the nature versus nurture arguments about thought disorders and affective illness and ego defenses. They take into account the potential for genetic or constitutional proclivities to operate, not directly, but through their impact on sensory processing and subsequent ego structures. In addition, they focus on the role of specific environment experiences in ameliorating or accentuating the maturational vulnerability.

The sensory, thematic, affective, deviational, and developmental aspects of early ego development have been discussed and a theory suggested of how the ego develops through a series of organizational structures. Freud's goal of pinpointing both biological and experiential contributions to ego formation and the selection and structure of defenses was discussed. Hypotheses were suggested on the relationship between early patterns of sensory processing and reactivity, and the development of ego deficits, character constrictions, and defensive patterns.

Chapter 3

The Application of a Model of Stages in Ego Development to Selected Aspects of Psychoanalytic Theory: Identification, Repression, the Dynamic and Structural Unconscious, Regression, Conflict, and Drive Theory

This chapter will consider selected aspects of psychoanalytic theory which require reexamination in the light of new developmental findings. The concepts to be discussed include identification, repression, regression, conflict and deficit, and the drives.

THE ROLE OF RECIPROCITY AND IDENTIFICATION

The levels of ego development discussed earlier may prove useful in reconsidering the role of identification in structure building. The concept of identification is heavily relied on in psychoanalytic theory. In fact the model of learning often applied to intrapsychic structure formation is one of taking in, or incorporating (a real or metaphorical swallowing of the object as a way of building up one's own internal world). Later identifications (and imitation) are often thought to be built on this oral incorporative pattern. In later childhood, with super-ego and ego ideal development, identification as a way of taking in the other is frequently postulated.

But is the model of taking in the other the most appropriate one? Perhaps another way to consider the building up and organization of internal experience is from the perspective of the infant and young child constantly elaborating, organizing, differentiating, and later transforming *experience*. Experience in this context is always subjective and internal (even when colored by objective reality). How then do early relationships become internalized? It is unlikely they become internalized in the traditional sense of a taking in. Rather, it is likely that the infant experiences himself in a relationship with an other, and as part of the relationship the infant is continually defining himself (at each level of ego organization referred to earlier). For example, a sense of pleasure and joy and eventually a sense of oneself as pleasurable and joyful is developed in part by the reactions and interactive patterns one experiences. Suppose mother is conflicted about joy. When the infant playfully reaches out to play with mothers' hair, she recoils in disquiet. The infant in this situation is likely to feel a variety of unpleasurable affects. Suppose the infant experiments with assertiveness and takes the spoon to feed himself, but this, is viewed as "aggressive," and he is yelled at. His definition of assertive experience will be colored by this reaction. (If an infant could create and use words, perhaps he would sense his adultomorphized sense of confusion and say, "I thought I was asserting myself, but it feels like I was being bad. Maybe assertion is aggressive and bad.")

In these interactions, the infant is defining himself in part by what he initially feels and intends, in part by what his feelings and behavior elicit in others, and what he in turn feels as a consequence of their affects and behaviors. At times this may look as if he is taking in the other, but in fact he simply may be evolving various drive–affect dispositions (e.g., around the themes of pleasure, dependency, assertiveness, curiosity, aggression, etc.) as these domains of experience are experienced in some preliminary form and then are harnessed and refined by the affective tone of his early relationship patterns. To the degree certain drive–affect dispositions are ignored, not perceived, rejected, or aggressively punished, various alternative patterns are developed, including chronic fearfulness, apathy, negativity, protest, and passive compliance (all commonly observed in stressed infants).

The infant's maturational capacities help him continually organize and reorganize "experience." The evolving organization of experience derives from the infant's own tendencies and reactions to others. The degree to which these experiential organizations become experienced as a self or an other (at various organizational levels) depends both on the infant's capacity to differentiate his own behavior and affects from those of others and the degree to which the significant others in his world differentially perceive and respond to the infant's full range of drive–affect colored communications.

Yet, there appears to be that special type of learning where the infant behaves just like his parent. It seems like he is "taking in" the parent. In fact one observes imitative behavior at each level of ego organization. In the first month an infant will stick out his tongue after his parent does. This appears to be a type of reflexive or preadapted perceptual motor schema, constant with what has earlier been referred to as the "somatic stage of learning." The nine-month-old will copy motor patterns including gestures as part of his cause-and-effect interaction patterns. The eighteen-month-old will copy abstracted roles; for example, put on daddy's baseball hat and try to hold the bat. This is consistent with the functional conceptual level of learning. And the two and a half-year-old will imitate a tea party or a space ship race he has observed and take it in new directions, reflecting imitative representational learning. The ability to imitate or copy, therefore, appears to be an important learning tool which can be harnessed by each level of ego organization.

But is imitation a type of oral taking in? Perhaps it is more a perceptual–affective motor capacity that helps a child learn a new behavior quickly. As the child observes a new behavioral and affective pattern, he tries it on for size so to speak. Through his own activity, that is, his continual reexperiencing of it, it becomes part of his experience. This is not a taking in, it is a unique type of perceptual–motor learning which then becomes colored with affect, depending on the child's and the caregiver's responses. If, for example, father thoroughly enjoys junior putting on his baseball cap, junior may feel it is fun to pretend to be like father. If father feels anxious and becomes aggressive, junior may feel it is scary to pretend to be like father. As a four-year-old, junior may even change father's scary behavior through a change of meaning and pretend he is a "nice" Smoky the Bear with a baseball cap on. The wish to copy, not copy, change, or transform experience with a caregiver is part of larger interactive pattern.

How does one account for those seemingly unintegrated aspects of one's self or object representation which is based on some global, often negative feature of an important other, as seen in identification with the aggressor or in the compulsive reenactment of traumatic experiences with the other? In such instances one experiences one's self in an interactive pattern with another. If there is extreme anxiety or fear, however, there is a tendency for there to be a relative dedifferentiation secondary to anxiety. In general, if anxiety is severe enough, it can be disorganizing in terms of the ego's ability to discriminate and categorize. In other words, there is less clarity regarding the boundaries of self and other and the boundaries between various drive–affect dispositions and their thematic derivatives. At the same time, as originally described in the accounts of the repetition compulsion, there is a tendency to replay experiences that are frightening or traumatic as part of an attempt to master and integrate them. The "replay," if not fostering mastery and integration, takes on a life of its own. Therefore, one sees the repetition or replay of experiences organized under states of anxiety or fear (i.e., undifferentiated patterns).

These undifferentiated patterns of experience remain uninte-grated with the rest of the personality, like a foreign body, because of their relative lack of differentiation in comparison to other self–object organizations that are more differentiated.

From this perspective, a seeming identification with the aggressor may have to do with reciprocal experiences of the self and object that are relatively undifferentiated. Because of the lack of differentiation, what is the self and other may change easily or at times become confused. The tendency for abused children to do to others what has been done to them in part reflects the tendency to replay undifferentiated patterns where the self and object representations are easily changed. The fact that most abused children replay both side of their interper-sonal drama further suggests boundary diffusion.

The identifications that characterize superego and ego ideal formation are thought to relate to the resolution of developmental conflicts. Consider another perspective. These developmental conflicts may be hypothesized to serve as moti-vation for the creation of higher-level abstractions to solve what initially seems like an unsolvable dilemma. A successful oedipal resolution is in a sense a high order synthesis of competing self–object representational characteristics abstracted out of their original context into general governing principles. In this view the oedipal boy does not identify with father, he abstracts a higher-level sense of self which includes aspects of his relationship with his father, based on their prior and ongoing experiences. His ability to simultaneously deal with his wishes to be close to mother and father, as well as his competitive strivings and fears in positive and negative oedipal triangles can now all be organized together. Incompatibilities are dealt with through a new sense of relativity.

The resolution of his conflicts, in this context, is only in part a sense of "I will be like Daddy and someday have a wife of my own." It is also, and perhaps more importantly, the ability to hold a series of relative relationships in mind, such as: "I can be competitive with Dad and still love him"; "He can be competi-tive with me and still love me"; "Love and anger can coexist";

"There are degrees and different types of love and anger";
"There is Daddy–Mommy love"; "But there is also father–son
love and mother–son love," and so forth. It is this ability to
construct a series of relative relationships between wishes and
feelings and classify them in different ways that allows the
oedipal child, as he moves through latency to find higher level
synthetic solutions to what initially seems to him to be an
unsolvable dilemma. After all, as a preoedipal and early oedipal
child, he does not have as full a capacity to see how gradations
of wishes and feelings can coexist. "Only one man can be in love
with mother at a time." With such polarized views, the only
solutions are either denial, splitting, avoidance, or grandiosity.
Global quasi-traumatic undifferentiated identifications may occur if new capacities for higher level synthesis are not possible.
Favorable development, however, makes higher level abstraction possible. Out of the construction of relative relationships
and classifications of wishes and feelings there eventually
emerges abstracted principles. From "I can compete with and
love father," emerges an abstracted principle about respecting
and empathizing with authority figures. From a sense of "If I
hurt father, he could hurt me, but if I compete and win at
baseball without hitting him, he will only be a 'little' rather than
'very' mad at me," emerges judgment about internal limits.
Therefore, it is not global identifications that signal an oedipal
(or other stage) resolution, but the ability to construct a higher
level synthesis out of conflict or competing demands (in part
related both to new maturational abilities and experiences).
This new synthesis in turn leads to new abstractions or governing principles.

　　There are now generalized patterns of behavior in a
continuing dynamic relationship to the formative self–object
patterns and their drive–affect dispositions. But these experiential organizations are also sufficiently abstracted from its
origins that they perform functions such as self-limit-setting.

　　Therefore, what appears to be a taking in is, in fact, in the
case of pathologic identifications, a dedifferentiation of self–
object representations, and, in the case of adaptive structure

building, an abstraction of self–object characteristics to a level of function. It is not by chance that superego and ego ideal formation are not fully in evidence until early latency, and often not organized until late latency (ego ideal organization will go through additional reorganization in adolescence). It is in early latency that there is sufficient maturation of the central nervous system (CNS), and is concomitant cognitive growth (i.e., concrete operational thinking) for the ego to have the cognitive tools to construct derivative-expanded representational systems (Greenspan, 1979). Dynamic factors are instrumental in whether the ego uses its tools to resolve conflicts and create new structures under favorable circumstances. It is the nature of the conflicts themselves and the tools the ego has available that determines the solution. Relationships play a role in how the ego resolves conflicts. But it is not identifications that are pivotal, but rather the ego's ability (and motivation) for a "higher" synthesis.

PRIMARY AND SECONDARY REPRESSION AND THE DYNAMIC UNCONSCIOUS AND STRUCTURAL UNCONSCIOUS

The concept of levels of organization of experience provides another way to consider the concepts of repression, and more broadly, qualities of experience such as conscious and unconscious.

Primary repression usually refers to experience which is not remembered because it was never in symbolic form. Secondary repression refers to experience which was in symbolic form and became repressed because of dynamic considerations.

The concepts of levels of learning and levels in the organization of the ego provides the basis to explore another explanatory model. In this model experiences are organized according to the principles of learning and the characteristics of ego organization operative at the time they are learned. There is somatic experience, behavioral experience, functional conceptual experience, simple representational experience, differentiated representational experience, and structural or transformed representational experience. One may postulate a relative degree of "primary" repression between one level of organization and another. The mechanism by which the separation of memories in different states of ego organization occurs, may be understood in part in terms of the related concept of state-dependent learning.

There is some (but not consistent) observations that experiences learned during one mental state (e.g., under drugs, feelings of depression, hypnotic states) are remembered best during that state and only partially if at all remembered in other states of mind (Bower, 1981). Differences in the organization of experience, in terms of level of ego development, as well as differences in affective tone would certainly constitute a type of "state." Therefore the notion that learning which occurs in one "state" tends to remain organized and remembered in the context of that state, and not others, may have application to the concepts of primary repression.

In this model, there is a relative lack of access of experiences between different levels of ego organization. One may go beyond verbal and preverbal experience and consider each of the stages of ego development outlined earlier. For example, differentiated representational experience is (i.e., after age three) much more likely to be remembered than predifferentiated representational experience. Transformed differentiated representational experience after the age of six is more likely to be remembered than differentiated representational experience. Somatic, behavioral, and conceptual levels will likely be the most difficult to recall as they differ in form as well as degree of differentiation. Multiple extended representational organizations (i.e., adolescent level) are most likely to be remembered in adulthood. The closer the information is to one's current ego organization, the more likely information will be remembered. It is as though the "bridges" linking information follow the rules of the organizational level at which the information is learned, and therefore is most accessible in this state of mind. Under special conditions (e.g., hypnosis, drugs, sodium amytal), an earlier state of mental organization may be reproduced. It may be interesting to think of free association as an attempt to return to an undifferentiated representational state of mind, and at times through transference behavioral tendencies, affective tone, and empathetic relatedness, an even earlier somatic and behavioral level. A crucial ability learned in successful psychoanalysis, in this context, may well be to shift states of mind (e.g., from early representational to later representational levels) and create integrated "bridges" between different levels of experiential organization.

Secondary repression may be viewed as a related phenomenon. The traditional notion of "pushing an idea into the unconscious" may be better conceptualized in terms of levels of ego organization. Secondary repression may work as follows. Imagine that learning is occurring at a relatively high level of ego organization. Disruptive anxiety, however, temporarily leads to a regression in terms of the level of ego organization. Therefore, the new "anxious" experiences are learned under an earlier less differentiated ego organization. For example, as anger at a younger sibling leads to feelings of rage and fear of retribution, a seven-year-old experiences disruptive anxiety and regresses momentarily to an undifferentiated representational organization. This experience is organized as part of an undifferentiated representational organization. After the child recovers his usual latency level of ego organization (differentiated and transformed representational level), the feelings toward his sibling are not easily accessible because they reside in a different state of mind. This could well be an explanation for the simple repression seen in hysterical personality disorders.

What then about the need and purpose for a defense such as reaction formation or isolation of affect? There appears to be a general human tendency to make sense out of life at the level of ego organization available. Under the influence of a posthypnotic suggestion, for example, one usually invents a "rational story" to explain the seemingly irrational behavior (e.g., "I touched the top of my head six times because I was feeling for a bump"). The defenses of rationalization and intellectual-ization would certainly fit into this category of trying to "explain."

Defenses such as isolation of affect may well be related to general coping strategies used to deal with conflict or ambiguity. In an earlier section, a model for the selection of defenses was discussed. In this model, the "defense" may already be in place before the secondary repression occurs and may in part be responsible for it. In the above example of the rage against the sibling, suppose the child did not tolerate feelings of anger. In this example, anger against a sibling is not tolerated because in earlier interactions with his parents, this type of aggression was not only forbidden, but representational access to it was limited. There was no parental engagement of this feeling in a representational mode. Only "feeling loving" was encouraged in a representational mode. Feeling angry was engaged behaviorally with withdrawal. Consider further that this child is more oriented toward visual–spatial than auditory–verbal abilities, predisposing him (as discussed earlier) to isolation of affect as a defense. When the rage appears, therefore, there is already a tendency to isolate the affect (e.g., discuss anger philosophically). Only now, because anxiety leads the rage to become "repressed," that is, organized at an earlier level of ego organization, the general tendency to isolate affect and talk of anger in general terms helps to make sense out of vague feelings of ambiguity and distress. The mechanism of secondary repression, it is suggested here, therefore, is not simply a "pushing the rage into the unconscious," but an organization of the "rage" experience at an earlier level of ego organization; the level is, in part, determined by the nature and intensity of the disruptive anxiety. Defenses in this model may set the stage for disruptive anxiety as well as provide a way to deal with the vague sensations only partially available from other states of mind.

This model has interesting implications for traumatic experiences as well. Nightmares and experiences during sleep are at a different level of ego organization than those that occur during awake time. During wakefulness, the intense affect of the dream state may be present but is often only experienced in a vague, yet intense undifferentiated manner, like intense somatic sensations, frightening but hidden from the ego's interpretive power. Different stages of sleep in fact may be viewed in the context of different levels of ego organization (e.g., the differences between REM and deep sleep may correspond to undifferentiated representational levels and prerepresentational somatic and behavioral levels).

In this model, the notion of unconscious processes may be thought of not as simply an undifferentiated organization of experience but existing on many levels. Each level has different organizational characteristics. The levels would include all of those organizations that are not part of or come after the stage of representational differentiation. The levels of unconscious experience would therefore include undifferentiated somatical behavioral levels, differentiated somatic and behavioral levels, and undifferentiated representational levels.

DRIVE REGRESSION

As part of this discussion of traditional ways of thinking about compartmentalizing experience (i.e., primary and secondary repression), it may be useful to also comment on the concept of *regression*. Regression is usually thought of in terms of level of drive development (e.g., regression from oedipal to anal levels, etc.). At times, regression is also viewed in terms of ego functioning (not in terms of levels of organization), but in the context of a breakdown in basic ego functions such as reality testing or impulse control. In its more widely used "drive" context, regression refers to going back to an earlier point (i.e., a fixation point) in psychosexual development. There is an assumption that this earlier point in psychosexual development was part of a *normal* developmental sequence (i.e., oral, anal, phallic–oedipal, etc.). This model was derived from clinical work with neurotic disturbances, character disorders, borderline states, and psychotic phenomena. Patients with these disorders functioned in a regressed manner. From their regressed behavior, wishes, affects, and thoughts, one obtained a picture of a presumed normal aspect of earlier drive development.

It may well be, however, that fixation points are not "normal" early levels of drive organization. Fixation points may represent early deviations in drive–affect disposition in relationship to evolving levels of ego organization. For example, the extremely and chronically negative two-year-old who is already showing behavioral and representational constriction in the elaboration of pleasure and assertiveness may be evidencing a pattern quite different from the age-expected norm. Even if later on this situation improves but then, under the pressure of conflict, there is a regression and the negativism comes out again and leads to a "learning problem in school," it would not necessarily be appropriate to view the negativism as a sign of a normal anal drive organization. Most likely it is a drive and ego organization that has already deviated that becomes part of a regressive pattern. It was perhaps once thought that those early deviations were only manifested in later neurotic structures or ego distortions seen in character disorders. Our observations of infants, however, suggest that these early deviations are clearly seen in one infants behavior, affects and relationship patterns. It is likely that healthy development minimizes fixation points, whereas early intensification, inhibitions, or constrictions are associated with a greater number of fixation points. Later regression, therefore, reveals early and clearly manifested deviations of drive and ego development, not healthy drive development.

CONFLICTS AND DEFICITS

The presumed differences between conflict and deficit models of the mind have led to differences in opinion regarding etiology and treatment of a number of disorders. For example, in conceptualizing narcissistic disorders, Kohut (1971) highlighted deficits (lack of empathy) and focused on the early "lack of a gleam" in the parental eye (i.e., on the missing experience and the sense of loss and rage that follows).

Kernberg (1975) has focused on conflicts, the defense of ego splitting in dealing with primary aggression, and the goal of helping patients integrate aggressive feelings with other feelings. Different treatment approaches have evolved from these different theoretical positions.

A consideration of emotional development in the second year of life may provide useful insights into this controversy. In the early part of the second year the toddler is experimenting with assertiveness and is organizing a higher level behavioral organization, an initiating self. At this time, the toddler is also quite capable of experiencing conflicts between different behavioral tendencies, including the desire to be close and the desire to be independent, anger, the desire to be in control, and the desire for security. As the toddler progresses toward eighteen months, he is able to integrate behavioral polarities, such as passivity and assertiveness, love and hate. Earlier in the second year, there is a normal tendency toward a lack of integration akin to ego splitting. In other words when the thirteen-month-old is angry, it feels as though "he could kill." When the eighteen-month-old is angry, he seems to also know at the same moment that he is angry at mother, that mother is also a figure of love and security. It feels as though he could hit but not kill. Perhaps there is a shift from a normal phase of behavioral ego splitting, or rather lack of integration, to behavioral integration. As this potential shift is becoming possible, however, intense conflict between emotional polarities may maintain the earlier splitting mode. For example, parents may take the child's anger too literally and "blow it up" and not foster comfort and closeness. They undermine the opportunity the child may have to experience anger and love in the same interactive sequence, and therefore the child cannot abstract both as emotions which are part of the human condition. To the degree emotional polarities are seen as separate behavioral self organizations, there is a tendency for conflict to be maintained in a primitive state. One can, in such a situation, observe conflict in formation.

At the same time, we may look at the types of parental

experiences that foster deficits. Withdrawal, rather than engagement, misreading of affective cues, envy rather than admiration, overcontrol and projection rather than empathy, or overexcitement rather than comfort (i.e., the parents are unable to provide the core needed emotional experiences or the integrating emotional experiences) may undermine the toddler's capacity to organize a sense of an organized self. Yet many toddlers are fragmented, negative, angry, or impulsive in part due to their own constitutional maturational tendencies. With such toddlers, even average "expectable" parents would likely get caught up in the child's conflicting needs and therefore fail to provide the necessary relationship and empathetic experiences. Deficits are likely in such circumstances.

How do deficits and conflicts relate to one another? During psychic structure formation there is an intimate interplay between conflicts and deficits and deficits and conflicts at each level of ego organization. Conflicts are not the province of the representational stage, and deficits not the province of prerepresentational levels of ego organization. Severe prerepresentational conflicts invariably create deficits, however subtle (e.g., self-esteem maintenance), because at this stage a conflict will undermine a piece of structure formation. However, deficits invariably create conflicts (the uncontrolled or disorganized rage of the undermined toddler conflicts with his security needs). The lack of structure leaves competing needs unintegrated, unsolved, and therefore exposed and intensified. Therefore clinically one looks for both the deficits and conflicts.

As a potential guide to where to put one's emphasis, the following suggestions may prove useful. Where there is a clear history of sensory reactivity or processing difficulties and/or constitutional maturational difficulties with self-comforting and self-regulation, and a tendency toward aggressive affective or motor discharge, there is a high likelihood the individual will experience prerepresentational conflict at each early level of ego organization. In addition, it is likely that subsequent deficits (if the environment is unable to provide the special needed experiences) will in part be experienced by the individual as secondary to his own primitive (and often negatively perceived) feeling states, including aggression, greed, and overexcitement. It is important, in such cases, to also tease out the constitutional and maturational components so that the individual can see how these contribute to his sense of himself and others. As adults, these individuals often have great fluctuations of mood, affect, and behavior and an underlying sense of "badness."

Individuals who have had good, early regulatory capacities but who, as toddlers, experienced severe parental overcontrol, envy, and/or competition (rather than empathy and admiration) due to parental misperceptions of the toddler's healthy assertiveness are likely to experience their deficits as being due to deficits in the environment, which later in life may be compensated for with a search for the "perfect" environment or partner. These individuals are likely to have more stable narcissistic character traits with an underlying depression, but without a great deal of intense fluctuation of affect and behavior, except in reaction to profound loss, illness, or other experiences which undermine their attempt to find the "perfect" set of circumstances.

While clinical emphasis may in part be determined by the relative degree of the patient's own constitutional maturational contribution and his environment's contribution to his early conflicts and deficits, it is important to highlight that during phases of rapid structure formation, as the ego is developing, deficits and conflicts operate in a chain reaction with each other. Reconstructive work must focus on the relationship between both types of experiences. The inability to create an internal sense of security and self-worth leads to conflicts over aggression and loss. And conflicts over aggression, loss, and security undermine the organization of an internal sense of security. In other words, as structures are forming, intense conflicts undermine their formation, and deficits in structures leave the ego without tools to absorb the flames of conflict, and find higher-level synthesis.

PSYCHOANALYTIC NOSOLOGY

This model of ego development provides a basis for a framework of psychoanalytic psychopathology based on constrictions, deviations, and deficits in ego development. This framework is closely tied to phenomenology rather than unconscious mechanisms, and therefore might provide a useful bridge to psychiatric nosology.

At present psychoanalytic diagnosis is based on the classification of a mixture of phenomena, including unconscious conflicts, defense mechanisms, and aspects of ego and superego structure. A model based on the ego's capacity to organize experience which, at the same time, was consistent with presumed unconscious conflicts would have an important advantage. It would offer a potentially verifiable psychoanalytic nosology (i.e., based on observable phenomenon). This nosology would be tied to explicit hypotheses regarding unconscious conflicts. The distinctively unique features of psychoanalytic inquiry would therefore be maintained.

This model of psychopathology looks at the way the ego organizes experience into adaptive (as outlined earlier) and maladaptive structures. At each level of ego organization certain maladaptive experiential organizations are possible. Deficits in basic ego functions generally derive from failures in organizational adaptations.

There may also be constrictions in the range of experience organized at each level (e.g., no pleasure, no assertiveness, no sense of loss, as seen in character disorders). There may also be encapsulated constrictions relating to narrow bands of dynamically relevant experience (e.g., difficulty with certain types of authority figures, as seen in the neurosis). The following figure (Figure 1) highlights the broad categories of psychopathology that can be related to levels of ego organization (with implications for drive and conflict organizations).

As the figure indicates, these can also be seen in a relative scale of degree of psychopathology. Figure 2 outlines the relationship between the stages of ego development and the maladaptive organization of experience.

FIGURE 1

Scale* **Most Maladaptive**

10

Ego Defects

Basic physical organic integrity of mental apparatus (perception, integration, motor, memory, regulation, judgment, etc.)

Structural psychological defects and defects in ego functions

Reality testing and organization of perception and thought and capacity for human affective engagement

Perception and regulation of affect

Integration of affect and thought

7.5 **Defect in Integration and Organization and/or Differentiation of Self- and Object Representations**

6.5 **Major Constrictions and Alterations in Ego Structure**

Limitation of experience of feelings and/or thoughts in major life areas (love, work, play)

Alterations and limitations in pleasure orientation

Major externalizations of internal events, e.g., conflicts, feelings, thoughts

Limitations in internalizations necessary for regulation of impulses, affect (mood), and thought

Impairments in self-esteem regulation

Limited tendencies toward fragmentation of self-object differentiation

5 **Moderate Constrictions and Alterations in Ego Structure**

Moderate versions of major constrictions listed above

3 **Encapsulated Disorders**

Neurotic symptom formations

Limitations and alterations in experience of areas of thought (hysterical repression, phobic displacements, etc.)

Limitations and alterations in experience of affects and feelings (e.g., obsessional isolation, depressive turning of feelings against the self, etc.)

Neurotic encapsulated character formations

Encapsulated limitation of experience of feelings, thoughts, in major life areas (love, work, play)

Encapsulated alterations and limitations in pleasure orientation

Encapsulated major externalization of internal events (e.g., conflicts, feelings, thoughts)

Encapsulated limitations in internalizations necessary for regulation of impulses, affect (mood), and thought

Encapsulated impairments in self-esteem regulation

2 **Age- and Phase-Appropriate Adaptive Capacities with Phase-Specific Conflicts**

1   **Age- and Phase-Appropriate Adaptive Capacities with Optimal Phase-Expected Personality Flexibility**

Most Adaptive

* This framework may also be used quantitatively. For example, a scale from 1 to 10, as illustrated in this diagram, may be used to reach an approximation of degree of impairment. See column at left (scale), where 10 indicates the most severe psychopathology. It should be noted this particular quantitative scale represents the author's clinical impressions regarding relationships among different levels of impairment, in terms of degree of severity, and is presented for illustrative purposes only.

FIGURE 2

Developmental Levels and Adult Psychopathology

Developmental Structural Levels of Personality Organization	Illustrative Derivative Maladaptive (Psychopathological) Patterns in Adulthood
Homeostasis	Autism and primary defects in basic integrity of the personality (perception, integration, motor, memory, regulation).
Attachment	Primary defects in the capacity to form human relationships, internal intrapsychic emotional life, and intrapsychic structure.
Somatic-Psychological Differentiation	Primary ego defects (psychosis) including structural defects in: (1) reality testing and organization of perception and thought; (2) perception and regulation of affect; (3) integration of affect and thought.
Behavioral Organization, Initiative, and Internalization	Defects in behavioral organization and emerging representational capacities, e.g., certain borderline psychotics; primary substance abuse; psychosomatic conditions; impulse disorders and affect tolerance disorders.
Representational Capacity	Borderline syndromes and secondary ego defects in integration and organization and/or emerging differentiation of self and object representations.
Representational Differentiation	Severe alterations in personality structure.
Consolidation of Representational Differentiation	More moderate versions of the personality constrictions and alterations, for example, character disorders such as moderate obsessional, hysterical and depressive.
Capacity for Limited Extended Representational Systems	Encapsulated disorders including neurotic syndromes.
Capacity for Multiple Extended Representational Systems	Phase-specific developmental and/or neurotic conflicts with or without neurotic syndromes. (This pattern can also occur during earlier phases.)

In summary this approach to psychopathology focuses on clinically observable aspects of the organization of experience, and therefore provides a psychoanalytically based approach to psychopathology which is potentially verifiable. It is rooted in developmental principles and is consistent with hypotheses regarding conflict and unconscious phenomena.

IMPLICATIONS OF A MODEL OF EGO DEVELOPMENT FOR CONSTRUCTS RELATING TO THE DRIVES

Psychoanalysis has been struggling to find an appropriate construct for understanding the relationship between the mind and the body. Some have advocated doing away with motivation. But to ignore motivational constructs or to attempt to deal only with the mental representations of bodily sensations without understanding the functional relationship between the two is akin to throwing out the baby with the bath water. Yet the controversy regarding the clinical usefulness or the validity of anergic motivational hypotheses creates a challenge. Newer constructs are needed which deal with the relationships between bodily sensations and their mental representations.

From the perspective of the ego, one can postulate two central tendencies that seem to govern mental life. The tendency to use new maturational capacities to engage in experience (e.g., sucking, looking, listening, crawling, walking, feeling, masturbating, holding, etc.) and the tendency toward self-regulation and self-control; often these two tendencies work together. Vision, hearing, and motor planning capacities are used by the infant to both engage the world and calm down or achieve self-regulation. For example, it is not unusual to help the crying infant calm down by offering visual or auditory information, thereby gaining his attention. In the second year of life, the toddler can look across the room and experience mother's "pride" by understanding her gestures, and can feel as if he is in her arms from afar (distal communication modes are being used for comfort and self-regulation). In the third year of life, the representational child can create comforting fantasies.

But, as is well known, fantasies can be scary (e.g., nightmares) as well, and the legs that carry one toward new experiences and provide security by bringing one back can also get one lost in a store.

The tendencies toward regulation and exploration of new experiences most of the time are in a relative state of equilibrium. (Interestingly, this model of central tendencies of the ego is close to Freud's concepts of eros and thanatos [Freud, 1920]), which have been relatively ignored because of their level of abstraction, and the assumption that they reflected Freud's thinking late in his career.

As one views the ego's tendency to use its equipment to engage in experiences it becomes useful to consider experience from the perspective of the drives and from the perspective of the ego. It is useful in this context to partition experience into levels of organization of experience and thematic affective areas of experience as discussed in chapter 1. From looking at types of experience, one can infer the degree to which there is a balance between the "use what you have" part of the equilibrium and the regulation and self control part. A full range of age appropriate experiences suggests an adaptive balance. Constrictions or intensifications suggest difficulties.

To facilitate observing how affective–thematic experiences are organized a number of categories have been formulated that have been found to be clinically relevant. With these categories it is possible to look at the degree to which all or only some affective–thematic areas are organized in the context of phase-specific tasks. Conversely, it is possible to see how certain affective–thematic proclivities when not present may hinder the full attainment of an expected level of organization.

This approach involves elucidating defects (when an age-expected level is not attained) and constrictions (when the full range of affective–thematic inclinations are not present). The categories were therefore chosen on the basis of areas one would expect to be present, the absence of which would have clinical significance. There was an attempt to avoid double referencing (e.g., assertiveness and tendency toward avoidance). Either assertiveness was present or absent, and if absent one would assume that something else, such as avoidance or withdrawal, was in its place. Similarly, certain affects related to specific phases (e.g., wariness or stranger anxiety) were not included because we found clinically that infants who did not progress to this level of differentiation reflected their limitations in other more generally observable ways (e.g., a general lack of pleasure or comfort with dependency).

The categories we found clinically useful include (1) interest and attentiveness; (2) relaxation and/or calmness; (3) dependency (including holding or comforting-type behaviors); (4) pleasure or joy (including enthusiasm); (5) assertiveness–explorativeness and curiosity; (6) protest or other distinct forms of unpleasure, including anger; (7) negativism or stubbornness; (8) self-limit-setting (often not seen until children are in the middle of the second year of life); and (9) after the age of three, empathy and more stable feelings of love.

Each affective–thematic area may have many distinct contents. One two and a half-year-old will evidence assertiveness or anger by shooting guns, another by "beating up" his father, and another by winning a car race. Similarly, pleasure may be reflected in the excitement of feeding and undressing the dolls or in the joy of building a huge tower. The contributions of psychosexual theory toward understanding the phase-specific organizing fantasies or "dramas" are of inestimable importance in the study of what contributes to distinctly human experience.

It is interesting to note that while in the first month or two it is difficult to observe all of these affective–thematic areas, by four months of age, it is possible to clinically observe each of these affective–thematic areas in a series of free exchanges between mother and baby. A healthy four-month-old, for example, often has no difficulty showing focused attentiveness, particularly to mother's face and voice. He will use this focused attentiveness to be relaxed or calm. He will contribute to dependency by holding and finding comfortable positions (the infant holds mother's neck and even begins directing her toward the type of rhythmic movements or sensory experiences that are most comforting). He will evidence pleasure and joy by smiling in synchrony with mother's smile or vocalizations. He will show assertiveness and curiosity by somewhat chaotically but purposely moving his arms to grasp an object. He will evidence anger, frustration, or protest with a distinct cry, angry look, and a flailing of arms and legs when a desired object is taken away. He will evidence negativism and even belligerency by refusing to open his mouth or by spitting up what he does not like. These affective–thematic dimensions, which are differentiated during the first and second year, have been partitioned by investigators into subcategories and subtle gradations (Charlesworth, 1964; Ainsworth, Bell, and Stayton, 1974; Stroufe, 1979). Interestingly, adaptive toddlers appear to have all the "moves"; that is, they have the subtle affective expressions, including bewilderment, surprise, anticipation, and even a little smirk as they deliberately behave in a provocative or negative fashion. The disturbed toddler's emotions, in comparison, are somewhat global and dampened.

Therefore from the perspective of the ego, drive derivatives become organized, together with the ego's relationship to all its other experiences, as part of an integrated experimental matrix, and these matrixes can be described according to the developmental level, thematic–affective inclination, and range.

Yet this still leaves open the question of the mind–body relationship. How does drive related experience become integrated with other aspects of experience. Stated differently how does experience at one level relate to experience at another level? Here too the concept of levels of ego organization and levels of learning may prove useful.

To understand the relationship between prerepresentational learning and representational learning, it may prove useful to postulate three types of learning by which the ego organizes information—somatic learning, consequence–behavioral learning, and representational–structural learning.

Somatic learning. Somatic learning may be seen as an organizing principle for understanding learning that occurs in relation to the human body, in particular the bodily or biological functioning which is accessible to variations in organization in the context of environmental experience. Such phenomena as general arousal patterns, overall interest in the world, specific autonomic nervous system patterns, and bodily rhythmic processes (sleep–wake cycles, alert cycles, hormonal variations) are determined in part by this very early type of "somatic" learning.

Consequence–behavioral learning. Consequence–behavioral learning may be seen as the organizing principle for behavioral change. It may also be involved at both the somatic and the representational levels. This type of human learning, evident in the stimulus–response approaches such as the operant learning paradigms (Skinner, 1938), is particularly powerful, however, in demonstrating how learning of new behaviors and discriminatory capacities can occur as a result of behavioral consequences (the contingencies of reinforcement). While consequence learning can be applied to the level of ideas and meanings, its explanatory power is most useful when applied to observable discrete behaviors. In this context it is not surprising that operant approaches, developed from experiments with animals, where discrete behaviors are easier to observe and control than in humans, help us understand a different level of human experience from experiences at the level of meanings. The reorganization of meanings into new meanings differs somewhat in character from the changing of behavior through altering consequences.

Representational–Structural Learning. Representational–structural learning may be seen as the way to account for "higher-order" learning involving the formation and organization of mental imagery and symbols which ultimately fit into configurations that permit us to think and learn. This level informs "awareness" in the traditional sense; that is, awareness of ideas or representational awareness.

It is no longer necessary to conceptualize mind–body relationships and levels of awareness in terms of totally different realms of functioning, and therefore in terms of different conceptual contexts (e.g., neurophysiological, psychological). It is now possible to view mind–body relationships within a uniform framework of human learning in which somatic or psychological events occur on a continuum (i.e., somatic to representational learning) in a constant relation to each other. The particular processes occurring at each level and the relationships among the three levels determine the nature of an individual's experience.

We must consider in more specific terms how the three levels relate to one another; in particular, how do somatic patterns relate in an ongoing manner to representational patterns?

Somatic patterns relate to representational patterns in three crucial ways. First, somatic patterns form part of the basic structure of the representational system. Second, somatic patterns are part of the experiences that eventually become organized (internalized) at a representational level. Third, somatic experience is constantly perceived in the context of the representational structure and is interpreted and transformed just as external experience.

Somatic patterns are part of the basic structure of the representational system because of the constitutional and early developmental somatic differences that account for the individual way in which infants process experience. For example, the early somatic pattern of arousal may form the basis for later intensity of internal representation. The early stimulus threshold (somatic pattern of shutting out stimulation) may form the foundation for later tendencies of the representational system *not* to experience certain noxious sensations. In her work on anorexia nervosa and obesity, Bruch (1973) postulated that, because of experiences in early life, certain infants, toddlers, and young children never become aware of such basic bodily sensations as hunger; on the other hand there are children who may respond hyperreactively to minimal stimulation. Due to interactive patterns in the second and third year certain bodily feelings and impulses may or may not come to be available to representational awareness or may be altered or distorted.

During the second year of life, when complex interactions

are becoming organized and internalized, somatic patterns involved in these interactions may become organized and internalized at a representational level. The toddler who experiences intense somatic patterns of irritability upon stimulation (based on earlier somatic learning) may come to experience stimulating human relationships as "irritating," thereby forming mental images (representations) which build the earlier somatic proclivity into the later complex human experience. A personal "meaning" is thereby established (human relationships provoke irritation) which incorporates the earlier proclivity.

Another example: the somatically very active infant may, in the second year of life, use this activity in the service of expressing rage. If, as a consequence of this rage, mother or father withdraws, the toddler may organize a representation associating activity and rage with loss of human contact. Again, a meaning becomes organized which includes both the original somatic proclivity and the later interaction (activity and withdrawal). Similarly, early somatic pleasure patterns may become involved in complex human relationships which become internalized and reach a representational level.

In this regard, it is interesting to consider defects in the transitional experiences leading to a capacity for representation or internal imagery (e.g., work on alexithymia [Nemiah, 1977]). If, for example, by being overly intrusive, parents undermine the toddler's tendency to organize behavior and experience complex emotional interactions, and the toddler turns away from the human emotional world to the inanimate world where his initiative is not undermined by intrusiveness, opportunities for experiencing and internalizing ideational and affect proclivities may be missed.

As indicated earlier, the representational system, once organized, may act to modify experience. Once there is the capacity to alter, recombine, and later transform internal representations (imageries) in accord with defensive and adaptive goals, we observe such events as the following: A vague sensation associated with protest behavior comes to be expressed as an angry feeling. This feeling may then be transformed to a "loving" feeling. Fears may be displaced from one object to another, and new fantasies may evolve from old ones. Through this process, the original somatic experience may be hardly recognizable and its role in early development obscured.

In summary, then, the relationships between the somatic and representational levels of learning involve the somatic foundation of the representational system, the organization of complex interpersonal experiences involving somatic proclivities, and distinct styles of perception, interpretation, and transformation of the representational system in relation to somatic experience.

ISSUES OF SPECIFICITY, INTENSITY, AND AWARENESS IN MIND–BODY PHENOMENA*

Freud's (1915) theory of instincts was an important contribution toward delineating the relationship between somatic or biological processes and psychological processes. By postulating psychic energy that could be transformed into drives and become attached to wishes and ideas, he advanced a theory of a relationship between physiological and psychological phenomena. The use of these anergic concepts (from early psychoanalytic theory) has been seriously questioned, however, and psychoanalytic ego psychology has attempted to resolve these questions by placing an emphasis on the formation of ego substructures that evolve through early object relations. Psychic structure, rather than being seen as evolving from the transformation of drive energies, is viewed as existing from the beginning as part of "an undifferentiated matrix," while drive–affect dispositions are acquired through maturation and the accumulation of human experience (Hartmann, 1939). In a sense this approach begs the issue of transformation of drive energy by taking as its starting point mental representations with drive–affect dispositions accruing to them (Kernberg,

---

* This discussion was originally presented in *Intelligence and Adaptation* (Greenspan, 1979) and "Three Levels of Learning," (Greenspan, 1982).

1975). Neither early instinct theory nor the more recent developments in ego psychology and object relations theory, however, have accounted for the clinical phenomena Freud was attempting to explain. How does one account for the intensity of excitation or the degree of pleasure? How does one account for zonal preferences?

Early in his theorizing, Freud postulated hypercathexis, investments of larger amounts of energy, as a way of explaining intensity of sensation as well as "awareness." He also postulated that different zones of the body or different modalities could become hypercathected. The skin can become "libidinized," for example. He postulated that at different stages of development different zones become cathected (the oral zone, the anal zone, the phallic zone). Though Freud's theory of instincts cannot be recapitulated here, it is worth noting that models which have attempted to ignore Freud's theory of instincts have had difficulty finding a useful way of accounting for the phenomena Freud was trying to understand. For example, Klein (1976) proposes a model involving cognitive schema, but in so doing, does not deal with precognitive somatic levels of excitation and other neurophysiologic events. A theoretical model which posits representational capacity and with somatic events experienced in their representational or symbolic form overlooks the issue of mind–body relations that Freud was struggling with, as well as much of the prerepresentational aspects of early development in the first years of life.

The model of three levels of learning offers an alternative. With this model we can understand the observations relating to intensity and awareness, and those relating to zonal or modal preference in the following manner. Early on, somatically based schema stemming from the earliest experiences with the environment may establish both intensity and zonal specificity. Each baby has his own individual maturational pattern, and these innate givens in part account for intensity of sensation and zonal preferences. There may, for example, be individual differences in the number of nerve fiber endings in different zones. It is maturation, together with enviromental experiences in the earliest stages, however, that establishes these early somatically based schemata. A mother who sensitively and pleasurably breast-feeds her baby may help consolidate the baby's already pleasurable experiences around the oral zone. One can envision repeated stimulation of certain zones at pleasurable levels, leading to a schema that represents this early experience. This does not postulate that psychic energy is disposed at a location in the body; it merely postulates that certain repetitive patterns of experience become organized into a somatic schema. (This may be similar to Piaget's early sensori-motor schema formed through repetition in the cognitive realm.) The repetition itself sets up the consolidation of an organization of early experience. To the degree that this early experience is highly pleasurable, the schema consolidates the physiological and emerging affective components.

At the level of consequence learning, further differentiation of these schemata may occur. For example, a mother may selectively reinforce pleasurable experience around certain parts of the body. These body parts may become experienced not only as zones of pleasure but as zones of attachment and contact with the nurturing object.

As experience begins to shift to the third level of learning through the organization of imitative and identificatory processes seen in the last half of the first year of life and into the second, we may observe another process which accounts for the phenomena of intensity and zonal specificity. As discussed earlier, during this period experience is becoming more organized or internalized and takes on meanings. The interaction that initially was recorded purely at the somatic level of learning (a mother strokes her infant's body and the infant begins to organize schemata of pleasure around bodily stroking), now becomes an experience of social interactions. Both the emotional experience and the cognitive schema of how this experience occurs become part of an organized system. Eventually, an organization of experience emerges that becomes identified as the "self," perhaps initially a "body self." The self that becomes organized is *the self that has been experienced*. This self representation need not be an accurate perception of the way the person actually is. It is the self of perception and sensations. Thus, if a bodily zone has been an intense focus of experience (either of pleasure or pain), it may assume a relatively prominent place in the initial self representation. At the level of meanings, therefore, we may see special emphasis and/or zonal specificity. With continued maturation, the development of the CNS (e.g., sphincter control) in interaction with environmental experience further determines zonal configurations.

But once the mental representational system is formed, how are variations in intensity (for example, excitement) explained? How does one account for the relationship between changing somatic experience and representational experience without using a concept such as transformation of energy? We can postulate that the representational system, just as it organizes itself in order to perceive the external world, organizes itself to perceive sensation from the interior of the body. How and what it perceives depends on earlier learning as well as on constitutional and maturational patterns.

Sensations in the somatic sphere of the body are experienced and organized into somatic schemata. The representational structural level of learning then perceives these experiences and, depending on its dynamic relationship to earlier somatic levels of learning, may perceive accurately, perceive inaccurately, "downplay," "hyperreact," or in other ways distort what is going on. For example, one youngster may deny pleasure because mother withdraws when he is feeling excited. Once this pattern becomes organized at the level of representation, it may foster a tendency to ignore certain kinds of sensations from the interior of the body. Another toddler, whose interpersonal relationships are minimal, may develop relationships mostly to the inanimate environment. In this instance, interpersonal, emotion-laden somatic schemata and representations are barely formed. Or, if a youngster's explorative and assertive behavior is undermined by a mother who is overly controlling and belittling, he may turn toward the

inanimate world which he can control and over which he can
feel a sense of mastery. In another situation, a youngster's
discomfort may generate exaggerated responses that facilitate
the organization of experience to the point where he feels every
minimally uncomfortable sensation from within to be of major
significance (internal sensation is exaggerated). In yet another
situation, a youngster may, for defensive purposes, begin to
split and change certain feelings into others, such as hate and
love (e.g., ego splitting, and later, reaction formations).

The intensity of the somatic patterns themselves also
determines the resulting experience. The importance of somatic dispositions, as illustrated by the different drive proclivities that are related to constitutional, maturational, and
developmental factors is well known and need not be further
elaborated.

Thus, the issues of intensity and specificity can be accounted for under the rubric of the three levels of learning.
They are related to the vicissitudes of the initial somatic
schemata that are laid down, the experiences that lead up to
interactive behavioral organizations, the structure and character of the representational system itself, and the later somatic
shifts and transformations that representations can undergo.

This discussion has suggested a model for the relationship
between the physical and mental aspects of drives consistent
with recent observations of infants and young children. It may
also prove useful to speculate on new ways to conceptualize the
bodily contribution to mental functioning. Is the dual instinct
theory still the best way to view the psychically important bodily
sensations? There may be, as indicated earlier, a general
tendency (which may be true for all living matter) to use new
maturational functions (to "use it or lose it," so to speak). There
are different aspects of the infant's maturation. Pleasure seeking or orality (referred to under the umbrella of the sex drive)
in early life certainly involves the mouth or oral cavity, but it
also involves the entire tactile system as well as sound, vision,
smell, and motor patterns. Whether the oral, anal, phallic
designations of levels of organization are the best ones to

capture the essence of early drive and pleasure activity, or whether a new designation relating to the way in which pleasurable sensation is organized may provide the topic for useful interdisciplinary dialogues. From infant observation it would seem that the terms *oral, anal,* and *phallic designations,* while certainly highlighting important areas of the body for the growing child, may be too restrictive to categorize the complete progression of the organization of bodily pleasures.

Considering another aspect of experiential organization, aggression (the aggressive drive), leads to a great deal of debate. There are attempts to separate constructive aggression from destructive types (Parens, in press). There are no comparable steps to go along with to the stages of psychosexual development in terms of the organization of aggression. Because aggression makes use of the voluntary motor system, this system may provide clues for a useful model of the organization of aggression. From observations, one might postulate aggression as organized according to overall developmental levels of the motor system, including (1) somatic proximal (e.g., physiological activity, mouth); (2) intentional distal (e.g., actual movement of arms, legs); (3) derivative technological. The latter would include: type I—extension of self (e.g., guns), type II—extensions of self displaced in space (e.g., remote control guns, bombs, etc.), type III—extensions of self displaced in time (e.g., a time bomb), and type IV, using technologies displaced from self in time and space (e.g., automated or computerized weapons systems); (4) gestural (e.g., vocal–affective and motor gestures, intended to convey intentions) but not actually destroy; and (5) representational (e.g. ideas, words, meanings), which symbolize aggressive intentions and feelings and permit further reasoning and elaboration in relative safety.

It is also interesting to speculate that the organization of pleasure may be related to maturational and developmental patterns of the autonomic nervous system and smooth muscles (sphincters, penis, etc.) and that the organization of aggression may relate to maturational and developmental patterns of the voluntary aspects of the nervous system and striated muscles.

These are speculations of the sort that may lead to further attempts to classify those critical bodily experiences that have special psychical importance in motivating psychological activity.

To return to the main point of this section; it is possible to study drives as they relate to the ego as part of a model of ego development and functioning. In this context, it is useful to consider two observable central tendencies, to use new maturational capacities in terms of seeking derivative experience, and to remain regulated and in self-control. The equilibrium between these two tendencies creates a motivational force for the progressive organization, differentiation, interpretation, and transformation of experience.

Chapter 4

The Psychotherapeutic Process with Adults and Children: Developmental Perspectives

The sequence of early ego development leads to suggestions for general principles of the psychotherapeutic process. This process involves to some degree four levels of development and relatedness, (derived from the six stages of ego development), at the same time. One is always dealing with issues of engagement and disengagement, preverbal presymbolic organized, intentional signaling and communication, symbolic affective–thematic elaboration, and symbolic–thematic and affective differentiation.

THE FOUR LEVELS OF DEVELOPMENT AND RELATEDNESS

Involvement at the four levels of development provides critical ingredients for growth, communication, and resolving difficulties. Difficulties in any of these four levels may play an important role in symptoms, special challenges, and problems.

131

The first level, which comes from the stage of regulation and interest in the world and attachment, involves engagement, and has two components—shared attention and engagement proper. Simply stated, the principle that all communication must involve both persons' attention, sounds obvious. Yet, not infrequently clinicians try to get a "tuned out," inattentive child to verbalize rather than first to simply attend. This step cannot be skipped over for the sake of expediency. Attention depends in part on the ability to take in information through each sensory modality. Overreactivity, underreactivity, or processing difficulties in any sensory pathway will affect attention. Muscle tone, motor coordination, and motor planning will also influence attention.

Engagement, or a positive sense of relatedness, requires that both parties be engaged with positive expectations. This also sounds self-evident. But not infrequently indifference, negative feelings, or impersonal or aloof patterns continue longer than necessary. And pleasure and engagement are not even close at hand.

The second level comes from the stage of purposeful communication and a complex sense of self. It involves a more critical, often ignored, aspect of all human communication—intentional nonverbal gestures. These include facial expressions, sounds, posture, arm and leg movements, and so forth. From the middle of the first year of life through adulthood, individuals are always using gestures to communicate. This preverbal system is perhaps more important than one might think. The basic emotional messages of life, safety and security versus danger, acceptance versus rejection, approval versus disapproval, are all communicated through facial expressions, body posture, movement patterns, and vocal tone and rhythm. Words enhance these more basic communications, but interestingly we all form quick, split-second judgments regarding a new person's dangerousness or safety or rejection or acceptance of us before the conversation even gets started. In fact, if the person looks dangerous and says, "You know I am quite safe," we tend to believe the gestures and disbelieve the words.

People can fool us, to be sure. But that doesn't change the fact that we all rely on gestural communication for a sense of security, safety, acceptance, and approval.

At a more subtle level, gestural communication also relays to us what aspects of our own emotions are being accepted, ignored, or rejected. The looks and head nods as we are communicating about closeness, curiosity, anger, or excitement quickly tell us how the person feels about our message. More importantly, our emerging definition of the uniqueness of our very self is dependent on how others react to our own special tendencies with preverbal gestures. We are differentially responded to as part of the process which refines and defines our emerging behavior and sense of self. How is our mischievous behavior and smile responded to—with a smile and grin of acceptance or a head-shaking frown of disapproval? Our natural inclinations are in part either accepted and supported, or refined as part of this nonverbal communication system.

This gestural system, which is so important in human development, is perhaps the one aspect of communication most frequently ignored. For example, in the understandable eagerness to teach new words or even numbers and letters to a child, many a parent will focus on the child repeating the word or letter or number. They say it over and over again, feeling frustrated if the child looks dazed, or satisfied if the child, after five minutes, says the magic "word." The fact is missed that this same child marches to his own drummer, floats in and out of the room, does not respond to the parent's facial expressions with his own facial expressions or the parent's sounds with his own (each and every time), or follow the parent's arm and hand gestures with his own. Similarly, clinicians often focus on changing isolated behaviors or symptoms and ignore the foundation needed for interpersonal processes. The very process of interchange that goes on every second that two people are near each other and that binds people together in an organized, intentional manner may be missing. Organized, interactive communication, rather than splinter skills, a word here or there, is the foundation for language reasoning and emotional adaptation.

The third and fourths level come from the stages of representational elaboration and differentiation. These levels involve the elaboration and sharing of meanings. The functional and interactive use of words and pretend or symbolic play are used interactively to communicate wishes or intentions, feelings and thoughts. At this level, there is a balance between fantasy and reality. Shared meanings are used to both elaborate wishes and feelings, as in pretend play, and to catagorize meanings and solve problems, as in logical conversations.

Shared meaning involves the communication of ideas, not just the having of ideas. Some children are great at pretend play and talking, but only like to, or are able to, communicate with meanings down a one-way street. They talk and they play out dramas, but they do not easily take in or use someone else's ideas and comments. For example, whenever Sally came home from preschool she played out scene after scene of being a queen, letting mother hold her cape, but not answering or even reflect on minor questions like "How did school go?" or "Who did you play with today?" Other children are just the opposite, diligently following the parents' instructions, listening to every word, but rarely elaborating their own understanding of events.

Obviously, children are only capable of the levels they have gone through. By eighteen months, all but the level of shared meanings should be mastered and by age three and one-half, all the levels should be well established.

As tempting as it might be, one cannot skip levels. This is especially true for the child who is delayed in any of these abilities. Skipping levels is akin to building a house on a weak foundation. For example, for a child or adult who has not mastered the intentional gestural communication of basic needs, words may only be empty concepts devoid of function or purpose.

It may appear obvious that the levels just described are always involved in all psychotherapies. After all, the patient comes in and seeks help. There is always some rapport or some emotional relatedness that develops; hence, the stage of engagement. As soon as the therapist opens the door and the patient sits down as the therapist's gestures toward a chair, and the patient makes eye contact, perhaps makes a few facial or arm gestures which are reciprocated by therapist, we have an intentional, preverbal communication system going. (Of course, some patients may already evidence some difficulty in the preverbal communication system, or even difficulty at the earlier level of engagement. But most patients establish these first two levels rather easily.) As the patient begins telling the therapist why he is there, we have further intentional communication, now using words. But even before particular themes or meanings are elaborated, the use of intentional vocalizations indicates further intentionality. To the degree the patient evidences the ability to put feelings into words and elaborate themes, the next level is reached—the level of representational elaboration. Typically, the patient will focus on some relevant themes in his life—boredom, apathy, frustrated passivity, impulsive anger, overexcitement, distractibility, fearfulness, anxiety, sadness, and so forth. The fourth level will be reached when the patient not only elaborates his themes, but is able to put them into some context which shows an ability to shift between subjective states (how the patient feels about being dependent, angry, or passive) and his view of external reality. The ability to shift gears between subjective elaborations and contructs of external reality signal the capacity for representational differentiation. Representational differentiation is also indicated by the ability to categorize experience (There is now a symbolic "me" and a symbolic "you" and "I always get so scared of everything") and construct bridges between domains of experience ("I am scared when I'm mad"). Most importantly the capacity for catagorizing experience helps the patient "Share meanings." He can elaborate his feelings and build on another's communications. The exploration of meanings becomes a two-way dialogue.

Different types of pathology suggest the need to focus

more on one or another aspect of the early ego development in therapeutic work. We can also follow how the therapeutic work progresses from one level to another and within each level across a greater range of thematic–affective domains.

In order to visualize this approach, picture these four levels: engagement; purposeful, organized communication; representational elaboration; and representational differentiation. Then visualize alongside each level the different affective–thematic domains that characterize the human drama, including dependency, pleasure, assertiveness, curiosity, anger, self-limit-setting, and, for the stage of representational differentiation, empathy and more consistent forms of love. One can then picture the degree to which a person has established a certain level and the range of the human drama (i.e., thematic areas evidenced at that level). The different thematic areas are in part related to drive–affect derivatives and interpersonal patterns.

The therapeutic goal is to help a person function optimally at all levels at once in the context of the full range of thematic–affective domains. For example, a person who is capable of functioning at all levels, but at the level of representational elaboration and differentiation is constricted and therefore cannot apply his representational elaboration and differentiation to issues around intimacy, has a clear therapeutic challenge. The therapeutic work will focus its energies on applying their representational capacities to a new domain.

Another patient may come in capable of engagement of purposeful communication, but not capable of representational elaboration or differentiation (in any of the emotional areas). This patient can describe relatively impersonal interactions representationally, but cannot describe any major emotional themes. He can describe action patterns, but not abstractions of emotions. He says, "I held her hand" or "I gave her a hug," when he is talking of dependency, and talks of hitting or biting the other person when angry. He does not talk about abstracted feeling states such as "I felt angry" or "I missed her so." In this case, the goal would be to help the person begin embracing new developmental levels and then increase the affective–thematic range at the new levels. To do this, one may have to first increase the thematic–affective range at some of the levels already mastered. Such a person may already have difficulty with his thematic–affective range at the level of intentional communication or at the level of engagement, even though he is solidly at these earlier levels.

Therefore, we can profile the patient's capacities for these four levels of ego development and begin targeting our therapeutic goals. The targeted goals would include increasing the range at each level to incorporate thematic–affective domains that were missing and mobilizing progressive development to reach the most differentiated stages of ego development.

Interestingly, by using such a model one avoids getting lost in amorphous therapeutic goals. Most patients, for example, will need to master the issues at one stage before they fully master the issues at the next stage, even though they are partially involved in the issues at all stages at the same time.

Consider a patient who comes in and can engage, but only partially. When anxious or frightened he quickly disengages and becomes aloof or withdrawn. Also, let us consider that this person at the same time gets disorganized and can't even gesture purposefully and intentionally (e.g., he gestures and talks in a disorganized way). His capacity for representational elaboration is limited to either disorganized emotional communications or organized descriptions of impersonal events. There is little capacity for subjective elaboration of feelings in the context of shifting between subjective elaborations and an appreciation of reality. This person then uses words in a fragmented way, tends to be concrete and impersonal in his descriptions of the world, signals in a disorganized and chaotic way, and is capable of engaging with others, but easily disengages and becomes aloof.

The first goal with such a person is to try and establish more effective engagement. Such a person may come in to a session and start talking, but the "chit-chat" needs to focus on the ability to broaden his capacity for engagement, the first step in his potential therapeutic progression. As the person talks about furniture in the office or the ride on the bus to the office, the therapist, as he listens will be especially alert to eye contact, emotional tone, the patient's feelings of satisfaction or pleasure, an emerging sense of synchrony evolving between the therapist and the patient, and the pattern of connectedness and disconnectedness throughout the session. The therapist may have to work hard not to be too intrusive (e.g., ask questions that are too personal or provocative) or too disinterested (e.g., appearing to be too casual or aloof). Most experienced therapists have encountered this type of patient and have intuitively found the right pattern of engagement. The attempts to find this pattern should be elevated from the intuitive, nonspecific aspect of therapy to the explicit, systematic aspect. The therapist may deal with many issues without addressing them verbally. But instead of feeling nothing is going on, he will feel quite satisfied when, over a period of weeks, the patient is able to remain affectively engaged for 50 percent of the session in comparison to when they first started and it was only 20 percent of the session. The therapist will also feel progress is being made when the patient is able to tolerate as part of his system of engagement, patterns which suggest warmth, assertiveness, or even anger. The quality of engagement begins to tolerate a full affective and thematic range, even though the affective and thematic range is neither symbolic nor even intentional or purposeful. For example, such a patient, frustrated with the therapist's inability to take away his pain, may initially withdraw. But then he manages to stay engaged with impersonal verbalization, eye contact, a sense of affective connectedness, and rhythmic synchrony, in terms of motor movements, gestures, and the like. If at a later time in the therapy there is a sense not just of the patient's frustration and anger, but of disappointment and loss (e.g., the patient's reaction to the therapist having been absent), it may indicate a further broadening of the range of affective themes that can be incorporated into the quality of engagement.

The same process may then occur for the level of intentional communication. Once the patient begins feeling more secure and broader in his quality of engagement, we often see him begin communicating more intentionally through gestures and other preverbal methods. This level, then, begins to organize a larger range of affects and themes. The therapist can note how intentionality is maintained or lost during times where the issues are dependency, assertiveness, anger, excitement, and so forth. The therapist is always keeping an eye on the developmental level and the thematic–affective range. To the degree the patient incorporates an increasing range of themes and greater intensity of affect, there is a more stable structure at that developmental level.

One may think of stability as involving the range of different thematic–affective domains that can be organized at each stage. One may also consider stability in terms of the ability to recover the capacities associated with a developmental level after it has been lost; that is, the ability to become reengaged or intentional again. The affective intensity that can be tolerated before a disruption of a stage-specific capacity occurs is another indication of stability. The range of themes and emotions, the intensity of affect tolerated, and the ability to recover are all obviously related to one another, and together they provide a picture of the range and stability of a particular stage of ego development.

In addition to problems in the engagement and purposeful communication stages, many patients, as this patient did, will evidence compromises in the capacity for representational elaboration. As indicated earlier, some patients will not have much of this capacity. These patients will tend to be concrete and describe action patterns, rather than abstracted feeling states; for example, if angry, "I hit her," if longing, "I hugged her," rather than: "I felt like I needed to give her a hug because I felt so lonely," or "I felt so mad I wanted to punch him in the mouth." Such patients who tend to deal with the world concretely when upset will tend to act out in action modes either by physical acting out (hitting, pinching, grabbing), or by massive inhibition and passivity. Such individuals have little ability to transform behavioral and physiologic aspects of affect and drive into their representational components. This is evidenced with adults, in language, through expression of abstracted feeling states and with children in pretend play, or through forms of complex gestures, drawings, other visual–spatial constructions, or other forms of symbolic communication.

For the patient who hasn't achieved this level, the therapist will be impressed with progress simply by that person shifting from describing an event in an action mode—"I walked out of the room"; "I hit my wife," to an abstracted description of a feeling state, "I *felt* mad and *wanted* to hit," or "I *felt* like *wanting* to walk out of the room." This shift represents a significant structural change and is a sign of enormous progress. The way that the therapist can foster this shift is to focus with the patient on their initial description and then help the patient elaborate it. For example, to the patient who says, "I walked out," the therapist might say, "Oh, you walked out. Gee, it sounds like there was something important or serious going on." Then the patient will describe in greater detail what was happening. As the patient describes this in detail, the therapist will be curious to know of other such similar events where the patient has walked out. When the patient describes a situation with his wife, his boss, or his best friend where he has walked out, the therapist may then ask whether such things have anything in common. As the patient tries to find some common link between all these situations where he has walked out, he is trying to abstract across many behavioral situations. As he learns to abstract common behavioral features (and the therapist helps him with pattern recognition type questions and clarifications), he may learn to elaborate and abstract behavioral or somatic themes (e.g., "Yes, in all these situations I felt terribly uneasy and couldn't stand being there"). The patient still isn't talking about a feeling, he is talking about a physiologic state of discomfort. Over time, though, as he continually abstracts common behavioral and somatic states, the patient will gradually be able to learn to abstract feeling states. He may talk about all the situations where he feels the specific state of "discomfort." The therapist may want to hear more about this state of discomfort: "What does it feel like? Where is it?" "Oh, it's in my stomach. My stomach gets queasy"; "It's in my shoulders; they get tight." The therapist may wonder, "This tight feeling is like . . . ?" The patient may then realize there is a thought of "hitting someone." Associated with this somatic state of "tightness," the patient may spontaneously conclude that he feels "angry." He is putting together his thought of hitting with his physiologic discomfort. Slowly but surely, a feeling state becomes abstracted.

This feeling state doesn't become abstracted unless there is engagement, security, and purposeful signaling. The foundations of the ego, the engagement, and purposeful communication must be present to organize the person and help the person feel secure. In time, this organization, intentionality, and security provides the confidence to jump to a new level of emotional elaboration where feelings are identified for the first time.

Often, however, true intentional signaling, as a foundation for representational elaboration, is not present and a seeming problem in representation and elaboration will alert the therapist to focus on this earlier stage. In all relationships, certain parts of ourselves are acknowledged and supported and other parts are undermined, unsupported, or unacknowledged, through preverbal interactive processes.

Consider an example from a recent session between a child psychiatrist and a child he was treating. The child was making things with clay. He would show his accomplishments to the therapist and then get provocative. The therapist kept interpreting the child's discomfort with showing him things and the need to then sabotage his own best efforts. The therapist's affect was mostly one of criticism, "Why do you always ruin a good thing?" The therapist's gestures were also critical. Before the child would get provocative and disorganized, however, for a brief moment, he clearly wanted the therapist's admiration and support for what he had done. The therapist missed the patient's fleeting proud smile (a gesture) and only tuned in to the second half of his communication which admittedly came so fast it easily obscured the anxious and quickly denied beam of pride. The child was saying, nonverbally, "Hey look!" and the therapist responding, nonverbally, with "You are ruining everything." There was a powerful nonverbal communication going on. When the nonverbal message being received is negative, it can become quite disorganizing. Imagine what negative feedback does to a toddler when he is going "Wow!" and everyone else in the room is communicating nonverbally in a negative way. Picture yourself talking to 500 people. You are anxious and wanting approval, much the same way that a toddler feels when he is talking to only one "big" person. He is a tiny little guy talking to a big person, just like you are when you are talking to a large audience or an admired, but potentially critical authority figure. Your audience starts shaking their heads "no" when you expect a "yes." They look bored, angry, and tune out. How disorganized does your thinking become? The child experiences the same process.

I suggested to the therapist that he empathize gesturally (as well as verbally) with the prideful feelings of the child. Even though the child only looked prideful for a few seconds (and then got provacative), "Harness it," I suggested. "Expand it. See if he tolerates the pride a little longer and develops the provacative behavior." In this way the child might well learn to become more comfortable with his own pride. In a subsequent session, for the first time the child and the therapist beamed with joint pride. The child then got anxious (after five minutes) and began trying to sabotage the mood. The child didn't lose his need to sabotage. It was already an internal process. But he went from tolerating about two seconds of pride in himself, to a good five minutes (and later fifteen minutes) of pride in himself. This gave the therapist enough time to then anticipate with him and say, "You are showing me stuff you are really proud of! But what I can tell from what you did yesterday is that in another minute or two I bet you are going to start throwing things. Let's look at why you might want to do that." The therapist had now acknowledged the anxiety-provoking behaviors and gestures, and the difficulty with feeling "pride," rather than just highlighting the need to sabotage. They could later figure out why the youngster's self-pride was so obviously in conflict by representationally elaborating it. The first step is to establish *preverbal recognition* of all the natural inclinations of the child (i.e., both sides of the conflict).

The child at the behavioral level also pieces together how "I make dependency happen." He is developing a style of going up to mommy and giving her a hug, a style of teasing daddy. He is also developing styles of aggression and self assertion. Either these patterns are supported through the nonverbal communications of the parents or are undermined. If they are undermined, the child may become anxious and withdraw from the undermined behavioral realm (become provocative, disorganized, passive, compliant, negative, etc., the symptoms of later character pathology in adults). The child's environment does not confirm the child's pattern through an acknowledging set of nonverbal interactions. This critical part of early personality development is often overlooked in adult psychotherapy. In the adult psychotherapeutic relationship, preverbal experiences can be understood in verbal, symbolic, or representational elaborative modes.

Consider another example. A very disturbed patient was telling me about her desire for an extra session. It wasn't possible to have an extra session and her face looked very sad. I said, "I can see by your facial expression how it makes you feel to not be able to have a second session this week. Can you tell me how it feels?" She said, "Well, I've been looking at a knife in my house and at my own fingers." Often at this point we begin supplying the feelings. But the patient who is at the late behavioral stage of development (intentional but not representational), will keep giving you poignant behavioral descriptions. These descriptions of knives and fingers have affect implied. As I proceeded with this patient, I said, "You are telling me the behaviors that come to mind and I can see the emotions in your face, but can you describe the feeling tone in your body." She said, "The only thing I feel is a sense of empty, vague frustration." She could not elaborate more well-defined affect states, such as anger, loss, futility, fear, loneliness (i.e., any typical feelings that one would normally empathize with). She could continue to elaborate vivid behavioral sequences, all of which had a desperate self-destructive and painful quality to them. In such circumstances, as indicated above, we often put words into patients' mouths. Sometimes they parrot these words back to us. We have an illusion that they are at the stage of representational elaboration. If and when they get there a year later, it will be a major therapeutic success. The patient finds herself locked into behavior pattern modes because the signal of a potential affect doesn't make it to a core abstracted affect state, like anger or sadness. Instead, it triggers only a series of images, in terms of behavioral patterns, that have affect implied. As the patient is beginning to progress to the next level, one may hear of vague affect states—emptiness, diffuse frustration, frenzy. These are vague and generalized. Slowly, this patient verbalized some of these very vague affect states. The best she could do at this time in her therapy was to elaborate very painful, diffuse affect states. Yet she found it helpful that empathetic understanding was negotiated. She found some temporary relief and made a small step forward as we understood the juxtaposition of self-destructive behavioral images, vague feelings of frustration, and not having a second session.

In the past when I tried to supply the feeling, the patient often felt unconnected, rejected, and controlled. Her self-destructive images would become more intense. It is important to pay attention to how to help patients get from the behavioral stage that implies affect to vague affect states that are very painful—frenzy, emptiness, hollowness, deadlike feeling inside—to more differentiated affect states, such as anger, sadness, excitement, pleasure, closeness, or loss.

In many therapies, this step of abstracting feeling states is mistakenly assumed to be present. As indicated, the therapist fills in the missing pieces—"You must have felt angry"; "You must have felt sad"; "You must have felt mad." The therapist feels the patient has the capacity to abstract feelings, but is simply not willing to do so. The therapist even gets mildly annoyed with his "resistant" patient who won't talk about feelings. The therapist must realize that while his assumptions may be true for some patients, for others his assumptions are incorrect. His patient may be learning to elaborate and abstract feelings for the first time and may not have reached this third stage of development. The therapist must work patiently with abstracting different behavioral patterns and physiologic states of discomfort, and connecting these with fleeting thoughts. Out of this work central feeling states may become abstracted.

At the stage of representational differentiation, the therapist also should not assume that the patient has this ability, but is simply not using it. Some patients will have this ability and some will not. Some will have it in certain thematic areas, but not other areas. The goal is to help the patient to develop one step further. He is already now elaborating feeling states about anger, dependency, curiosity, sexual interest, but cannot necessarily shift gears easily between fantasy and reality, and cannot categorize experience or interpret his fantasies or feelings by making connections between different elements of his fantasies.

CONSTITUTIONAL-MATURATIONALLY BASED DEFENSES AND REPRESENTATIONAL DIFFERENTIATION

For some patients representational-differention and integration do not come naturally. This is expecially true for individuals who have difficulty "seeing the forest for the trees." They are often gifted verbally and may be quite bright. They lack the ability, however, to see the big picture. In some cases, this is related to a relative lag in visual–spatial abstracting capacities (in comparison to advanced verbal–symbolic capacities). As described in chapter 2, it may be associated with a tendency toward affective lability or mood disorders. One man with this pattern required a great deal of work simply on the issue of "seeing the forest." He learned that he had had a cognitive or intellectual preference for verbal detail since he was five years old, but had difficulty with the "big picture." He intensified this pattern for defensive purposes. "I could never figure out my parents' relationship," he would naively state. He always felt "helpless" and "needy" and never saw his own anger or demandingness or greediness. For him, each state of mind was quite independent. The left hand never knew what the right hand was doing. It was essential to address this pattern, understand its maturational–cognitive components, its defense uses, and its adaptive value. Then it was possible to begin the more traditional work of learning to differentiate representations. Skipping over this step often results in the therapist *doing* the differentiating work for the patient and the patient improving symptomatically but remaining naive and at a level of representational elaboration.

The approach to defensive patterns which are related to the constitutional and maturational patterns described in chapter 2 requires helping the patient comprehend his own "processing tendencies" and the way he uses them for defensive purposes. Both children and adults appear to favor their relative vulnerabilities when under stress unless they have specifically learned to do the opposite. Children who tend to become fragmented and not see the forest for the trees become more fragmented when anxious. Those who have trouble decoding auditory, verbal, and affective meanings become even more unsure of their emotional meanings under pressure. The tendency to go with your own maturational style seems to be almost a biological principle, as children with motor planning problems become more clumsy, children with tactile oversensitivity become more cautious, and children with word retrieval problems more uncommunicative.

How can the constitutional maturational aspect of defensive functioning be examined and ultimately, if necessary, compensated for with a more flexible and representationally differentiated coping style? As indicated above, when there is a deficit in visual–spatial processing, as seen in affective disorders, hysterical patterns, and anxiety disorders, the goal is to help the patient learn to shift from a tendency to see each element but miss the pattern to observing the entire pattern.

To facilitate this capacity for representational integration, the patient first needs to see how they use this pattern defensively. One affectively labile and often depressed woman came to see that whenever she felt competitive, sadistic, or grandiose, she dealt with her fears of losing a love object (originally mother, now husband), by losing sight of her competitive goals and feeling overwhelmed, fragmented, and helpless. She would literally only be able to "keep track of what I need to do each half hour." Each issue of the moment would overwhelm her and her longer range goals and life patterns were obscured. In session, she would lose sight of what we discussed from the early part of the session to the latter part, and from session to session. As we focused on this tendency to "lose the big picture" and how this in itself made her feel panicky and clingy to either me or her husband, she saw that the "loss" of her sense of herself in terms of goals and patterns often preceded her anxious, empty, or depressed feelings. There was therefore a feeling such as competition or sadism, a loss of "the big picture," and then dysphoric affects.

While examining how this pattern operated in many contexts and exploring its historical roots, the patient also began to focus on how to keep herself from getting lost in this defensive pattern which would take on a life of its own. Whenever she began feeling "lost," instead of getting further lost, she stopped whatever she was doing and literally forced herself to answer a series of rhetorical questions such as, "What's going on with my husband, boss, children, etc.?" "Am I dealing with competition or anger, rejection, etc.?" She was quite intuitive and this simple cognitive exercise helped her identify the "big picture." She had to go against the grain, so to speak. The recognition that an aspect of her defense was a constitutional and maturational style made it possible for her to realize that she had to develop a compensatory capacity. Only the understanding of how initially she used her maturational style defensively, however, made this step possible.

The patient with a different constitutional maturational style also may benefit from this approach. We also discussed in chapter 2 the relative deficit in auditory–verbal–affective processing associated with thought disorders, schizoid, and obsessional–compulsive personality patterns. Here, the challenge is helping the patient identify moment-to-moment affective meanings so that his superior capacity for pattern recognition is built on real interpersonal affects of the moment rather than on meaningless or highly personalized idiosyncratic (however creative) cues.

A young man with this tendency first learned how he "spaced out" and became superabstract in his ruminations after feeling slighted or rejected. He saw how he tried to use abstract logical reasoning, building hypothesis on hypothesis, to figure out emotions he could not detect such as how he or a new girl friend felt after a date. This man learned to interrupt his highly abstract reasoning about simple emotions. (He continued to use his abstract capacities in his work as a physicist.) Instead, he tried to give himself more information based on real interpersonal cues. Instead of ruminating about "what she meant," he recreated what she did and said and tried to identify points of feeling including pleasure and anxiety. He, for example, focused on "how she held my hand," "How much she told me about her former boyfriend," "How my body got tense when she kissed me," and so forth. With these interpersonal details in mind, he could then permit himself the luxury of his abstract thinking. Rather than "obsessing" he also learned to pay extra attention to his and her feelings and their dialogue when they were together, and even ask her questions about what she meant if he was confused.

There are, therefore, two aspects to dealing with constitutional maturational aspects of defense and personality: (1) to discover how and in what contexts it is used defensively (e.g., response to themes of aggression or dependency or as a general strategy to deal with all challenges), and (2) to recognize its constitutional and maturational basis and learn in a way consistent with one's own individual differences to develop compensatory coping strategies (e.g., to see the big picture or identify moment-to-moment affective meanings).

Understanding more about the biological–maturational aspects of defenses and personality may also shift the way we view the effects of pharmacologic agents. For example, perhaps antidepressants work not on mood, per se, but on the individual's ability to integrate and abstract visual–spatial–affective patterns (i.e., be less fragmented and more "big-picture" oriented). Interestingly, the antidepressants work for many overly active, distractible children. They tend to help these children be more organized, have more stable moods, and to be toned down a bit. The hypothesis, in keeping with the model presented here, is that the positive effect of medication is in its ability to help the individual organize their perception (self and other) of affective patterns. Secondary to this improvement, one sees less dysphoric affect (the person has a more stable integrated sense of an affective self). This explanation begins to tie together observations of the impact of antidepressants on affective disorders, learning, attention, and activity level problems, and even anxiety and phobic conditions. (Individuals with anxiety and phobic conditions, as described earlier, also tend to use fragmentation rather than pattern abstraction and integration.) These hypotheses are sufficiently specific to suggest potentially useful further research.

The identification and work on maturational style is part of the overall therapeutic effort toward furthering representational differentiation and integration. Differentiation and integration occurs hand-in-hand. Representational differentiation focuses on how the sense of representational self is separate from nonself or other; how dependency is separate from aggression; and how the past is separate from the present. Representational integration is implied by representational differentiation. Integration focuses on how each representational island is part of a larger pattern (true differentiation also suggests relational bridges between each piece). It is easy to see how the difficulties with either pattern construction or identifying individual meanings will compromise the process of forming higher level representational structures.

The capacity for representational differentiation and integration is achieved in a steplike progression. It is learned through elaborating different feeling states. The therapist is curious to know more about these feelings. The patient is also curious and reveals more and more about them. As the patient reveals the contours of dependency feelings, aggressive feelings, assertive feelings, curious feelings, sexual feelings, and the like, he begins seeing, through his own associative process, some natural connections. At such junctures, the therapist supportively and empathetically wonders about the nature of these connections. For example, as the person talks about wanting to be close to people but always being upset and anxious and scared of being rejected, the therapist begins wondering out loud about the person's desire for closeness and experience with rejection. As the patient elaborates both sides of the equation and fills in the historical elements of the wish for closeness and the fears of rejection, the therapist wonders how these elements go together. At some point, the patient may begin associating to angry feelings. The angry feelings may serve as a bridge in helping the patient understand the connection between some of the longings and desires and some of the fears of rejection. The patient may realize that his desire for closeness becomes so intense (and when frustrated, these desires become even more intense) that he becomes scared that their very intensity could hurt somebody, or he may, because of feeling frustrated, even want to hurt someone. This capacity for bridging requires empathetic elaboration of each thematic area as well as looking for connections between the different thematic areas. The therapist's ability to shift gears from empathy and engagement to self-reflection helps the patient make these shifts.

We have not yet discussed how one increases the thematic–affective range at each level. Let us take an example from representational elaboration: Not infrequently, a person comes in able to elaborate themes of dependency but not anger. The person talks about his desire for closeness and how people don't give him what they want. In child work, the child plays out a scene of two dolls hugging each other and wanting to be close, but anger never comes into the scene. Over weeks and months there is no spontaneous elaboration of themes of anger, either in the verbal deductions of the adult or the pretend play productions of the child. As the therapist plays with the dolls with the youngster or talks about dependency, separation, hurt, and pain with the adult, the therapist begins to wonder more and more about the nature of the pain and how it feels. How does the doll who has been rejected feel? Slowly but surely, feelings of frustration come in. The therapist is looking for an opportunity to wonder out loud whether the patient ever feels anything other than hurt or rejected. Slowly but surely, inklings of assertiveness or anger may creep in through behavior (body posture or grimace) or behavioral description. Initially, the anger is not representational. The anger must first be communicated at earlier levels before it can be represented. Some patients, if they have the earlier level, may begin at the representational level. The therapist can nurture the anger along by empathizing with the person's tendency at their developmental level. The key is not to force the anger, not to provoke it by saying, "Aha! You must feel angry sometimes," but rather to empathetically wonder about tendencies and inclinations. Eventually, as behavioral tendencies are seen in patterns, together with security, engagement, and purposeful communication, the tendency to empathize with the verbalization of feelings helps the patient further abstract and spontaneously laborate new feelings such as anger. The job of the therapist is to be aware of which feelings are missing. Often therapists only delve into feelings that are present. One mental health professional who had been through a lengthy analysis dealt in detail with her dependency and anger. She did not bring up sexual feelings and her analyst assumed that if sexual issues weren't being elaborated, they weren't caught in conflict. Quite to the contrary, this patient was so anxious around sexual issues, especially sexual feelings toward authority figures, that these were "walled off." A model where one listens for what is being excluded as well as what is being included, would prevent these types of therapeutic limitations. The therapist supports spontaneous elaborations when they occur and further encourages them along. Sometimes the therapist can continue to make comments about how only certain feelings seem to be brought up and wonder about aspects of the patient's life they seem to be more private about. Other times, the theme being elaborated will provide a clue and a bridge to the "walled off" area.

At each stage, but particularly in the stages of representational elaboration and differentiation, one wants to help further support new thematic–affective areas. In terms of differentiation, one may hear areas being elaborated, but only in a relatively undifferentiated manner. The person, for example, doesn't distinguish between subjective and objective reality around intense dependency longings. One would bring the interpretive tools to the area of "longings." One would wonder about the patient's inability to figure out "what you think versus what someone else is thinking when it comes to intense longings in comparison to anger where you are always clear in what you think in comparison to what someone else is thinking." Similarly, where certain thematic–affective areas are poorly differentiated from one another, interpretive work is needed ("You have a hard time knowing if you feel needy or angry"). In the differentiating work, just as in the representational elaborative work, it is often necessary to differentiate at early levels of behavior and behavioral description before truly representational differentiation can take place. "I seem to squeeze my wife in a hurting way when I haven't seen her for a few days" may precede "I often feel *angry* at my wife when I *miss her* the most."

In accomplishing the tasks of shifting from one developmental level to another or broadening the affective–thematic range, it may sound as if these are intellectual or cognitive endeavors. It should be clear, however, that as one elaborates the different themes at each developmental level, one is always engaging the person in the first two levels of ego structure. One is engaging the person at a level of relatedness. One is also organizing communication in a highly intentional manner so that there is an organized signaling system going back and forth at the preverbal–affective level and at the emerging verbal–affective level. Therefore, for example, when somebody is talking about aggression either in action words ("I hit that person") or talking about it in emerging feelings ("I felt like I wanted to hit that person"), they are in the presence of another human being who is not withdrawn, aloof, or intrusive or changing the subject quickly by saying, "You must be hungry" or "You must have to go to the bathroom." At the same time they are talking about an area that is hard for them, they are experiencing an enormous amount of personal engagement. They are feeling the therapist's sense of interest, positive regard, respect and concern, and highly intentional counterresponses. The therapist, in addition, asks intelligent questions, clarifies, furthers the elaborative process, provides a balance between respect for the person's need to elaborate in their own way, and, at the same time, offers clarifications, structure, and limits as appropriate. In this way, the therapist is highly active in terms of engagement and purposeful communication. It is interesting to consider that purposeful communication at the gestural level, involves both the elaborative side of the equation and the structuring, limit-setting side of the equation. In very many nonverbal, purposeful communications, in fact, we see both the support for the elaborative process and also limit-or structure-setting. If you watch two people carry on a conversation, without listening to the words, you can see how they support each other's elaborations and also structure and limit the nature of the discourse.

When we talk about engaging a person, we are talking about a highly emotional process. The person may be, for the first time in his life, feeling a sense of relatedness and a sense of interactive purposefulness around certain formerly avoided thematic–affective areas.

The transference relationship is well known and will be discussed in chapter 5 on the therapeutic process in psychoanalysis. Even in supportive psychotherapy, however, the transference brings alive the patient's themes and affects at each developmental level. Regardless of the degree to which the transference is central to the therapeutic work or "worked through," it provides a personal emotional saliency to the entire process.

The development of the ego continues well beyond representational differentiation. There is, for example, the ability not only to see connections between the core affect states, but to transform affect states into higher level affect states. One observes affect states, such as empathy, altruism, higher forms of mourning and loss, as well as the organizing structures of late latency and adolescence. New levels of elaboration, transformation, and organization of wish and affect build on core affect states and take into account emerging biological changes in the body, challenges for defining a psychosocial identity, and new capacities to anticipate the future and integrate elements from the past and present into expanding personal, social, and intellectual roles. A consideration of these later advances will be undertaken in a future work.

Looking at the psychotherapeutic process from a developmental perspective may change the way one thinks about how and why psychotherapy works with different types of patients. It is only a rare number of patients who come in already at a highly differentiated level. Different levels of empathy and psychotherapeutic process may need to relate to the developmental level of the patient. One may begin to explain why different psychotherapies work for different patients from a developmental perspective. Consider a person who is very concrete and has no ability to identify core affect states and see connections between affect states. He might be very attracted to a behavioral modification model which focuses on behaviors and then control. If you say, "Look here. The reason why you are having temper tantrums is that you get rewarded every time you have a temper tantrum. We have to change the contingencies of reinforcement for you to make sure you don't get rewarded." The patient may say, "You're absolutely right! In fact it's not every time I throw a temper tantrum that I get a lot of attention, it's every fifth or tenth or fifteen time. The schedule is a *random ratio*, one which only increases the frequency of my tantrums because I never know how many tantrums I have to throw to get reinforced." In this humorous example, the person is not denying his psychoanalytic heritage. Behavioral constructs make emotional sense to him because of his developmental level. The person who is interested in relationships among affect states, who can abstract affect states, finds behavioral explanations meaningless. To a behavioral explanation, he might say, "But before I have my tantrum I have all these different feelings—loneliness, anger, guilt. I need to know my feelings better."

Not only does the person become attracted to the approach that fits his developmental level, but the metaphor of the therapy becomes a shared meaning between the patient and the therapist, whether it is a psychoanalytic set of metaphors, behavior modification set, or cognitive–behavioral therapy set. (The cognitive–behavioral therapy, for example, would rely on the stage of representational elaboration as well as some aspects of representational differentiation.) The shared metaphor consolidates the earlier stages and provides a sense of shared attention and engagement. In order to have a sense of engagement with a mature cognitively sophisticated adult one may need shared metaphors. Perhaps the attraction to different religions relates in part to the types of metaphors that become part of a symbol of engagement. The religion or the therapeutic philosophy becomes the vehicle for a sense of feeling connected or engaged in a highly meaningful relationship.

But in therapy, it is important to go beyond the stage of engagement, however blissful or meaningful it may be. Different therapies may work for symptom relief because anytime one is engaged and feels understood, symptoms are bound to improve. If different therapies work for symptom relief, the question is: Are certain therapies intrinsically and potentially more helpful than other therapies?

Perhaps there are advantages to therapies that come closer in their own complexity to mirroring the complexities of the human condition; namely, those that focus on all the different developmental levels. They facilitate shifts from one level to the next, whereas a therapy that is focused on only one level will be more limited. With many current therapies, some tend, in many hands, to operate at the higher levels and ignore the lower ones, and vice versa. Psychoanalytic and psychodynamic approaches, it will be suggested in subsequent chapters, need to focus more on the earlier stages in development. Behavioral approaches in contrast require a developmental, not just behavioral, frame of reference to be able to group behavioral patterns and "discriminating" and "reinforcing" experiences in terms of naturalistic human capacities.

Chapter 5

The Psychoanalytic Process
with Adults and Children

We have looked at the general model of the psychotherapeutic process. Now we will look at the psychoanalytic situation.
We will see how the developmental model plays itself out in the
psychoanalytic situation. This is a model which views the
different levels at which therapeutic experience takes place,
including regulation and engagement, intentional signaling,
representational elaboration, and representational differentiation. To do this, we will consider a number of characteristics of
the psychoanalytic situation and look at how the developmental
perspective sheds light on these characteristics.

The psychoanalytic situation makes use of an intense
relationship between patient and therapist in which the patient
uses free association to help make available information about
his current and past emotional patterns. Through the working
alliance, the therapist and the patient collaborate to explore the
meaning of these patterns. As they understand these meanings
in cross-sectional (i.e., current), historical, and genetic contexts,
they attempt to work through the repetition of older patterns
and help the patient gain freedom for new patterns. In working

through the older patterns, they "tease out" the conflicts that operate both currently and historically, by making use of the transference relationship. This includes the patient's tendency to reexperience with the therapist the same emotional patterns they have historically experienced and now experience with others. These emotional patterns are brought into the transference with intensity and economy due to the nature of the transference relationship. This relationship crystallizes these patterns in the here-and-now. The transference is therefore used as a window into the emotional patterns of the patient, including the conflicts the patient experiences. The working alliance facilitates the working through. As these processes occur, we hope to see overall personality growth and change. We expect to see the very structure of the ego advance to higher developmental levels. The resolution of conflicts which were associated with repetitive neurotic patterns and restrictions to further growth and development, now makes it possible for the ego to advance in its growth and development.

FREE ASSOCIATION

In free association, with the adult patient lying on the couch, or with the child patient talking and playing in the playroom, the patient says and/or does (with the child) whatever comes to mind. The key is to have a noncritical, facilitating atmosphere for the spontaneous emergence of emotional themes.

Free association is usually thought of as a verbal phenomenon. Representational life is elaborated freely in the safety of the analytic relationship. In other words, the patient and the analyst agree that there will be no acting in, such as translating thoughts into destructive behaviors to self or to others. Within this safety, and with the further safety of lying down so motor control is partially suspended, the patient has the freedom to literally put whatever he wants into words. However, the focus on words and representational life, in the traditional use of the concept of free association, may be too narrow. A developmental perspective would build the concept of free association into a broader concept. It would include communication at each of the developmental levels as part of the free associative communication system.

For example, free association would include the patient's tendency for patterns of regulation and disregulation, interest in sights and sounds of any kind, tendency for engagement, and the subtle shifts of engagement, and gestures using motor patterns, posture, and vocal tone and rhythm and facial expression. Some patients will respond to the sound of the analyst's voice and find it soothing, others may find the analyst's voice too high and experience it as nonsoothing. This may be an early regulatory issue. The patient's reaction is part of his free association. Even though the patient at times may describe his reactions in verbal forms, the analyst may also observe the reactions in terms of the patient's activity level, movement patterns (i.e., the way the patient lies and shifts), breathing rhythm, and attentiveness to the analyst's voice or certain inanimate objects in the room. The sensory affective level, as indicated, involves not only verbal but also preverbal mechanisms, such as posture, gesture, and movement.

The level of engagement would monitor the quality of the patient's relatedness, lack of relatedness, and all states in between. It would monitor the way the patient deals with transitions at the beginning and end of the session (in terms of reengagement), the way the patient modulates engagement in relationship to frustrations, anger, and deprivations during the hour. It would monitor the way the patient deals with distractions such as the telephone ringing or noise (in terms of the quality of engagement); and the way the engagement is influenced by higher level processes involving emotions, wishes, and ideas at the representational level.

One would not usually think of the quality of engagement as being a free associative vehicle. But, after all, the way the person engages and disengages from the therapist (e.g., various types of aloofness and withdrawal or types of demandingness), is a channel of communication that in part is not often in the person's representational or verbal awareness. The patient may say: "I tend to withdraw under these circumstances" or "I feel distant from you." At this point, it is a representational obser- vation. More often, the pattern is subtle. The patient is not aware of a pattern of aloofness and to the analyst he feels a little "spacey" and unengaged for a period of time. The analyst should not view this as simply a separate issue, but as a communication from the patient, and, in fact, quite a free communication, or a free association. Often, it is a motor and/or gestural type of communication.

At the third level, we see organized, intentional behavioral patterns. Here, the patient uses hands, vocal rhythms, eye contact, body posture, and other devices for intentional ges- tural communication. When angry, the person may move his hands in one gestural pattern; when feeling loving, in another. This pattern of intentional communication is going to be limited with some adults because they are lying on the couch. However, such communications may be exceedingly varied in children who are moving around the office—yet another pat- tern of free association. The patient will communicate many issues at this presymbolic level. It is important to highlight here that gestural communication is closely tied to later symbolic communication and is a direct precursor of it. The use of the gesture precedes the use of the word and, in many respects, the word becomes an abstraction of the gestures that preceded it. The patient will communicate a wide variety of feeling states and emotional patterns through his preverbal gestural commu- nication. Through angry gestures, loving gestures, dependent gestures, independent gestures, and sexual gestures, an entire dialogue will be taking place at the preverbal gestural level. At times, these will be in synchrony with verbal communication. At other times they may have a life of their own. The patient may verbally be saying, "Nothing comes to mind. My mind is a blank," and yet may be writhing in sexual ecstasy at the gestural level of communication. A person may be saying they feel loving and yet communicating gesturally their strong anger. This gestural level therefore must be viewed as an important vehicle of free association. It need not be viewed as a defense against, avoidance or denial of, or some less worthy method of communication, in comparison to words. It should be viewed as an important, developmentally based level of communication. We will discuss later how one integrates the different levels of communication. For example, how does one deal with an issue that is free associated about at the gestural level, but not at the representational–verbal level.

At the level of representational elaboration, we observe free association as it is traditionally thought of—the patient's ability to put into words various thoughts, feelings, wishes, inclinations, and the like. Here, we notice the different themes the patient verbalizes about—dependence, assertiveness, pleasure, anger, and so forth. It is important to note that the level of representational elaboration has been reached when the patient's free associations involve the identification of "core" feeling states through the use of words. A person who says, "I am furious at my wife because she . . ." and then later says, "Yet I felt loving toward her after she apologized," is elaborating representational affect states. A person who says, "I hugged my wife" and then "I hit my wife," is not abstracting affects of love or anger, but is only describing different behavioral states. He has not yet made it fully to the stage of representational elaboration. He is using words to describe the stage just preceding representational elaboration; that is, the stage of behavioral organization. This could be viewed as transitional to representational elaboration. It is a common mistake to assume that descriptions of behaviors mean the person has abstracted feeling states, such as anger, love, pleasure, excitement, and the like. The behavioral describers usually act out and, in fact, do not have the labeling ability that would suggest a representational elaboration of affective states.

As one listens to the patient's associations, one can look for the range of emotional themes which are truly at the representational level—which themes are representational, which are still action patterns, which are somatic descriptions ("My muscles ache"), and which are simply avoided entirely. Here, one can monitor, cross sectionally, the different potential affective themes, including dependency, pleasure, excitement, assertiveness, anger, love, empathy, and self-limit-setting, as well as the opposites to each of these themes (e.g., dependency–separation anxiety) and observe which themes are present at which level and which are not present.

The fourth level is representational differentiation. The free associations at this level involve spontaneous back and forth communications between verbal elaboration of the different themes in one's life and exploring connections and relationships between these themes. It involves attempting to examine subjective feelings from a reality point of view, as well as making here-and-now dynamic and genetic–historical connections. It also involves cross-thematic connections (seeing the bridges between pleasure and dependency, anger and pleasure, etc.). Here we see not just thematic elaboration, but thematic differentiation in terms of cross-thematic, temporal thematic, spatial thematic, and in terms of subjective–objective and intrareality thematic bridges. The ability to engage at this level of the analytic process signifies a high level of free association.

At this level, we also look for the emotional range of these "differentiating free associations," and in which thematic sectors the person is or is not capable of them. Some people will have this level of differentiation in terms of dependency, but not aggression, and vice versa. One person, for example, will see connections between his behavior and different feeling states around anger. However, when it comes to dependency, he may operate in a more undifferentiated manner.

We can therefore look at free association in terms of each of the levels, and see how the patient communicates at the level of his early regulation and interest in sensation, at the level of engagement, at the level of organized purposeful behavior, at the level of representational elaboration, and at the level of representational differentiation. Tuning in to all these levels vastly enhances recognition of the patient's free associations. Simply looking at the levels of representational elaboration and differentiation alone, as is traditionally done, with fleeting attention to posture and nonverbal communication as a kind of inferior form of communication, in part addresses these levels, but only in part, and with a clear bias toward the representational level. It is suggested here that if we use a developmental context, we will want to pay attention to free association in a fuller sense. We will want to use Freud's admonition of even, hovering attention in a truly even, hovering way. If we only look at the verbal elaborations, our attention will be quite narrow. And as we all know, our attention is only as good as our listening abilities. We must not only train ourselves to listen for words, but equally have to train ourselves to listen for these earlier levels of free association.

One may ask at this point, "How do I use my awareness of these earlier levels even when they do occur? Do I simply try to put them into words for the patient?" This is an important question. How does one relate to the levels of free association? If one simply says to the patient, "I can see you are disengaging from me every time there is ten minutes to go in the hour. What is going on here?" one is assuming that the patient has the ability to communicate his feelings around engagement in a higher form, such as a highly representational elaboration or differentiation. The person is not simply doing so out of habit or for purposes of defense. Such a comment may facilitate the person saying, "Yes, I do that because I am so angry at the impending separation I can't bear to talk about it," and so forth. If the patient could elaborate that easily, in all likelihood they would make some verbal references to their feelings and one could deal with the verbal system directly. More than likely, the patient is not verbally describing his feelings because at that moment the issue around engagement cannot be communicated in the mode of representational elaboration or differentiation. The feelings do not have access to that system.

To be sure, it is a goal to eventually help the person develop representational access. With the representational system, and particularly with the system of representational differentiation, the patient can comprehend patterns and find better solutions for his conflicts. In the short term, however, it may be most essential to relate to the person at each level of his communications. The key may not be the technical issue of "what do I say," but, "How do I maintain engagement and truly even, hovering attention at each of these levels." The analyst who is sensitive to the issues of engagement (to continue the example of the patient who disengages ten minutes before the hour ends) will often indicate his awareness of a pattern to the patient through his own preverbal processes. Some analysts may find themselves becoming more active and wooing the patient into more consistent engagement. Other analysts will find themselves becoming aloof, disengaging alongside their patient. Other analysts may find themselves getting angry and making their more aggressive, intrusive interpretations to the patient during this period of disengagement. Still other analysts may find themselves going after sexual material at this point, covertly thinking that this will excite their patient and keep him or her involved. Much of the analyst's response will be unconscious and will have to do with the way he has dealt with subtle disengagements throughout his own life. The analyst will often be unaware of his counterreaction to the patient's reaction. In a sense, we will have what we will describe later as a preverbal transference and countertransference at the level of engagement. The patient acts out one pattern and the analyst acts out (or in) a counterpattern, often based on his own personal reactions.

It is unreasonable to assume the analyst will be sufficiently well analyzed to see this pattern quickly and therefore not have his own empathetic counterreaction to the patient. These preverbal patterns, I believe, happen too quickly and are so embedded in the character structure(s) of the individuals involved that only their repetition over time makes them accessible to analytic scrutiny. The goal, then, is for the analyst to recognize at the level of representational elaboration and differentiation the patient's pattern of disengagement, recognize his own counterpattern, and comprehend what they have been doing together. In doing this, the analyst, in the process of reflection, will be maintaining his engagement with the patient.

The analyst who had been overcompensating by attacking the patient or bringing up exciting material or overwooing the patient, will probably return to a baseline of even hovering attention where engagement is maintained, without defensive maneuvers. Similarly, the therapist who disengages (begins getting sleepy with ten minutes to go) because of the patient's disengagement, will likewise maintain a state of even attention.

Against this more neutral but engaged posture, the patient will have a new experience. In the past, he in all likelihood will have engendered a counteraction in others and the analyst, either similar to, or opposite from, what he had grown up with in his family. He will now have a new experience where the expectable counterreactions are not forthcoming. It will be interesting to observe how he deals with this. Needless to say, as information is building up and as the patient experiences a new reality, the analyst may try to help him put his perceptions into words in terms of representational elaboration and differentiation. In the short term, however, it must be emphasized that the ability to remain engaged with the patient and to come to grips with countertransference patterns of compensatory engagement is a critical first step. As indicated, this work often goes on preverbally and, perhaps, often intuitively, though usually not consciously. For the analyst to raise this to consciousness is the critical first step in the process.

The processes described for engagement apply to issues involving sensory–affective, reactivity and receptivity, behavioral organization, and intentional preverbal communication. The analyst, in each of these situations, will find that he has a preverbal counterreaction to the patient's communications. Understanding the counterreaction will help the analyst to move from a position of countertransference acting in to a position of engaged, interactive neutrality.

Engaged, interactive neutrality is never a state of apathy or withdrawal or lack of affect. It is a state of affective, intentional, engaged involvement which facilitates the patient's communicative freedom. Lack of involvement, engagement, or empathy, however well disguised as abstinence or "neutrality" is almost always sensed by the patient, and is therefore a clear affective communication and serious countertransference problem. The concept of analytic abstinence and analytic neutrality is sometimes used to justify the state of relative nonrelatedness. It should be pointed out that this state of nonrelatedness can often be a preverbal countertransference quality of disengagement, which not only restricts the patient's freedom for free association, but in fact interjects a very powerful affective state which leads the patient into dealing with issues around deprivation (somewhat iatrogenically). The concept of even, hovering attention in a developmental framework, suggests a state of affective involvement which maximizes the patient's freedom and his ability to grow and further develop. Active listening, with empathy and engagement, is very different from apathetic withdrawal.

ANALYTIC NEUTRALITY (AND RELATEDNESS)

Because neutrality as a style depends so much on the personality of the analyst, it is often hard to define in practice. For example, often one refers patients to another therapist based on the latter's temperament and the kind of a "fit" the patient requires. Here, one is making a judgment about the quality of neutrality or relatedness of a colleague. For some patients, one will recommend a more reserved analytic posture; for others, a more actively wooing posture. These issues should not be left to intuition or ill-defined qualities. They should be articulated clearly as part of a more integrated concept of analytic neutrality. The concept of analytic neutrality, from a developmental perspective, includes not only avoiding getting caught up in the patient's conflicts but also providing those minimal experiences that every human being needs to grow and develop. These would include an environment which is sufficiently protective and interesting so that the patient feels both calm and interested in the environment around him. Second, it should provide the opportunity for engaging with a sense of connectedness that has some positive emotional qualities to it. (This becomes the baseline for which the patient can distort or change the relatedness.) Third, this analytic relationship should have a quality of intentional communication where the analytic environment can engage and purposely interact with the patient so that his preverbal gestures are responded to in an organized, intentional manner. From the gesture to lie on the couch and the occasional comment, clarifying or interpretive, to the more ill-defined body movements and breathing rhythms, this purposeful system underneath the representational system gives a sense of safety, logic, and reality to the quality of engagement. The analytic relationship must have the capacity for engaging at two additional levels—representational elaboration and representational differentiation. This includes the ability to listen to all the themes present, understand the verbal symbolic patterns, and later to be able to shift gears and look at relationships between the different themes, in terms of temporal, spatial, and intrathematic and intrareality bridges. These last two capacities depend on the analyst's empathetic ability and technical skills. The technical skills are an important part of the ability to do the work of representational elaboration and differentiation. Neutrality at this level means the analyst does not become more interested, insightful, empathetic, verbal, humorous, supportive, understanding, confronting, and so forth, with dependency themes than with aggressive themes or sexual themes and so forth. A tall order! It means equal ability to engage, intentionally signal, and symbolically elaborate and differentiate material for each domain of experience.

Therefore, one can define analytic neutrality from a developmental perspective. It need not be a sterile concept described in negative terms. It may be described in active terms involving attention, engagement, purposeful communication, symbolic elaboration, and differentiation.

THE WORKING ALLIANCE

Traditionally, the working alliance is conceptualized as the ability to engage the patient in a collaborative effort to look at the experiences becoming elaborated through free association. It suggests that a part of the ego of the patient and of the analyst are working in collaboration. The working alliance suggests a highly differentiated ego structure in which the patient can experience and elaborate experiences through free association, and at the same time take a step away and observe experiences in collaboration with the analyst through the working alliance. This definition would suggest that only a fairly mature patient is capable of analytic psychotherapy or analysis. Only a highly differentiated ego structure that, for the most part, has entered into the stage of representational differentiation would be capable of a working alliance of this kind.

Our developmental perspective would suggest that this is much too artificial a description. In fact, the working alliance exists in a developmental context, as do all other experiences of the patient. There is "more or less" of a working alliance, depending on progress along a certain line of development. The earliest aspect of the working alliance relates to the patient's earliest level of ego structure having to do with regulation and interest in the world. It relates to the patient's ability to recognize patterns. The parallel is the baby's ability to begin abstracting verbal and visual–spatial patterns in the first few months of life. It is the interest in decoding patterns and comprehending them that is one important component of the working alliance. This constitutes an important function of the collaborative ego of the patient and the therapist.

At a second stage, the stage of engagement, we have a most important foundation of the working alliance—a relationship (with the analyst) that can tolerate transference reactions and distortions, including disappointment, anger, and loss, as well as excitement. This stage is based, in part, on the quality of engagement between the analyst and the patient. Some "engagements" can survive disappointment and frustration; other patterns of relatedness and engagement do not survive such stresses and tension. The working alliance, the ability for an on-going sense of relatedness in spite of emotional variations of great intensity, is part of the quality of engagement.

At the level of purposeful, organized communication, the patient is beginning to differentiate "me" and "you," different emotional themes, and different relationships. This preverbal, prerepresentational behavioral differentiation is a third contributor to the working alliance. It suggests that the patient can behaviorally relate to the analyst in different ways. The patient can differentiate different emotional polarities, themes, and aims. The analyst can be the analyst of strongly held feelings and the analyst of security and reality at the same time, just like the mother of the eighteen-month-old can be the mother of security and the mother of enormous rage or excitement. Interestingly, at eight and twelve months the infant is likely to be still experiencing emotional polarities in all or nothing forms, all good or all bad. Only by sixteen to eighteen months are the polarities integrated. At this level, the working alliance is based initially on concepts of splitting and then on concepts of integrated preverbal behavioral organization.

At the fourth and fifth levels (representational elaboration and differentiation) there are the more traditional notions of the working alliance. The patient representationally and verbally organizes his descriptions of his own feelings in terms of subjective states, transference patterns, and the reality of the working relationship with the analyst. The patient may say, "I feel enraged! I never want to see you again! But, of course, I'll be back tomorrow." Now feelings are symbolized and differentiated. The angry feelings can be experienced together with a sense of security in the working relationship. This developmental approach to the working alliance allows one to see how the working alliance operates at each level of development. For example, there is the person who talks a good game at the level of representational differentiation and says, "I don't really hate you because I depend on you for understanding things, but I feel like I never want to come back." He then misses three sessions. He also evidences a pattern of disengagement with people whenever he is frustrated or angry. For this person, the therapeutic alliance is compromised at the level of basic engagement. He may have never learned at the preverbal level of engagement to sustain frustration without disengaging. Even though he talks a good game, he may have a vulnerability in his working relationship at an early level of development. If this person tends to have short-term relationships, and when frustrated tends to opt for complete disengagement, one may be quite concerned about the analysis surviving serious disappointments or frustrations. On the one hand, this is a transference issue, on the other hand, it is an issue in the early development of the working alliance. When such an issue in the preverbal engagement phase of the working alliance reveals itself, it must be dealt with early in the analysis. One must deal with one's counterreaction to the patient's disengagement. Does the analyst "woo," overexcite, disengage, or become hostile? Or can the analyst maintain a posture of engaged analytic neutrality as a basis for trying to work this issue through and help it become elevated in an emotional sense (not in a contrived intellectual sense) to the level of representational elaboration and differentiation.

CONFLICTS

Like each of the other subjects discussed, conflicts, too, can be thought of in traditional terms or in the context of the developmental model being described here. Usually, we think of conflicts between certain wishes and certain internalized fears or prohibitions. For example, the wish to hurt someone may be in conflict with the fear of injury or loss of love and approval. The two sides of the conflict, postinternalization and consolidation of the superego, are mostly internal. Early in life, the two sides of the conflict feel internal, but one-half of the conflict is based on external reality. The presence of the parents, for example, confirms the fears.

This section will outline some of the early stages at which we can observe conflicts. These early stages will be seen to relate to the type of internalized conflict that is central to both normal functioning and psychopathology.

At the level of regulation and interest in the world, we will often see what appear to be conflicts in the infant between the interest in certain sensory stimuli and the tendency for being overly excited. Here, there is a conflict between the need for calm and regulation on the one hand, and the excitement with the world of sensation on the other hand. In fact, one will often see babies overexcite themselves when given the opportunity to. They will then overcompensate with extra calmness, only again to overexcite themselves.

At the level of engagement, we will see conflicts between the wish to be engaged and the tendency for the sameness that results from disengagement and total control over one's environment. At the level of organized, purposeful behavior, we will often see conflicts between the aggressive side of organized, purposeful behavior (being the boss, taking charge) and the tendency for compliant passivity, and/or the need for admiration and approval, both of which maintain an unchallenging interactive flow with the love object.

At the level of representational elaboration, we will often see conflicts between the independence that this stage offers (to now carry one's world with one inside in terms of symbols) and the need for dependency on the actual object. At the level of representational differentiation, we will often see the conflict between more differentiated phallic–assertive inclinations on the one hand, and undifferentiated self–object connectedness (i.e., fear of separation). The phallic–assertiveness, which defines self along thematic and gender-sexual lines, may be contrasted with a passive, nongender, nonthematic differentiating self.

Therefore, for each developmental stage there may be an inherent structural conflict as part of the organization of that particular phase. Conflict is not simply an organizing structure at the level of mental representation, or representational elaboration and differentiation; it is part of each stage of development.

TRANSFERENCE

The transference also plays itself out at each developmental level. Traditionally, transference is thought of in terms of representational levels: there are oedipal transferences and preoedipal transferences. Oedipal transferences have to do with triangular conflict involving sexuality, aggression, and negative and positive oedipal strivings. Preoedipal transferences involve issues around anger, dependency, separation, and control. The capacity for representational elaboration and differentiation is the vehicle for exploring the transference and for ultimately resolving it.

Prerepresentational transferences are less obvious and are based on the earliest levels of development. As was described earlier in examples for free association, the patient relates to the analytic situation in many ways at once. The patient engages the sensory environment, tries to balance self-regulation and interest, engages, disengages, and establishes various subtle relationship patterns, and communicates with gesture and sound intentionally quite separate from his verbal productions. These examples illustrate different transference fragments at each level of development. There is, for example, the person who feels that no environment will be able to offer comfort and regulation; the person who has always engaged rather tentatively and disengages readily to create a sense of sameness outside the human relationship; the person who communicates somewhat chaotically and unpurposefully. The latter person may be in a state of mild frenzy due to experiences of disregulation, a lack of consistent engagement, and as a way to deal with the anticipation of disregulation and disengagement. It is as though he is saying, "at the level of behavioral disorganization, I will disorganize before my environment disengages and ceases to provide me protection." An infant may try to create a sense of mastery through chaos and disregulation. That infants could establish such a pattern prior to the stage of representation by anticipating disregulation and therefore creating it should not be surprising. Toddlers are quite sophisticated and can anticipate expectable patterns, and generate many different behavioral patterns—negativism, disorganization, engagement, warmth, and security—based on their own inclinations of the moment. One only has to see an eighteen-month-old double back in a chase game or make fun of father by putting on his hat backwards as he imitates father coming home from work. One can see intricate interrelationships among patterns in infancy. A transference configuration may, therefore, emerge in someone's life prior to any capacity for representational elaboration and differentiation. This pattern may then be played out yet again at the level of representational elaboration and differentiation. Or one may later on initiate other patterns which interact with these prerepresentational patterns.

Let us take the example of an eight-year-old girl, Molly, currently in analysis. She was born with a tendency toward disregulation, where even minimal levels of noise or light would overstimulate her and she would become difficult to console. It was hard for her to engage in a consistent way, and she frequently disengaged. Mother recalled how difficult it was to find synchronous rhythms, however hard she would try. At seven or eight months, mother mentioned how her little girl would become disorganized and chaotic and it was hard to read her behavioral signals. Mother sensed her daughter deliberately became chaotic when she wanted to engage her, and she felt pushed away. Fortunately, however, mother kept trying to reengage, though often unsuccessfully. Molly did not have a very deep engagement, but only one which could exist fleetingly and then she would go into patterns of disorganized activity (she would be incapable of controlling her motor system and her preverbal vocalizations). This girl's pattern of distancing herself and then elaborating these distancing maneuvers through patterns of disorganized activity had interesting implications for her representational stages of development. I should mention that this was an extremely bright little girl whose motor and cognitive development was proceeding on schedule, in part due to mother's ability to do the best she could and maintain some emotional relatedness in spite of the patterns being described. At the representational stage, this little girl became quite interested in themes of aggression and destruction. In pretend play, the animals were often hurting one another. The scenes themselves would get chaotic. Whenever mother would try to introduce nicer themes, "Don't the dollies want to hug one another? Don't they want to have a tea party?" the little girl would acquiesce for a minute or two, become anxious, and then substitute themes of anger. Soon the dolls were in each other's mouths, biting. Frequently, she would then start laughing and giggling excitedly. As sexual issues became of interest at around age three, she played with her dolls' bottoms. But organized, intentional play and accompanying verbalizations were fleeting, and quickly shifted to the dolls having their legs pulled off.

As Molly went from the stage of representational elaboration, where themes of aggression and destruction were dominant and themes of warm collaboration and engagement were only minor notes, to the level of representational differentiation (and began getting into triangular patterns) she would, in her verbalizations and play, promote herself as the "one and only, the best." If she was trying to sing, she was the "best" of all the children. She would imitate actresses she saw on T.V. In her emerging competition with mother, she liberally verbalized that father preferred her to her sisters or her mother. She established her victory by fiat, rather than by active involved competition. Mother vacillated between trying to contain her active little girl and feeling intimidated by her. Mother's own fear of not being loved, often made it difficult for her to deal with Molly's behavior. She tried to use what she described as "reasoning approaches," where she would cater to her "little devil" as a way of developing a closer relationship so that the child wouldn't feel "rejected." This only seemed to further antagonize her "little tyrant" who finally became involved in treatment at age eight. At this time, she wasn't able to play with other children. She needed to be first, "the best," and could not share or deal with disappointment. She was destroying property at home and in school, and was often involved in frenzied, excited activity where she could not control her disorganized behavior.

During the first year of her analysis, the themes character-izing her early development readily emerged. She would dom-inate the analytic hour, had to be the boss, number one. The analyst was frequently "disappointing her, not doing things right." Whenever the analyst attempted to find the right rhythm of engagement, she would find something wrong with it and scold or discipline him. At times she tried to physically abuse him. She was readily distracted by sights or sounds in the analytic environment and whenever there was a short period of engagement and collaborative work around exploring themes or playing a game, she would quickly disengage and become involved in disorganized, behavior with the clear intention of "driving you crazy." Yet, the behavior itself had a life of its own independent of the verbalization which she attached to it—"driving you crazy." The themes of aggression and the desire to destroy everyone who got in her way (other children, her mother, the analyst, but not her father), were dominant in her verbalizations. The insistence that her father was her protector and would "do in" mother, the analyst, and anyone else who didn't give her "what she wanted," was of paramount impor-tance.

Here, we saw in the transference how Molly was elaborat-ing elements from different stages of development: There was the sensory reactivity to the analytic situations, the disengage-ment after engagement, the disorganized behavioral activity, the representational elaborations around themes of anger and destructiveness. There was the theme in the stage of represen-tational differentiation having to do mostly with being the winner and the best, and having daddy as an ally to make everything okay. However, along with this she was not dealing with the fact that other children were mad at her, that she couldn't get along with mother, and that she was frequently, herself, feeling out of control and distraught. A series of transference fragments began organizing themselves at each developmental level. It would be a mistake to think of this entire pattern as existing at the levels of representational elaboration and differentiation, although it is interesting to see how the levels of elaboration and differentiation create a representational life that is consistent with the prerepresentational patterns and add on new pieces of it. In this situation, the representational levels did not create and organize a sense of integrity for the earlier patterns, as they would with an organized transference neurosis. This little girl evidences far too much disturbance in early ego development for this kind of an organized, integrated pattern.

In the case of an organized transference neurosis, one might see less severe earlier distortions in ego development manifested as representational fragments. Earlier prerepresentational patterns get expressed through representational access. Here, a person could engage fairly well, communicate in a purposeful, organized way, represent his anxieties around engagement in terms of fears of loss, and represent the anxieties around behavioral intentionality in terms of fears of being disorganized and hurting others. Here, one might see fears of loss and fears of hurting others playing itself out as part of an organized transference neurosis. Earlier fears would contribute to the foundation in the structure of the person's primal scene and oedipal fantasies and be available to analytic scrutiny in representational forms. However, where the transference elements cannot be harnessed and organized at representational levels, it is important to see how they exist at levels of homeostasis, attachment, somatapsychological differentiation, and behavioral organization as well as representational elaboration and differentiation.

Therefore, with the girl described, the strategy involved dealing with her behavior at each level, making sure to engage each level of the transference. While engaging each prerepresentational level it was important not to enter into a countertransference acting in by compensating for her tendencies. Analytic neutrality included in her case engagement at each level; attention to the basic rule of not allowing injury to self or property; and eventually, through this process of engagement and reworking at the prerepresentational levels, to help her find verbal forms for these prerepresentational patterns. It was recognized that she would experience these patterns as emotional and behavioral urges, not strictly as abstracted affect states, as would a person who had worked through these earlier stages.

In other words, the person who works through these stages experiences the fear of loss of engagement or the fear of going out of control as they abstract an affect state strictly in a representational form. The person who disengages in reality and disorganizes in reality tends to experience the tendency to disengage. The patient is in the process of doing so, is beginning to throw things around the room as he learns to attach representational meaning to these patterns. The person can then sort of "catch themselves" and perhaps talk about the behavior rather than act it out. This step alone may take many months. The behavioral tendency to enact directly is quite different from the abstraction of the behavioral tendency as an affect state.

The difference between abstracted affect states and behavioral tendencies should be highlighted. In dealing with deviations in early ego development, we are dealing with behavioral and somatic tendencies, not abstracted affect states. As part of the analytic work (i.e., creating a situation of analytic neutrality rather than countertransference behavioral acting in) one tends to allow the working-through of these behavioral and affective inclinations which then eventually find representational forms. This in turn helps the patient limit the acting in. Eventually, through this process, representational elaboration permits the abstraction of certain affect states. We then see the development of ego structure.

The process of creating abstracted affective states is a critical part of the analytic work. It is essential for structural growth from prerepresentational to representational patterns. It might be just as central as the interpretation of oedipal transferences are for structural growth.

The repeated description of the prerepresentational patterns of attention, engagement, and intentional behavioral
organization (in multiple contexts) as well as their anticipation,
allows the patient to begin abstracting certain behavioral and
affective features across different behavioral states. He begins
to see that whenever he wants to behave in a disorganized way,
he is feeling a sense of physiologic discomfort. He begins to see
that this physiologic discomfort relates to the anticipation of
disengagement in the quality of relatedness: "You leave me, I
leave you," as Molly came to say. She doesn't say, however, "I
feel like you will leave me and I feel like I will leave you," she
says, "You leave me, I leave you." She experiences this behavior
in the reality of the current situation, not in terms of abstracted
feeling states. The repetition of this description, enables her to
not actually take the "leaving me" as literally as she once did. She
leaves a little bit, but doesn't actually have to walk out of the
room or hide behind the chair. She leaves in terms of her
affective involvement and then describes it, and then feels the
tendency to want to throw things at the can, rather than at me.
In describing this, she connects up the "leaving and throwing."
The state of leaving and the behavioral disorganization then
becomes observed as part of a pattern. As she observes these
behavioral inclinations and patterns in multiple context (before
vacations, when frustrated, when she comes a few minutes late
for a session, etc.) she begins abstracting these patterns. Eventually, she abstracts a feeling state of discomfort and the
accompanying disorganization. This leads the way to a truly
representational elaboration of this pattern. She can eventually
say, "I feel empty, wild, like I will never be able to get close again
and like I want to destroy everything." She begins to tease out
an affect state which elevates her to the stage of representational elaboration, and eventually to the stage of representational differentiation. The abstraction of affect states is the key
developmental accomplishment between the prerepresentational and representational patterns (sixteen to thirty months of
age). This is similar to another critical juncture—the internalization of superego functions around the oedipal stage.

In fact, in terms of the development of the transference, the critical junctures involve the establishment of a pattern of human engagement at the three- to six-month level, the capacity for abstracting behavioral patterns at the eight- to eighteen-month level, the capacity for abstracting affective states at the eighteen- to thirty-month level, and the capacity for internalizing triangular conflict at the three and a half- to six-year-old level.

Therefore, we can now see the transference as existing on many developmental levels each meriting its own consideration, each providing different insights into the patient's normal and pathologic development, and each needing different therapeutic principles, in terms of analytic inquiry and analytic understanding.

THE WORKING THROUGH PROCESS

This leads us, naturally, to a discussion of the working through process. Traditionally, working through involves the understanding of conflicts and their derivative feelings, thoughts, and behaviors in multiple contexts of the patient's life. Once understanding is achieved through the transference relationship, one must apply this understanding to situations with family, work, a reexamination of one's history, as well as applications to current areas of functioning.

The developmental perspective can broaden the concept of working through to involve each level of development and the range of behaviors and themes the person is capable of at each level. We can look at the working through of a core issue, in terms of its ramifications for the level of engagement, behavioral organization, and representational elaboration and differentiation.

Assume, for example, that the core issue has to do with the inhibition of aggression because of fears of loss of love. It has now been understood in the transference at multiple levels, in terms of genetic representational material, and cross-sectional representational material. The patient is now attempting to work it through. Also assume for this example, that this pattern

has critical elements in prerepresentational as well as representational life. The core difficulty did not just result from
representational conflict, but came about because of earlier
issues. At eight months of age, when the patient would try to
assert himself, often mother would disengage rather than to
urge him on. At eighteen months, he further experienced this
pattern of withdrawal from his assertive behavior. At twenty-six
months, it was connected with verbalizations dealing with anger
and loss of love. In the oedipal situation, assertiveness was
caught up in triangular conflict where competition and castration fears were intensified by fears of loss of love and abandon-
ment.

The first element in the working through may revolve
around the person maintaining or understanding why its
difficult to maintain a quality of engagement while being more
assertive. Or do they become more tentative after assertion,
expecting loss of love and disengagement? Part of the working
through will involve monitoring the security of the engagement
as an assertive act and attempting to elevate subtle prerepresentational patterns to levels of representational awareness.

At the level of purposeful communication, we want to see
if the person can be behaviorally assertive in multiple contexts
to learn that the behavioral loss of engagement and love does
not in fact occur. They may have already decided at the level of
representations that it won't occur, but are now working it
through prerepresentationally. Similarly, at this (second) level,
we want to look at whether they can assertively pursue all the
themes of their life. Can they assertively pursue dependency
needs? (For example, when wanting closeness, can they reach
out or do they expectantly wait, whine, or passively demand?)
Sexual excitement? Curiosity? Anger? Can they, as they get
older, assertively pursue empathy? In other words, to the
degree that assertiveness has to do with self-starting and taking
charge, it covers the full gamut of themes and can be applied to
each of the thematic realms that cross sectionally characterize
the level of behavioral organization and, then again, the level of
representational elaboration and differentiation. We look for

the developmental level and then we look for its application in each theme of the patient's life.

Now, if we jump to the level of representational elabora- tion and differentiation, we look at whether the person can represent assertive wishes without inhibition around fears of loss of love and, later on, castration. Moreover, we look to see whether the person can do this in multiple settings, and multiple contexts in those settings, related to dependency, sexuality, curiosity, anger and competitiveness, and empathy and love. Can they pursue each of those themes without the fear of loss of love? Not infrequently, we feel satisfied that a patient is comfortably assertive in some area (e.g., sexuality), but overlook the fact that he hasn't worked it through in terms of dependency. We assume he was generalized his gains. One monitors the working through at each developmental level in the context of each thematic area.

For example, one patient in working through such a conflict, applied it to all areas except sexual behavior. She had become assertive in her sexual fantasies and was assertive at work. But when it came to sexual behavior with her husband, an area she avoided thinking and talking about she still remained inhibited, passive, and fearful, often feigning or- gasms to please him in fear that he would leave her if he knew just how hard she was "to please." This represented a last ditch effort to retain some degree of symptomatic behavior and retain some degree of her conflict. She was persuaded by her own reasoning that if she tried to work things through in this area, it would surely result in true loss of love and perhaps even disengagement in terms of her key relationships. In looking back historically, it turned out that this feared loss of engage- ment around pleasure and sexual excitement was particularly difficult for this patient for a variety of reasons, including her parents' difficulty with "cleaning my bottom" as an infant. (The patient, curious about her earliest experiences, asked her mother about diaper changes, and so on with regard to her own baby, and learned of her mother's disgust for this activity.) This led to an awareness of a general feeling of maternal withdrawal around body functions. Her mother became "aloof" around her puberty and was always distant while either she or her mother was menstruating. In this case, it was helpful to have a model which looked at each thematic area and each developmental level so that assumptions were not made that a problem was worked through in all areas just because it had been worked through in some areas.

With this model, one can observe that many patients hold on to resistances around certain thematic areas. Often these will go undetected unless one is listening systematically for what is *not* being said. It is assumed when the representational or fantasy level is worked through, let us say in terms of sexual excitement, all other levels are worked through. One may assume that the behavior level of sexuality is worked through, too. One may be reluctant to ask about this out of concern for guiding the patient too much. However, as part of the patient's free association one would expect all areas of his or her life to emerge spontaneously. If an area does not emerge after a reasonable period of time, it is useful to comment, not as a question or an intrusion, but simply as a statement of clarification, "I don't hear much about area A, B, or C," and then listen for further associations. Often, this type of intervention will reveal the remaining area of difficulty.

As a more subtle example, one often sees working through at the engagement, behavioral, and representational elaboration levels. But there remains a lack of full differentiation at the level of representational differentiation. Dependency with one's real parent stays shielded from the otherwise expected differentiation of the ego which has been in evidence. Thus, the relationship with the real father or mother surprisingly retains a childlike undifferentiated quality, while all other areas of dependency have become more differentiated. This remaining difficulty often becomes revealed when one systematically looks at the patient's abilities to make connections between different realms of experience related to that relationship. One has only to look at one's notes from the last six months to see which areas are often missing, or if not missing, retain a more primitive quality. (The primitive quality is not in the nature of developmentally early drive derivatives or affects, but in the inability to integrate these contents in a differentiated manner.)

The concept of working through, from a developmental perspective, offers a systematic way of understanding the working through process by looking at developmental levels and thematic affective areas at each developmental level. One can construct a grid as a way of checking one's own memory and seeing if each area has been worked through to the same degree.

In this chapter a number of concepts central to the psychoanalytic process have been considered from a developmental perspective. Viewing the psychoanalytic process in the context of the stages of early ego development identifies the different ways the analytic relationship may promote understanding and growth. These developmental considerations also raise questions regarding which patients are most suitable for psychoanalysis. Understanding the stages of early ego development may facilitate the treatment of patients with defects, distortions, or compromise in early ego development. The foregoing discussions, however, also raise the question of whether psychoanalysis should be reserved for a narrow group of patients who have reached the stage of representational differentiation and developmentally informed analytic psychotherapy, in some instances four—six times per week, should be the treatment of choice for patients with moderate to severe difficulties in the stages that precede representational differentiation. Stretching a treatment that focuses on representational life and deliberately reduces prerepresentational forms of communication (e.g., lying on the couch or minimizing face to face contact) to include patients whose difficulty cannot yet find representational access may be less wise than using the principles of analytic treatment in a form that lends itself to working at the early levels of ego development. As indicated, however, the principles described earlier regarding free association, neutrality, transference, and working through are equally important in working at the early as well as late stages in ego development.

Chapter 6

A Developmental Model of Therapeutic Change

The theory of change is probably the most complex of the issues central to the analytic and psychotherapeutic process. Current theoretical notions lack a truly developmental perspective, such as the notion of mutative interpretations where elements of the superego, ego, and drive derivatives are all manifested simultaneously (Strachey, 1969), or the traditional notion of making drive derivatives available to the ego so the mature ego can organize new compromise formations and sublimations. A developmental model of therapeutic change may prove even more revealing.

The theory of change is among the most controversial in psychoanalytic theory. This is, in part, because explanations of how conflicts get resolved have never been clearly tied to a more general learning theory of change. Traditional psychoanalytic notions of change have focused on helping unconscious conflicts become conscious. Through the interpretative process, including mutative interpretations, a new equilibrium is forged between unconscious drive derivatives and superego prohibitions, as well as the subliminatory capacities and de-

185

fenses of the ego. Through the simultaneous experience in the transference of drive derivatives, superego prohibitions, and maladaptive ego defenses, the ego has a chance to find a new level of equilibrium where either less debilitating defenses or new subliminatory channels are used to reorganize the relationship between drive derivatives and superego prohibitions. In this way, the ego finds a new equilibrium and structural change is possible.

This traditional way of looking at change, while in keeping with the central role of conflict in psychoanalytic theory, nonetheless fails to adequately explain change and does not address the issue of why some patients who go through this process change dramatically in terms of their intrapsychic and adaptive capacities and other patients change little (even though they seem to have insight into their difficulties). As indicated, what is missing is a more general theory of learning. A developmental perspective will provide some ideas regarding a general developmental theory of learning and change.

THEORY OF GROWTH AND CHANGE IN THE THERAPEUTIC PROCESS

Understanding the normal course of the ego's growth should have implications for understanding the advances in ego development during the therapeutic process. Perhaps there are general principles which describe the ego's growth.

One may postulate a tendency to balance an interest in engaging in and organizing new experiences consistent with maturational achievements (e.g., taking in sights and sounds, object seeking, purposeful interaction, representing experiences, etc.) and maintaining self-regulation and control. Occasionally, when experimenting with new capacities and experiences such as using representational capacity to create a nightmare, one side of the equation overwhelms the other. This may also be the case in the opposite direction. A child who is excessively sensitive to sensory experience withdraws to achieve regulation. Most often these tendencies may be viewed as part

of an equilibrium. Sometimes, however, there is constant difficulty in balancing these inclinations. When some relative balance is achieved, there is a general tendency to embrace and
organize new experience in accord with maturational capacities
and attempt to organize and interpret the new experiences to
achieve a higher level of self-regulation and control.

Central to the ego's ability to organize experience is having
phase appropriate experience available. Phase appropriate
experience, as outlined earlier in terms of the features of the
adaptive environment (experiential nutriments), refers to specific types of experience which are geared to emerging developmental capacities (e.g., love, cause-and-effect interactions,
symbolic or representational interactions). These experiences
also must take into account the person's individual differences.
Loud sounds are great for some two-month-olds and interest
them in the world of human sound. But for a child with an
auditory hypersensitivity a loud sound may lead to withdrawal.
For this child a low-pitched soft sound may encourage interest
in the world. Therefore, both the appropriate developmental
level and individual tailoring of the experiences must be
available for ego growth to occur.

In addition, in order to engage in new experiences, there
must be some degree of mastery of the prior level of experience. For example, one must represent experience before one
can differentiate represented experience.

In addition to mastering prior experiences there must be
the capacity to let go, to some degree, of the gratification
associated with the earlier level and embrace the new level and
its new gratifications; (e.g., generalized and differentiated
attention is usually relinquished for the satisfaction of respect
and mature love). In this context potential fear of the new level
of experiences or its gratifications or challenges must be dealt
with.

Therefore a number of parameters necessary for ego
growth may be postulated: (1) the tendency to use maturational
equipment to engage new experience and organize and integrate new experience to achieve self-regulation; (2) the avail-

ability of phase specific experiences tailored to the individual's maturational differences; (3) the mastery and integration of one level of experience in order to establish a readiness for the next level; (4) relinquishing, to some degree, gratification associated with the level of experience just mastered; (5) dealing with potential fears associated with engaging the new level of experience and its gratifications and challenges.

These principles of ego growth and development will now be briefly discussed in the context of the psychotherapeutic process and the psychoanalytic situation. First, consider the "ideal" analytic situation where classical technique is applied to an individual with an adaptive ego structure and a well-organized neurotic configuration. In this situation the individual is clearly attempting to move on in development (principle 1) and is trying to engage in new experience and organize it (principle 2). His level of interpersonal relationships do not limit him in finding access to age-appropriate experiences. But he may be having difficulty in integrating a narrow band of dynamically relevant experience from an earlier phase and establishing a readiness for his current phase of development in this area (e.g., relationship to controlling authority figures). He may also be having difficulty in relinquishing a narrow band of earlier gratifications and in dealing with current fears. In this context the formation of a transference relationship will bring alive the earlier conflicts, anxiety, sources of gratification, and current fears. Interpretation, reconstruction, and working through will permit the individual to deal with his fears, relinquish older sources of gratification (facilitated by analytic abstinence), and attempt to engage in the full range of age-appropriate experiences. The individual's level of overall ego development makes it possible for him to create his own opportunities for a range of adaptive new experiences while facilitating the working through process. In this "ideal" case the analytic situation only needs to provide a process whereby the patient can master conflicts and their related encapsulated structure. He can then move on under his own steam.

But such "ideal" prototypical cases are only a small part of analytic practice. Most severe character disorders (ego constrictions) involve a situation where early in life an important aspect of experience (e.g., assertiveness) was *never* fully engaged and therefore never organized at a level of representational differentiation and representational transformation. Here the challenge is more complex. It is not simply that a "psychological hurdle" must be mastered and that having done so the patient can move on under his own steam. In this case, there are major challenges to ego growth involving each of the five steps outlined earlier. The tendency to use maturational equipment for engaging new experience is limited by the avoidance of certain areas of experience. The availability of phase appropriate experiences is limited because of chronic patterns of avoidance. The integrative tools to master one level and move on to the next are compromised by the fact that early in life flexible integrative structures were not formed due to a constricted range of experience. There is enormous reluctance to relinquish early forms of gratification because "higher level" gratifications have never been experienced, even in transformed (i.e., defended) ways (as is the case with the healthy neurotic). The patient therefore feels as though he is giving up the old tried and true, however painful, for the feared unknown. The fears of new experiences in the realm avoided may be enormous and associated with the anticipation of various degrees of ego disorganization. Core human experiences were avoided initially, most likely to protect the integrity of the organization of the ego at that time.

A similar but even more challenging situation is present when there are ego deficits, however subtle or contained (e.g., borderline conditions involving compromises in basic ego functions relating to organizing thought, organizing and regulating affect and self-esteem, and modulating impulses and behavior). These may be related to compromises at both prerepresentational and representational levels.

In these situations, as indicated, one cannot assume an adaptive ego structure which can do the necessary work for its own growth once a "psychological hurdle" is mastered. The ego cannot easily avail itself of the types of experiences necessary for its own growth. In this circumstance, it may prove especially useful to consider both the therapeutic and the analytic process from a developmental perspective.

From a developmental perspective the therapeutic process creates an opportunity for the patient to create a transference relationship whereby gratification is sought and constrictions and conflicts (including fear and anxieties) are evidenced at the level of ego organization characteristic of that individual. In the context of "bringing alive" a primitive level of ego organization, the therapeutic process must attend to all five elements that characterize ego growth. As indicated, it can no longer be assumed that the ego itself can mobilize the necessary phase appropriate experiences and organizational and integrative tools.

Does this mean analysis is not possible and only advice and relationship oriented dynamically informed psychotherapy is possible? Not necessarily. In many respects an analytic posture, in either formal analysis or psychotherapy, is even more important in such instances. Only it must be a "developmentally aware" analytic posture. For example, the patient is likely to engage in and form a transference around pre- or early representational levels of ego organization with areas of inter-personal experience entirely "walled off." Here the analyst lends himself to the transference through his empathetic relatedness. Subtle transference and countertransference tendencies of avoidance, withdrawal, rejection, passive compliance, envy, competition, intrusive overcontrol, or symbiotic projective identification may easily mimic the individual's earlier object relationships and can become either a form of acting in or an introspective tool in maintaining a balanced empathetic relatedness. This relatedness can in turn be the basis for clarifying and interpretive comments. At each level of ego development the self–object patterns must be replayed through the transference patterns with special attention to the five steps in ego growth outlined earlier.

While, as indicated, this does not mean creating a "corrective emotional experience," it does mean paying greater attention to a number of tendencies than is usually necessary with a healthy neurotic patient. The patient, because of his maturational equipment, may not engage a full range of experiences due to phase specific fears and anxieties including early somatic sensory hyper- or hyposensitivities. He may use the analytic relationship initially as a basis for phase needed experience (i.e., experienced via the patient's behavior and thought and the analyst's empathetic, but not acting in engagement). For example, simply feeling "engaged" while angry or competed with while competitive may provide trial experiences in the safety of the analysis. Long periods of empathy and clarifying may be necessary. Countertransference tendencies may include premature activity, disinterest, or boredom. The patient may need to progress up a sequence of self–object relationship patterns characteristic of each stage of ego organization. The analyst must not falsely assume either developmentally more advanced capacities or more regressed ones. The analyst must use interpretation and reconstruction together with empathetic availability. The empathetic availability permits "higher level" engagement to facilitate relinquishing no longer needed gratifications. It permits clarification and interpretation of fears of new experiences.

These new sequences may be approached for the first time in the analytic relationship and therefore are truly new in the patient's life. The patient who has never represented a feeling of aggression may do so for the first time with the analyst. The patient who has never represented a feeling of love may do so for the first time with the analyst. For example, a patient who experienced anger only as a vague state of excitation where he felt "overwhelmed" and felt like "hitting or kicking" (and sometimes did this to his spouse) may for the first time symbolize a feeling state called "anger" which can subsequently serve as an intermediary state between perception and action. In this context analytic empathy is a "trial experience," so to speak. It allows the exploration of the fears and excitements anticipated and provides a bridge for new experiences.

As a general model (which can only be discussed briefly here), this developmental perspective suggests greater respect for the analyst's empathetic understanding of the patient's developmental level, the sequence of steps necessary to shift to higher levels, and the countertransference tendencies which can undermine these progressive shifts. Properly honed analytic empathy, it is suggested, provides the substrate for transference explorations, "trial experiences," and higher level integrations. In essence, by not undermining ego growth and by providing a context for exploring the self–object patterns which originally undermined ego growth, the analyst provides an experiential setting where new growth can occur. The practice and "bridge" role does not demand analytic acting in an "advice type" activity. It does demand, however, an unusual gift for analytically informed empathetic availability at each stage of ego development and special awareness of nonverbal countertransference tendencies evidenced through subtle shifts in attention, interest, and analytic understanding. It is rare that a therapist is equally comfortable and respectful of the full range of human affective themes as expressed at different levels of ego organization including the somatic, behavioral, functional–conceptual, early representational, and later representational forms. Here, we may include expressions of dependency, pleasure, assertiveness, curiosity (including sexual curiosity), aggression (including envy, competition, etc.) self-limit-setting, empathy, and love. Given human limitations to engage equally well in all realms of experience, and the patient's considerably greater skill at drawing the analyst into a transference–countertransference acting out (after all, the patient has been doing his patterns for years and the therapist is only learning about this patient's tendencies), it is important for the therapist to pay special attention to his own introspective needs (and seek consultation as needed).

Often the pattern of the therapeutic process may well follow a certain form where the patient draws the analyst into a pattern, and there is an unintentional, but ultimately useful acting out/acting in where an early self–object pattern is reexperienced. Analytic introspection leads to somatic, behavioral, and representational clarification and/or interpretation as a replacement for the reenactment. Analytic empathy and respect for the full range of human experience creates the conditions for further ego growth (together with firm handling of attempts at recreating the older self–object pattern in an acting out/acting in configuration). Obviously this pattern of learning plays itself out repetitively and with a range of variations over a period of time. The patient does not relinquish the old or embrace the new easily or without a fight, or without feelings of loss and extreme fear.

In order to systematize the steps in ego growth from the perspective of steps in the therapeutic relationship which mirror the steps in ego development, the following outline may prove useful (table 6.1). The functions of regularity, attachment, and process are divided and each one is presented in terms of an expected sequence. Many patients can quickly demonstrate mastery of the early steps. It is important to emphasize, however, that there is a tendency to overestimate the patient's therapeutic relationship level (and level of self–object relatedness) and thereby deal with the patient at a representational interpretive level (e.g., process level) without sufficient attention to the earlier stages in regularity, attachment, or process. It is suggested here that understanding the early stages of ego development will foster attention to the stage the patient is at and not the stage one may wish he or she were at.

EARLY LEVELS OF EGO DEVELOPMENT AND THERAPEUTIC CHANGE

Understanding early ego development suggests that ego is capable of change and growth when it can avail itself of the normative experiences that were essential for its growth early in development. As indicated, early in development, the ego requires experiences of engagement with the human world without undue overstimulation or undue lack of sensory affec-

TABLE 6.1
Steps in the Therapeutic Process

Regularity and Stability	Attachment	Process
1. Willingness to meet with an interviewer or therapist to convey concrete concerns or hear about services.	1. Interest in having concrete needs met that can be provided by anyone (e.g., food, transportation, etc.)	1. Preliminary communication, including verbal support and information gathering.
2. Willingness to schedule meeting again.	2. Emotional interest in the person of the therapist (e.g., conveys pleasure or anger when they meet).	2. Ability to observe and report single behaviors or action patterns.
3. Meeting according to some predictable pattern.	3. Communicates purposefully in attempts to deal with problems.	3. Focuses on relationships involved in the behavior-action pattern.
4. Meeting regularly with occasional disruptions.	4. Tolerates discomfort or scary emotions.	4. Self-observing function in relationship to feelings.
5. Meeting regularly with no disruptions.	5. Feels "known" or accepted in positive and negative aspects.	5. Self-observing function for thematic and affective elaboration.
		6. Makes connections between the key relationships in life including the therapeutic relationship.
		7. Identification of patterns in current, therapeutic, and historical relationships to work through problems and facilitate new growth.
		8. Consolidation of new patterns and levels of satisfaction and preparing to separate from the therapeutic relationship.
		9. Full consolidation of gains in the context of separating and experiencing a full sense of loss and mourning.

From Greenspan, S.J., Wieder S., Dimensions and Levels of the Therapeutic Process; Psychotherapy—Vol. 21, Spring 1984/No 1.

tive input. Furthermore, it needs experiences with the affective human world with intentional means–ends relationships (purposeful communication in the full range of thematic–affective domains). Third, it needs experiences with symbolic or representational communications across the full thematic–affective range of experience. Finally, it needs differentiated representational communication also across the full range of thematic–affective domains. Where a developmental level is not achieved, we have a developmental lag in ego structure. Where the full range of affective–thematic domains is not mastered at a given level, we tend to have a constriction of the flexibility of the ego at that level (because it cannot apply its capacities to the full range of affects and themes).

One can postulate that in the analytic situation it is possible for the patient to engage at these developmental levels in the context of a full range of affective–thematic domains. In so doing, the patient is engaged in the types of experience that provide growth for the ego. To facilitate this process, particularly at the prerepresentational levels, the analyst must engage the patient fully in *active, engaged neutrality*. This allows the patient to avail himself of the developmental experiences, in terms of level and range. For example, the patient who has always associated assertiveness with loss and disengagement will experience, through the analysis of the transference–countertransference tendencies, that the analyst does not disengage after aggression nor does the analyst overwhelm the patient with anxious protective behavior (as the patient may have elicited from others in his environment). Let us suppose that this patient, who is anxious about disengagement, has either elicited actual disengagement or compensatory opposite reactions from loved objects in his life. Through the analysis of the transference, the analyst, although initially he may fall into one or another pattern, is able to maintain a posture of truly even, hovering attention. This posture of engagement, which neither fulfills the patient's expectation of disengagement nor compensates with overprotectiveness, provides an opportunity for the person to experience a truly growth-producing type of engagement. In other words, the analytic neutrality sets up, at the prerepresentational level, a quality of engagement which facilitates ego growth. Each time the person anticipates disengagement at a prerepresentational level, it doesn't happen. Each time they anticipate overprotectiveness, it doesn't happen. This anticipation is not at the representational level. This is initially a kind of bodily experience having to do with the rhythms of early relatedness. The patient is now experiencing a type of early relatedness which does not conform to formerly expectable patterns. What the analyst may hear in such a situation are attempts at representational elaboration of the physical surprise or discomfort associated with the lack of the anticipated responses. It is like a person who, down deep in his gut, anticipates constantly being rejected and does not find it forthcoming. The patient might feel frightened at first because a strange or unfamiliar pattern is occurring. The physical sense of fear may get translated into representational forms that seem distant from the actual physical experience. One patient, for example, when the expected disengagement did not occur, tended to become frightened of becoming ill. He complained of gastrointestinal upsets and headaches. When the analyst listened closely, he could see that during this state of vague, physical discomfort the patient seemed to be struggling to disengage. He seemed to be having difficulty with the analyst's empathetic availability, that is, the analyst's even, hovering attention (analytic neutrality), which translated into a quality of constant engagement. Over time, at a prerepresentational level and, I believe, somewhat independent of the analyst's comments which try to verbalize these patterns, the patient began experiencing a more consistent quality of relatedness with less physical discomfort. Although at a later point this pattern was verbalized, the early phases of this work might be viewed as a prerepresentational clarification (through the analyst's clarity regarding potential countertransference patterns, which, after a short period of time, he did not reenact). He was, therefore, able to provide the necessary experiences for early ego growth; that is, a more consistent quality of engagement.

Establishing a sense of relatedness provides one of the ingredients for ego growth. The analyst's provision of a capacity for intentional, organized, purposeful communication across the full range of thematic–emotional realms provides another of the ingredients. What seemingly gets taken for granted is the patient coming in and vocalizing and gesturing preverbally about issues ranging from dependence to sexual excitement to aggression to rivalry and/or competition. The patient's verbal and preverbal productions usually receive an organized, intentional response from the analyst, beginning with the analyst's attentiveness and empathetic listening, including movement patterns, grunts, breathing rhythms, the timing of questions and requests for elaboration ("What further comes to mind?"), summary comments, and so forth. The way in which the analyst facilitates the patient's further communications through gestural and verbal communication, sets up an organized, intentional system of communication which is based on prerepresentational reality. This system of communication, when adaptive, is not unlike the healthy parent–infant pattern between eight and twenty months of age. The analyst's intentional listening and responding fosters the patient's capacity for prerepresentational differentiation. Much as the infant needs an environment that differentiates dependency from pleasure, aggression from curiosity, so, too, the analyst's differential responses to the patient provide prerepresentational differentiating experiences. This type of communication often gets taken for granted and is thought to be intuitive. When the patient has severe difficulties in preverbal communication, the analyst may become aware of all that he or she is doing to maintain this system of communication.

The "intentional" level, as with the level of engagement, should be raised to a level of awareness, particularly so that countertransference–transference trends can be understood. For example, around the issue of angry dependency, one patient was able to get the analyst excited and agitated. The intentional communication system then became disorganized as the analyst and patient both became chaotic. This pattern began with the patient calling up at all times of the day for extra analytic chit-chats around feeling depressed, overwhelmed, suicidal, and so forth. The patient also often showed up at the office two hours ahead of her appointment and waited for her time because she was, "so overwhelmed and frightened." She also intruded into the analyst's life by pointing out how much she knew about him. Invariably, as she kept the pressure on in the sessions, the analyst became agitated and started speeding up the rhythm of his voice and gestures. He thought he was often making proper clarifications and interpretations and setting appropriate limits on the patient. The content of his words were in fact quite reasonable. But his expectable prever-bal gesturing system was completely chaotic. If one had a videotape of this analyst, and compared it to his normal work with patients, one would see that it was hard to read his communications if one didn't hear his words. His gesturing was fast. It was hard to see whether he was angry or trying to be assertive, whether he was trying to be warm and close, or whether he was pushing the patient away. The patient had succeeded in drawing him into her somewhat confusing, am-bivalent pattern. It wouldn't be hard to imagine, particularly if one has seen tapes of eight- to twenty-month-old babies with their parents, the parallel for this kind of communication. The system of intentional communication, through gesture and preverbal vocalizations, instead of being smooth and inten-tional, had become somewhat chaotic and disorganized, just as one sees in maladaptive family patterns.

In normal development, gestures communicate a sense of safety or danger, acceptance or rejection, admiration or dis-gust, pleasure and excitement, or pain and discomfort, as well as acceptance or understanding of specific themes and affects. When this system is nonfunctional, the basic emotional com-munications of life are undermined. This system is critical to the formation of an organized, intentional, preverbal sense of self.

This patient had a mother who had difficulty with this period in development. That the patient drew the analyst into

a similar style of relatedness is not surprising. What is important, though, is to recognize the kind of transference–
countertransference pattern which exists at the prerepresentational intentional communication level. In reenacting
it, the analyst was not providing the tools for ego growth. In
fact, he was undermining ego growth.

Once the analyst became aware of the chaotic, preverbal
signaling pattern (and aware of the feelings the patient was
engendering in him), and of how it was a reenactment, he was
able to engage the patient in an intentional, organized manner.
The patient, as expected, still tried to draw him into a chaotic,
preverbal pattern of relatedness, as it "is the only pattern I ever
knew. It is the only way I feel close." The analyst, though,
persisted in responding clearly and systematically to her intrusiveness, her underlying neediness, the sexualized excitement,
and so forth. As the analyst's preverbal communications syn-
chronized with his understanding of what was going on, slowly
but surely the patient began experiencing a clear separation of
her different wishes and intentions. What she called the
"muddle," began, at a behavioral level, to be differentiated. The
analyst's ability to tune in to the patient in terms of one set of
gestures for her anger and intrusiveness, and another for her
needy dependency, and yet another for her excitement, helped
the patient differentiate these different behavioral–affective
states. Initially, this occurred at the preverbal level through
active analytic neutrality which provided empathetic responses
to the patient's different somatic–behavioral inclinations. (By
definition, empathetic understanding will be reflected in different body postures, movement patterns, breathing rates,
timing of comments and questions, tone of voice, and so forth,
in connection to the patient's communications. These natural
listening and facilitating gestures often only become known
when they are disrupted. In this sense, they define what is
meant in a developmental sense by "neutrality" and "even,
hovering attention.") As the patient became more differentiated at this level, it then later became possible to articulate these
issues in a more representational form.

At the prerepresentational levels active analytic neutrality provides those ego-producing experiences that are essential for ego growth. These ego-producing experiences parallel the types of experiences that are necessary for ego growth in infancy and early childhood. Neutrality and even, hovering attention cannot be confused with analytic apathy, withdrawal, intrusiveness, or chaos. The quality of neutrality and even, hovering attention is defined by the experiences needed for ego growth and development. These are fortunately also the intuitive responses of analysts. Having a model of the necessary experiences for ego growth allows us to begin defining what we mean by active analytic neutrality, and also begin defining derivations for an adaptive analytic posture.

The preverbal experiences—the quality of engagement and the quality of purposeful reading of signals—also provides pieces of a general learning theory. As the human body matures and the brain develops, certain kinds of experiences are needed to match the child's maturational timetable. Psychological structures do not evolve independently of specific human relationships. In this sense, Hartmann's (1939) concept of an average expectable environment can be redefined as an environment which provides those essential "experiential" nutriments that facilitate ego growth and development. In the analytic situation, these essential ingredients emerge as part of the analytic situation, the engaging, listening, clarifying, interpreting, and questioning process. It is easy for this process, however, to become derailed by the patient's prerepresentational transference inclinations and the analyst's countertransference reactions or difficulties with the analyst's own early ego development.

At the level of representational elaboration, we again see some of the features that promote ego growth and development. Here, it is essential for the analyst to engage the patient representationally, that is, to help the patient elaborate different thematic–affective inclinations (drive–affect derivatives) in a representational form. The patient's ability to abstract feeling states: "I felt angry," "I felt excited and aroused," as opposed to just describing the behaviors: "I hit her," "I made love to her," and so forth, signifies that this level has been reached. The analyst's ability to engage in the feeling states, in terms of his empathetic availability as compared to being interested in only hearing behavioral details of the patient's exploits in sex, aggression, dependency, and the like, signifies the analyst's empathetic or countertransference tendencies. The analyst, free of countertransference tendencies, who has reached this level of representational elaboration, will listen for abstracted feeling states and help the patient articulate these. The analyst will also become aware of his ability to engage and listen empathetically across the full range of representational experiences. Does he listen more easily to sexual experiences than to aggressive ones, or to dependency, closeness, and separation issues more easily than assertiveness, curiosity, and competition? The ability to engage representationally is intuitive and goes without saying for most experienced analysts. Just as they engage the patient, signal intentionally (prerepresentationally), they also use even, hovering attention to engage in elaborating abstracted feeling states.

This normative capacity of the analyst can be easily derailed by the patient's transferences, the analyst's own countertransference difficulties, or the analyst's lack of ego development or other limitations. For example, an analyst who has had difficulty early in development with abstracting feeling states (having to do with dependency and closeness) may, with a patient who has a great deal of concerns around aggression, fears of being hurt, and a tendency to exploit others, tend to become invested in the patient's descriptions of drive derivatives and abstracted affective states having to do with the competitive, aggressive, exploitative side of life. The analyst's own difficulty with abstracting the issues concerned with dependency, however, may mirror those of the patient, and the two may unconsciously collude to *not* elevate the patient's dependency needs to the state of representational elaboration. The patient, for example, may deal with dependency by feeling close to the analyst, gesture his closeness, and even create a state of warm intimacy. The analyst may similarly enjoy this state of behavioral intimacy as he engages in understanding aggression and its associated fears. Years may go by. As the analyst looks over his notes he will see that there have been relatively few representational associations and comments around dependency and closeness. The analyst may assume that this is not an area of difficulty for the patient, but in fact it may be just the opposite. Such a patient may not be able to experience closeness at the stage of representational elaboration. This limitation may be part of the dynamics of the patient's difficulties. Uncomfortable with representing and verbalizing closeness, he feels frightened of being exploited and in great detail describes his exploitative and angry feelings. The analyst's own limitations may preclude him from easily recognizing what is missing from the analysis. In such a case, the patient would not develop new ego structure; that is, the capacity to representationally abstract affective states around dependency. Dependency concerns would stay as prerepresentational issues. On the other hand, if the analyst, through his own self-scrutiny or through supervision, became aware of his limitations, he might then begin engaging the patient representationally in terms of dependency issues (for example, wondering out loud about how the patient felt during the warm, intimate interchanges they had around anger). The patient might then begin struggling with these issues. Over time, the patient may learn to go from behavioral to representational levels. He may begin describing dependency and intimacy behaviorally (how he is with this person or that person and how he is with the analyst). The patient then begins, with the analyst's help, trying to tease out the feeling states from these various behavioral descriptions. Eventually, he may learn how to abstract the feeling states associated with dependency. As this occurs, a new ability, a new ego substructure develops. This ability to represent themes associated with dependency would provide the patient with the tools to look at relationships between dependency on the one hand and anger and exploitation on the other.

   In this example we can see how subtly the analyst and the

patient may collude to not create representational access to all affective–thematic domains.

The next level is that of representational differentiation. Here, the patient requires experiences that facilitate the ego developing its capacities for intrathematic, temporal, spatial, and self–object intrastructural connections. These connections between historical and current events, different emotional themes (in both cross-sectional and historical contexts), and subjective and objective parameters, require an active bridge-building capacity. It requires an active ability to both categorize (differentiate) experiences and then build bridges between these experiences (integrating them). The degree to which differentiation and integration occur determines, in some part, the flexibility and the overall health of the personality. It also sets up the basis for future differentiating and integrating capacities that will be important for superego development, ego ideal development, and a differentiated sense of identity during latency and adolescence.

To facilitate ego differentiation and integration, the analyst must be able to provide appropriate clarifying and interpretive experiences. In addition, the analyst must make sure that he or she is not misreading the patient's representational elaborations and providing appropriate representational feedback. The analyst, for example, who misreads the patient's verbal presentations and sees concerns with excitement and sexuality as concerns with dependency, will undermine the patient's ability to categorize sexual experiences and dependency experiences and see the differences and connections between them. Reading the patient's associations requires a high degree of analytic and empathetic ability.

Consider the example of the parent who distorts the four-year-old's pretend play productions. When the little boy is looking to undress the dolls and study the body, the parent says, "You're being aggressive." The parent then rejects the child for being aggressive. That child is likely to begin feeling confused about his representational meanings. Similarly, the analyst who misreads the patient's productions, through his clarifying or interpretive comments or through his affective availability, will undermine the formation of categories of, and connections between, experiences.

The baseline experience of analytic neutrality and even, hovering attention, therefore, means listening empathetically and with appropriate clarifying and interpretative comments. These must be accurate and, for the most part, reflect the patient's unfolding thematic–affective patterns. To the degree the analyst is "off" in a consistent manner, ego growth is undermined. The analyst is providing the experiences neces- sary for ego growth and development to the degree he is empathetically in rhythm with the patient and helps the patient articulate the different thematic–affective domains, differenti- ate them, and eventually see the bridges between them. We will come back to this last as we talk about the technical aspects of growth and change later on in this work.

As a general principle the analyst must at this level provide the essential baseline experiences for ego growth as he did at the earlier levels of development. The analyst's responses go beyond simple elaborative comments. They now have to do with categorizing experience, that is, see patterns (a traditional analytic goal) and, second, help the patient see relationships between patterns. (This would usually be part of the clarifying and interpretive work of the analysis.) The analyst helps the patient see these relationships and facilitates the patient's own discovery of genetic, cross-sectional, intrathematic, and intra- self–object/intrastructural patterns.

Therefore, we have a general model of ego growth which lends itself to being part of a general learning theory. This theory would state that at each level of development certain experiences are necessary to harness the individual's own tendencies toward psychological growth. The environmental experiences must be matched to the maturational needs of the individual. These experiences fall into four broad categories: Affective engagement, prerepresentational purposeful signal- ing, representational elaboration, and representational differ- entiation. These correspond to phases in the normal emotional growth of infants and young children. They provide a way of further defining what we mean by an average expectable environment, analytic neutrality, even, hovering attention, and analytic work.

SPECIAL TECHNICAL CONSIDERATIONS RELATING TO ANALYTIC CHANGE

Thus far, we have talked about the general principles of ego growth. We have not talked about the resolution of conflict and the special role clarification and interpretation, and in particular, transference interpretation, plays in creating change. While the ingredients described above provide the baseline for analytic change, in themselves, they may not be sufficient. Yet they can be viewed as the necessary ingredients without which change is impossible. Unless these baseline experiences fostering ego structural growth are there, no amount of correct interpretation or insight will create the opportunity for change.

In addition to these experiences, however, the ingredient which is necessary for growth and change is the resolution of conflicts which, at one developmental stage or another, is undermining the ego's own capacities for further growth and development.

To simplify the issue, consider a rather traditional situation of conflict at the level of representational differentiation involving wishes, prohibitions, and defenses. By definition, as we describe this type of internalized conflict, we are describing a reasonably differentiated ego structure because there are categories of experience and ego structure sufficiently differentiated from one another to be in conflict. Representational differentiation has already occurred. In order to have a highly differentiated conflict, a person is already at a relatively advanced stage in ego development.

Consider a case that, at first, will appear to be typical in how it unfolds. We will show how a developmental learning model of change adds to our understanding of change. This is the case of a woman who had a somewhat depressed, intrusive, controlling, and aggressive mother. She developed power struggles with her mother early on, but at the same time was very frightened of her mother's tendency to become depressed and withdrawn. She therefore became conflicted over her own aggression. During the oedipal phase, she fantasized using father as a weapon against mother and, in fact, taking father away from mother as a retaliation for mother having "overcontrolled" her and "been abusive." The thought of defeating mother with father as an ally (which father lent himself to, to some degree, through seductive behavior with his daughter) while leading to "appealing" fantasies of mother dying in a depressed state, was also quite frightening. They led to states of intermittent depression and work inhibition. The conflict was clear. The patient, at the preoedipal levels, tended to fear loss of her depressed mother and inhibited her aggression with passivity and compliance. She then fantasized an oedipal victory, intensified in part, to retaliate against mother. Here, too, the fear of losing mother and defeating her, as well as the fear of mother's aggression, became too frightening. The resultant conflicts and their compromise formations led to depressive symptoms and work inhibitions. In the work inhibitions, the nature of the conflict was clear. To assert herself at work and be successful was associated with an image of her mother "suiciding" and her "laughing" over the suicide. These images occurred often while she was enjoying drinks with a male authority figure (supervisor). This fantasy was juxtaposed with the depressive fantasy where the patient, herself, felt despondent and ineffectual ("I can never do anything right").

The patient could engage rather well and had a well-developed system for prerepresentational intentional communication; however, at the stage of representational elaboration, themes having to do with her own anger or assertiveness, she tended to remain at a behavioral level. They were not put into representational forms. In contrast, themes having to do with worry, compliance, closeness and dependency, taking care of others, and being a bad person had a great deal of access to representational forms. At the level of representational differentiation, also, there were highly differentiated bridges between different aspects of dependency, compliance, and caring, but relatively few categorizations and bridges in the areas of assertiveness, competition, and aggressiveness, especially if they had to do with women.

The patient had not developed representational elaborative and differentiating capacities in certain thematic–affective areas having to do with competition, assertiveness, and aggression (especially having to do with women authority figures) related to the paralyzing nature of her conflicts. Every time the patient tried to become aware of her angry feelings toward her female supervisor, she would immediately feel inhibited, passive, depressed, and, occasionally, suicidal. Therefore, attempts on her own to broaden her representational elaboration and to further differentiate were not successful.

Certain areas of the ego are highly differentiated, but other areas are poorly differentiated and may even have difficulty with access to representation. Yet there were indications that she had achieved a partial degree of ability to represent the affects around anger—there were fleeting aggressive fantasies. However, she was unable to integrate these aggressive fantasies into her other concerns and was unable to categorize, differentiate, and integrate aggressive experiences consistent with the stage of representational differentiation. For the most part, access to representational elaboration was limited and representational differentiation was unavailable for the patient's aggressive wishes and feelings.

How this pattern of ego development played itself out in this patient's analysis is instructive with regard to the technical level of change. It is important to go beyond the notion that the interpretation of conflicts, even in the transference, is in itself sufficient to help the patient resolve his conflicts and progress to structural change and structural growth. Instead, I would suggest that a few more conditions are necessary that help the patient resolve conflict and change. These additional conditions will put conflict resolution into a more general learning theory.

In the general learning model, as in the traditional psychoanalytic model, the patient would free associate and, over time, develop a transference relationship. Let us assume the analyst would be, at various times, both the preoedipal mother and the oedipal father. In this way, the patient would develop a relationship with the analyst where various patterns are reenacted. Let us take one of the early patterns where the patient behaves somewhat supportively to the analyst and is somewhat compliant to him. She follows the basic rules, free associating and treating the analyst nicely and with respect. Anger, disappointment, and outrage are rarely mentioned. Instead, the analyst is treated with kid gloves. The analyst, in turn, is expected to take a protective position, where he colludes with the patient to avoid dealing with the patient's angry, competitive, and controlling feelings. The analyst, aware of this pattern, repeatedly points it out to the patient. The patient agrees and they associate further, providing much elaboration of her sense of "loss and sadness." There appears to be insight, but there is no change.

What more than likely actually happens in the analytic situation is a little different. Initially the patient is somewhat successful at drawing the analyst into the transference relationship. After all, the patient is far more experienced at drawing people into her patterns than the analyst, who is just getting to know the patient, is at extricating himself from such a pattern. This is probably true of most neurotic individuals. Assuming this is true, let us say this patient succeeds in drawing the analyst into a relationship where he enjoys the patient's compliance, admiring glances when she walks in the door, and desire to please with her excellent dreams and emotion-laden free associations around the dreams.

At this point, the analyst is not aware that his pleasure is part of a countertransference tendency. He feels he has a "terrific patient." Having succeeded in drawing the analyst into this pattern, the patient secretly expects the analyst to (1) not become depressed as she feared her mother would be, and (2) be the oedipal father figure who is going to help her destroy this depressed mother. These expectations initially are not known to the analyst. He evidences his countertransference acting in by very subtly showing his pleasure through his broad smiles and eager listening. She senses his pleasurable interest in her. While the analyst thinks of this as just a "fascinating patient" who has interesting dreams, he listens to her more intently than his other patients. Over time, he laughs more heartily at her jokes and feels more empathetic pain for her disappointments than he does for most of his patients. This, too, becomes a signal of the active countertransference acting in (carried out very subtly, of course).

During the analyst's first vacation, the patient becomes quite depressed, and when the analyst returns inhibits her anger, but behaves quite helplessly and morbidly. The analyst becomes concerned. Perhaps more is going on in the transference than he had thought. Perhaps it is not just a "oedipally oriented" woman trying to please him, and him enjoying her associative abilities. Through her depressive elaborations, the analyst becomes aware of some of the themes concerning anger and loss and begins wondering to himself how these have been playing out in the transference prior to his going on vacation. After some consultation with a colleague, he begins seeing that he had been enjoying the patient so much that he had been overlooking the fact that alongside her trying to please him, there was a hidden, angry demandingness and fear of loss.

With this new awareness, the analyst begins to broaden his listening. His comments, which facilitate representational elaboration and differentiation and integration, now stem from a broader base. They are not limited only to oedipal transference themes. Now he is attuned to depressive themes, anger, and need, and fear of loss. In facilitating a greater range of themes for representational elaboration and differentiation, he begins to not enjoy the patient's jokes quite as much, listening instead for the hidden agenda of anger and disappointment and fear of loss. He also greets the patient warmly, but with less enthusiasm as he is expecting more of a challenge from the session than simply having his imagination sparked.

Much of what has just been described would go on in any analytic relationship. At this point, however, consider that the shift in the analyst's posture to some extent, creates the ingredients for change at a technical level. This change occurs, in part, because the analyst now begins interpreting the patient's broader thematic and affective concerns. But it also occurs, in part, because the analyst has now shifted. He was initially in an acting-in posture where the patient was partially gratified, unbeknownst to the analyst. Most patients have the capacity to draw their analysts in to some degree because initially they are more experienced than the analyst is at their patterns.

The countertransference acting-in pattern consolidated the infantile neurosis, to a degree, in the analytic situation. The patient's satisfaction entrenched her in wanting her aims met in the analytic situation. The analyst now shifts his posture. He now evidences even, hovering attention. At this point, the patient begins experiencing a sense of loss and a mourning process. There is a parallel in learning terms, an extinction phenomenon. In general learning theory, when feelings or behaviors are not reinforced, those feelings and/or behaviors may begin undergoing extinction. They do not continue indefinitely under their own steam. Part of a general learning theory would suggest that all behaviors and feeling states, in order to continue in the personality, must at least some of the time succeed in eliciting an object relationship which gratifies those behaviors and feelings (Greenspan, 1979). In this sense, one would not be hard pressed to assume that this patient could enlist many others in her life to gratify her feelings and behaviors. Most neurotic individuals have succeeded in involving their friends or spouses or children in various aspects of their own neurotic patterns. She even succeeded in involving the analyst, to some extent. But now the analyst, "wiser," responds more evenly and doesn't respond selectively to the patient's "neurotic" patterns.

We would, as indicated, expect to see anger and perhaps mourning, including sadness, in response to the patient not being able to revive this neurotic object relationship with the analyst. (Interestingly, during extinction studies in the animal kingdom, as the animal is lessening the frequency of the nonreinforced behaviors, one sees rage, chaotic behavior, and episodes of apathy. This is remarkably similar to the human responses to loss, although it would also be important to understand the history of each person's response to loss.) The analyst aids his nonreinforcing role through the use of clarifications and interpretations. He now points out to the patient when she is being overly compliant or when she is trying to "excite" him with new dreams. He facilitates the elaboration of her fear of loss and her anger for not having what she views as her needs met. The patient sees, in part, why she is so furious and feeling such a profound sense of loss; that is, why she is feeling some of the affects that traditionally go along with a behavior being extinguished. At the same time, the clarifications help the analyst be active while not falling into the "old" patterns.

What is critical to remember is that from a learning point of view, the analyst's verbalizations and the clarifications and interpretations themselves may not be sufficient for change. What is critical for change is that the analyst now does not participate in the old object relationship (which he had participated in for a time). The old patterns are, by necessity, given up because she cannot find the object tie in the analytic situation to support them. The old relationship is part of an object relationship and can only exist as long there is another player to play along with her. The accompanying insights help consolidate the change at the level of representational differentiation.

The analyst cannot be covertly supporting the old pattern while offering interpretations. In all likelihood, if you had to do one or the other, the lack of covert support, even without the interpretations, would result in significant change; but the interpretations alone would not. This is the contribution of a

more general learning theory to specific technical considerations.

An important question still arises. Other relationships
(with friends) still support the neurotic trends. But the analytic
relationship prevails. "Why does an old relationship pattern
that does not become supported in the analysis reverberate at
such a profoundly deep level, deeper than with a relationship
in life outside the analysis?" Here, we have to be aware of
another aspect of a technical nature unique to psychoanalysis.
The patient is asked to free associate, and, as such, to suspend
many of her representational differentiating abilities. Free
association facilitates representational elaboration and earlier
modes of communication including engagement and prerepresentational intentional communication.

Let us focus on the stage of representational elaboration.
As the patient associates freely, without trying to categorize
experience or create logical links, he is in a regressed state. His
own behavior, feelings, and self–object patterns are relatively
less differentiated than is ordinarily the case. The relationship
with the analyst is also experienced in a less differentiated
form. This relatively less differentiated, "more primary
process," pattern of drive derivatives, affects, and self and
object relationships permits the possibility of greater generalization than more differentiated forms of behavior. Picture the
personality as a hierarchy with undifferentiated patterns being
a foundation for differentiated ones. As one experiences less
differentiated forms, there is the potential for greater generalization across the patient's life (Greenspan, 1975).

Because of the basic rule of free association, the transference relationship tends to foster a relationship that is at an early
level of ego organization (less differentiated) and therefore the
patterns and changes in this relationship can be generalized in
its subsequent differentiated forms. In addition, the transference is a highly intense relationship because of the analytic
relationship (four or five times per week) and fosters the
emergence of intense infantile wishes. The transference relationship, on the one hand, promises nothing and on the other

hand promises everything. The ambiguity, combined with the intensity, leads to the peaking of drive–affect derivatives.

The combination of intensity, along with the relative lack of differentiation, facilitates behavioral generalization. It is possible to conceptualize this tendency toward behavioral generalization from the perspective of an integrated psychoanalytic learning theory. In this model (Greenspan, 1975), there are classes of behaviors and responses. The archaic transference relationship exists at a level of relatively undifferentiated classes of behaviors, and their accompanying affects. In addition, the discriminative experiences, which create both the circumstances for expected gratification and nongratification and may be thought of in terms of transference components related to each developmental level, may also be experienced in less differential ways.

The analyst initially experiences and clarifies the transference nature of the patient–therapist relationship as well as his own countertransference tendencies. Once identified and supported with clarifications and interpretations, the analyst ceases to reenact the transference pattern with the patient. The patient then goes through a process of giving up the archaic, primitive object tie.

This process occurs with each transference fragment. With the patient described above, this initially occurred around the preoedipal relationship with the mother. Subsequently, the pattern of oedipal expectations (the analyst being the father who would collude with the patient to destroy the mother) also played itself out. In each instance, it was essential for the analyst to maintain truly even, hovering attention and analytic neutrality. This meant paying attention to all the themes requiring representational access, representational elaboration, and representational differentiation.

The transference relationship permitted the analyst and patient to see these patterns acted out at the level of engagement, prerepresentational interaction, and representational elaboration. Then the analyst brings these patterns into the realm of representational differentiation through clarifications and interpretations. At the same time, the analyst refuses to engage in the defensive, archaic patterns and, instead, keeps facilitating a more broad awareness of all the affects and themes relevant to the patient's life. It is this combination of the refusal to continually engage in the archaic neurotic pattern and the persistent support of a more broad availability of themes and affects for representational access and representational differentiation that creates the opportunity for further growth and development. In general learning terms, there is not only the lack of gratification of the old pattern but also the continual discriminations of the old and new ones as well as the clarifications of the new patterns.

It is also important to recognize that many patients are frightened of engaging in new experiences as evidenced, initially, in their free associations and, subsequently, as part of their patterns of engagement with others. The person who has been fearful of competition and aggression will not only try to be passive and compliant in the analysis, but even after the passivity and compliance is understood will still be reluctant to engage the analyst competitively or be competitive at work or with a spouse. The experience that has existed in a relatively undifferentiated form and has not been part of the patient's conscious representational life, is often a feared experience. The patient still often fears "jumping in the water" by engaging in the formerly feared levels of experiences. Insight alone will not change this fear. There is no valid theoretical reason why it should.

A child, for example, often still avoids assertive behavior with peers even though symptoms such as sadness may have lifted due to the empathy and understanding of the analysis. With the patient discussed above, this issue became quite apparent when, after she got married, she was still quite uneasy about dealing with her husband around his work schedule. She chose, instead, the more compliant, "I'll keep my mouth shut" approach. She was able to use analytic understanding to feel less depressed, but was still fearful of engaging fully in new areas of experience such as assertiveness.

To some degree, engaging in new areas of experience becomes a lifelong endeavor. With children, the importance of not just resolving conflicts of the past, but helping the child jump into the next developmental level, is self-evident. With adults, it is less clear what these next developmental levels are. As one understands the psychology of adulthood and the importance of new levels of intimacy, competitiveness, and assertiveness, one can keep an eye on the importance of fostering, the full engagement in new levels of experience through clarifying and interpreting avoidances of them. In a sense, the analytic relationship provides the prototype for figuring out what has gone wrong in the past and for engaging in the present in a fuller range of (representational) elaborative and differentiating experiences. The patient will still need special work, though, to fully confront all sectors of his life.

In our technical model of change, we see change as occurring when the transference relationship brings into stark reality the nature of the patient's wishes, fears, and prohibitions. These play themselves out in the analytic relationship, with the analyst first, inadvertently, engaging the patient in the patterns because of the patient's greater skill at creating the transference and bringing the analyst into it. Initially, the analyst joins in and colludes with the patient due to countertransference problems. Together, the analyst and the patient replay the old object ties which contain defenses against both the wishes and the prohibitions. As the analyst comes to understand these patterns, he refrains from replaying them and, instead, substitutes a broad support for representational elaboration and differentiation across the full range of themes. In other words, he offers analytic categorization, clarification, and interpretation as a way of broadening the base of representational elaboration and differentiation. The formerly warded-off themes (in the patient's elaborative and differentiating structures) now begin to find representational access through the analyst's consistent scrutiny. At the same time that he is technically facilitating the formerly avoided areas, the analyst is refusing to reengage in the old defensive patterns, that is, the archaic patterns, that conspired to keep the patient from moving into a broader range of elaborative and differentiating experiences.

Facilitating this process is the fact that the transference occurs at a level of relative lack of differentiation. This lack of differentiation fosters generalization in terms of the hierarchy of behavioral and affective patterns in the patient's personality structure. The relatively undifferentiated experience of the transference, combined with the intensity of the transference (because of the ambiguity of the analytic situation), permits a profound learning to occur.

What must not be forgotten, however, is that ultimately the patient's boldness in jumping into the water, to embrace new thematic–affective realms in more differentiated ways requires a great deal of security in the analytic relationship. (In the case of the patient described above, this involved the ability to come to grips with her own competitiveness, her own desire to destroy her mother.) This boldness is encouraged, in part, by the prerepresentational experiences of constant engagement and prerepresentational reality-based communications which convey safety, acceptance, and respect (from the mutual reading of preverbal signals). These two foundations create the necessary security (which often is not completely available as the patient grows up). This security, in part, helps the patient tackle new affective–thematic domains at the level of representational elaboration and differentiation. The inability to retrieve the old object tie (i.e., the analyst will not reenact the old patterns) and avoid these new patterns, as well as the continuing interest of the analyst in engaging the patient in new thematic–affective areas, provide the ingredients for further ego growth and development. In this way, approaches to conflict resolution work synergistically with the experiences which support ego development. In general learning terms, new types of gratifications (e.g. respect rather than attention) are as important as new behaviors and provide the motivation for new patterns of adaptation. Overall personality growth, not just behavior change, is, therefore, important (Greenspan, 1975).

A further comment on mutative interpretation is in order, because it is often thought that this is the critical analytic learning experience. A mutative interpretation occurs when in the transference the patient's wishes, internalized fears, prohibitions, and defenses all emerge with great intensity in relative proximity to one another. This proximity provides the opportunity for a "reequilibrium" between derivatives of the id and superego in the context of a new stage of ego defensive–subliminatory capacities. It is useful to realize that leading up to such mutative experiences is second-by-second, month-by-month, even year-by-year work where the patient, through the free associative process, is gradually poking away at the barriers to increasing their thematic–affective range. In other words, they are gradually moving into new thematic–affective areas at higher developmental levels. The person who is fearful of aggression, for example, and who tends to have created depressive symptomatology as a defense (the patient described above), over time is slowly becoming aware, through the free-associative process, of some of these aggressive inclinations. This may take place first at the level of preverbal feeling states, then at the level of representational elaboration, and, finally, in the more differentiated levels. These inklings, piece by piece, all the time are creating new psychological structures. Facilitating this piece-by-piece work is the analyst's tendency to not reengage in the old archaic patterns (which support the constriction and/or avoidance) and his continually attempting to engage the patient in a broader range of affects and themes which are already, at some level, felt by the patient. (There is an assumption here that all human beings experience the full range of human inclinations at some developmental level or another.) The analyst must facilitate shifts from earlier levels to later levels and, at each level, facilitate the broadening of these themes.

At critical moments mutative interpretations appear. It is my impression that these interpretations are more of a confirmation of a learning process that has already occurred than the critical element in such a learning process. The second-by-second learning that has already occurred reaches a crescendo when the patient finally has enough access to representational differentiation and enough breadth at the level of representational differentiation to experience most of the affective–thematic domains, especially those concerned with both the full range of wishes and the full range of internalized fears and prohibitions. As the patient has learned to do this, he is then capable of juxtaposing and seeing relationships between the different elements of his personality. This capacity testifies to the learning that has already occurred and becomes a final confirmation of such learning. After all, a mutative interpretation is not possible until (1) the person is fully at a level of representational differentiation, and (2) at this level is already capable of being engaged in many age-appropriate thematic–affective domains. In this sense, the mutative interpretation would be "the icing on the cake" and an important consolidation and confirmation of change, but in itself would not be the primary ingredient of change.

In summary, our general learning model would explain why the patient is motivated to change after he has insights into his behavior and feelings. The analytic or psychotherapeutic situation provides critical learning ingredients in addition to insight. They are:

1. Baseline security through engagement and preverbal cuing.
2. An opportunity to engage in and describe the neurotic configurations.
3. An opportunity through free association to engage in the neurotic patterns at an undifferentiated level.
4. The opportunity to relinquish this pattern at this same undifferentiated level. This creates a tendency toward learning with *generalizations*. It also creates an opportunity for relinquishing these patterns at a similar level of generalization as they were likely learned in the first place.

5. The analyst's true neutrality facilitates the patient's relinquishing of old patterns. The analyst does not engage in these patterns once he is aware of them. He substitutes clarification and interpretation.

6. The avoidance of new age-appropriate patterns are dealt with via clarifications and interpretations of fears in a broad range of age-appropriate feelings and behaviors. The security of the analytic situation and the lack of engagement in old patterns provides the patient with the necessary motivation to try out new patterns.

In this model, we see the complementary roles of insight and transference interactions in the context of a general theory of learning.

Chapter 7

A Developmental Model of
Short-Term Dynamic Psychotherapy

A developmental perspective can provide a useful model for dynamic, short-term psychotherapy. This discussion will build on the earlier discussion of the psychoanalytic situation. A major difference between short-term therapy and the psychoanalytic situation is the difference in the way the transference, or the relationship between the therapist and the patient, is used in mediating important learning experiences.

In the psychoanalytic situation, through the transference relationship the patient learns to identify and work through conflictual patterns. In short-term, dynamic psychotherapy both pattern recognition and the experience of new patterns may be learned outside the therapeutic situation where real relationships with others provide the intensity and generalization of experience that, in the analytic situation, occurs between the patient and the analyst.

SUPPORTIVE SHORT-TERM PSYCHOTHERAPY

First, it is important to distinguish between two types of dynamic psychotherapy. One type is predominantly support-

221

ive. The patient's ego structure is sufficiently fragile so that the therapist feels that an intense analytically oriented experience of either analysis proper or intensive psychoanalytic psychotherapy would not be in the patient's best interest. The therapist's goal is to support basic ego functions and gradually help the patient form better patterns of adaptation. The goal is not to develop an intense transference relationship which will stir up the patient's conflicts. The patient's fragile ego structure would not necessarily be able to deal adaptively with such intensity of experience. Some patients, however, after periods of supportive work, experience sufficient growth to engage in an intensive psychotherapeutic experience.

The model of supportive work, based on our concepts of development discussed earlier, would take advantage of our understanding of the importance of engagement and preverbal intentional communication in the patient's life. A foundation is established by the regularity of visits, the fact that there is a relationship that does not become disrupted by affect storms, severe disappointments, or by the patient's rage being reacted to with rage, the patient's withdrawal with withdrawal, or the patient's jealousy with anger. The fact that the therapist does not give in to countertransference tendencies or meet the patient's expectations for difficulties in engagement provides a secure base of engagement for ego growth and development. Similarly, the fact that the analyst is able to read the patient's preverbal signals and create a prerepresentational basis for reality helps the patient feel that there are islands of logic and understanding in the world. This creates a sense of safety, approval, acceptance, and, most importantly, personal definition. One has only to imagine what it is like to be talking to someone who is shaking their head "no" when you are expecting them to nod "yes" in approval. This is disruptive even to the most intact individual. When a person does not have a firm sense of preverbal reality, this sense of preverbal chaos and unpredictability is only further disorganizing. Achieving this second level of preverbal logic further supports the patient's ego structure. The therapist's initial goal through support and clarifying comments is to encourage a wider range of engagement and a wider repertoire of behavior at the level of preverbal, organized, intentional signaling. The therapist then gradually tries to help the patient elaborate different behavioral and emotional patterns at the level of representational elaboration. The patient who is passive (as a way of holding a fragile ego structure together), may gradually try to increase range of behavior, including assertive behavior. Similarly, the patient who has been frightened of intimacy may, against the security of engagement and a preverbal signaling system with the therapist, try to be more verbally open, first with the therapist and then with other adults in his life. In this way, the security of the therapeutic relationship enables the patient to slowly but surely expand his behavioral and emotional repertoire. As this becomes possible, the therapist may supportively encourage representational elaboration and the abstraction of core affective states. Representational elaboration will become more available to the patient as he expands his behavioral repertoire. Similarly, expanding his behavioral range may, in isolated instances, help the patient see connections between different behaviors and/or different feelings.

The security of the relationship in its engaging and intentional communication capacities provides stability for current ego functioning and encouragement for expanding the range of experiences tolerated, first at the behavioral and engagement levels, and later at the representational levels. This then creates a basis for some work at the levels of representational elaboration and differentiation. If the patient becomes ready for more intense work at these levels, one may consider switching from a supportive approach to a more dynamic approach. While this switch does not mean an actual change in the relationship, it does mean some shifts in the concepts one employs. In the supportive approach, one is thinking mostly of

security, encouraging and fostering ego growth in its prerepresentational stages, and gradually, slowly, and patiently helping the patient elaborate his tendencies in representational
forms. The focus of the work, however, is on the security of
basic ego functions, avoiding fragility and maintaining stability
in the context of expanding the patient's prerepresentational
behavioral and emotional repertoire. The relationship with the
therapist is a model and an actual experience of security. It is
not used as a transference window for learning. To be sure,
transferences need to be dealt with, especially negative transferences. The patient who is angry or disappointed after a
vacation, or the one who becomes suspicious because of erotic
longings, needs to be helped to feel secure in the engagement
and to establish a logical and purposeful way of exploring their
angry or overexcited feelings. But the goals here are not so
much to establish links between the person's current feelings of
loss or excitement and all of the fantasies associated with the
feelings of loss and excitement, or the historical antecedents to
these, or to examine all contexts in which loss or excitement is
felt as a bridge to the transference feelings. Rather, the goal is
to help the patient understand why the feelings of loss or
excitement are frightening and why basic ego functions, such as
engagement or purposeful communication, can be disrupted
by these intense feelings. The focus is on how feelings can
overwhelm, not on expanding the nature of overwhelming
feelings. Yet gradually, tolerance for feelings and a wider range
of behavior will emerge. The patient learns to tolerate intense
feelings in a new relationship with the person of the therapist.
Together they begin seeing, against a background of security,
that intense feelings do not lead to isolation of the relationship
and, therefore, the tendency to distort is not needed. In
supportive work, the goal is to focus on increasing the security
of the basic ego structure and only gradually to expand its
horizons.

   To the degree that the security is sufficient to begin
expanding horizons in a number of areas at once, a shift from
the supportive work to dynamic work may be appropriate.

DYNAMIC SHORT-TERM PSYCHOTHERAPY

In contrast to supportive short-term psychotherapy, dynamic short-term psychotherapy is appropriate for patients who have relatively intact basic ego functions. They have established the early ego functions of engagement and intentional communication (communication around a prerepresentational sense of reality and logic). They also have the capacity for representational elaboration and differentiation. They are often confronted with a challenge, an illness in the family, change of job, difficulty with a child, marital problems, disequilibrium associated with life transitions, or new developmental demands (sexuality in adolescence, intimacy and marriage in adulthood, having children, aging). These are individuals who do not have long-standing character, or severe neurotic difficulties which would require psychoanalysis or long-term intensive dynamic psychotherapy. They have flexible, intact ego structures (their expectable neurotic conflicts do not significantly interfere with this flexibility), but are confronted with a new challenge that they cannot resolve on their own. They need short-term work to master the new challenge and learn what in their on-going adaptive capacities makes it difficult to get through this new challenge on their own. Understanding their neurotic conflicts, which have not impaired them in the past, may be relevant to understanding the current situation.

These are individuals who do not require supportive work because they have intact ego functions. They do not require either psychoanalysis or intensive analytically oriented psychotherapy because they do not have long-standing characterologic or moderate to severe neurotic difficulties. Instead they have relatively adaptive personality styles and are finding a challenge in their current lives difficult to resolve.

In assessing the patient's readiness for short-term dynamic work, it is important to make certain that they have already established good functioning at the levels of engagement, prerepresentational, intentional, organized communication, representational elaboration, and differentiation. They can abstract affect states and elaborate representationally in most of the areas of life, including pleasure, dependency, assertiveness, competition, aggression, and the like, and they have the capacity to differentiate experience in a range of thematic–affective areas and along dimensions of self and nonself, and time and space. In addition, they have a difficulty in representational elaboration and/or representational differentiation, in relationship to a current challenge in their life. This challenge, in all likelihood, is "teasing out" a past issue where the degree of representational elaboration and/or differentiation was less than optimal.

Consider an example of a mother who is quite anxious and depressed over her premature baby. She feels frightened that she will hurt her baby and feels very sad thinking she is responsible for her baby's prematurity, blaming herself for her prenatal diet and activity level. She comes for therapy because she feels unable to be as happy, spontaneous, and joyful as she wishes with her new baby and simultaneously feels worried, anxious, and intermittently despondent. While she is able to do her daily routines, including part-time work, she lacks "zip and spontaneity" and is preoccupied with thoughts of "What did I do wrong?" and feeling "I am a bad person." She evidences a solid capacity for engagement, an excellent prerepresentational, intentional communication pattern (also documented by history), and in most areas of her life has advanced through the stages of representational elaboration and differentiation. She has a healthy marriage, is assertive at work, warm with her older children and husband, and experiences a wide repertoire of abstracted representational feeling states, including love and intimacy, sexual pleasure, some limited competition, and qualified anger (especially when her oldest child or husband or other people close to her "annoy her"). The area of difficulty seems to be circumscribed, in part, to the unusual challenges around her new infant.

In the third session, she reveals a picture of herself as an individual who, while able to be competitive and assertive, was always concerned with hurting other people. "I always took special precautions not to be too competitive for fear I might hurt someone." Her mother was a controlling, aggressive woman who competed intensely with the patient. The patient enjoyed competing back, but as she got into adolescence she noticed that the marriage between her mother and father was not what it was portrayed to be when she was a young child. She realized her mother felt quite insecure about holding her father's attention. She became aware that she could elicit her father's pride and admiration far more easily than her mother could. Mother covered up her own apparent unease by being a successful businesswoman and in this way maintained her confident exterior. She also seemed to thoroughly enjoy competing with, and often beating, her daughter in tennis and in various intellectual pursuits. It was only with the patient's greater sophistication in adolescence that she could "consciously" see her mother's vulnerability. It was at this time that she realized she became concerned about hurting people as a way to soften some of her own competitive strivings.

The patient also realized that she intermittently worried about hurting herself when involved in highly charged, competitive situations. Furthermore, in having her third child she was going beyond her mother who had only two children (the patient had a younger brother). It had been a dilemma for her for many months to decide whether or not to get pregnant for a third time and challenge her mother's family pattern.

Aspects of the patient's worry about hurting her baby or having hurt her baby and her feelings of depression seemed related to some of her conflicts with her mother around competition and hurt. In this context, the short-term therapeutic work had two simultaneous foci. One, focus was to "tease out," be it in an intellectual sense, the dynamics described above as part of the early evaluation phase to see what we were dealing with. The second was to see how the patient could further representationally elaborate and differentiate the dimension of experience dealing with themes of competition and hurt originally related to mother and now related to her new baby. Her ego needed greater flexibility to deal with a challenging new experience. Further accentuating this challenge was the patient's realistic uncertainty of whether she could provide all the experiences her premature baby would need. She also recognized that in general in any new endeavor she often felt unsure of herself at first, but would then gain the necessary experience to feel "competent." Fortunately, there was no evidence that, other than expectable delays in some motor milestones, her premature baby would have long-term difficulties in motor, language, intellectual, or emotional development.

Short-term treatment would involve helping the patient further elaborate and differentiate representationally issues related to this narrow aspect of experience. We would not use the transference as a core learning experience, as we would only meet once every other week. Meeting infrequently would not permit the intensity and regularity needed for the transference to be the critical learning vehicle. Instead, we would take advantage of the most intense experience mother currently had available in her life—the experience she was having with her new baby. Other intense experiences related to her husband, older children, as well as to her own mother and father, whom she saw regularly, would also be utilized. We would take advantage of these natural experiences which had the qualities of intensity that sometimes is acquired by the transference. The intensity of feelings with her new baby led, at times, to a lack of differentiation (i.e., representational elaboration without representational differentiation). This dedifferentiation had qualities that are similar to what one sees in a full-blown transference neurosis. Not infrequently, a patient may have an intense relationship which is giving them difficulty and is similar to a transference neurosis in intensity and quality of differentiation. In short-term therapy, we try to help the patient use this intense relationship for learning about themselves.

The transference works as a critical learning experiences in part because of its intensity and its lack of differentiation. This provides both emotional saliency and the tendency for generalization. Of course, the transference provides other features which also make it a unique learning experience. It is a controlled environment where the analyst can be careful not to act out in the countertransference tendencies and reinforce old, maladaptive patterns. The analyst also provides the sense of security the patient needs for the early prerepresentational stages of ego growth. The analyst is constantly engaged and will not reject the patient. He pays attention to preverbal communication patterns to establish a preverbal sense of reality. Furthermore, he helps the patient with pattern recognition, modulation of intensity, perspective taking (i.e., while they are living the transference, they are exploring the transference), and a sense of professional competence, neutrality, safety, and privacy.

In dynamic short-term psychotherapy, we have the first two features—intensity of experience, and, at times, the undifferentiated nature of experience to promote generalization. We call on the patient's considerable ego strength to provide the other elements. In this respect, short-term dynamic psychotherapy is more challenging and taxing for the patient. It can only be done with a patient whose ego structure is intact and flexible. We are expecting the patient to provide the sense of security in prerepresentational engagement and purposeful communication. We are also expecting the patient to trust her own ability for pattern recognition on the "firing line," so to speak, when, for example, she is with her baby or her own mother. Furthermore, we are expecting the patient to trust her own ability to carry out pattern recognition in the context of intense emotional states. Just as in the analytic situation the analyst helps the patient experience and observe at the same time, the patient must experience and observe at the same time in the midst of the intensity of life itself. We are also expecting the patient to identify with the therapist's goals and professionalism and to incorporate certain of these skills unto herself. In this sense, many of the capacities which can be worked with daily in analysis or intensive analytic psychotherapy, must be accomplished somewhat independently by the patient.

The therapist does provide one critical function which aids

in this process. He is the consultant to the patient in what becomes a collaborative endeavor. As the consultant, the therapist is alert to transference feelings and clarifies both negative transference feelings and highly eroticized and regressive dependency-oriented positive transference feelings. The therapist is a coexplorer with the patient and helps the patient actively incorporate the self-observing tool into him- or herself to be applied in daily life.

The therapist encourages a general principle (much like the principle of "saying what comes to mind" in analysis). The central principle of short-term developmental dynamic psychotherapy is to engage in the sectors of life that are likely to lead to the required elaborative and differentiating experiences. When the patient is avoiding certain life experiences, there is little opportunity for self-learning and for applying the tools on the consultant–patient relationship. As the patient "jumps in the water," so to speak, with the strength of these new tools on board, she can, with the help of the consultant relationship, understand her emotional patterns.

The patient described above had begun avoiding her baby because the baby engendered strong negative and sad feelings and a sense of guilt. The patient was beginning to add another day to her work schedule and leave the care of her baby to a competent helper. This decision was motivated, in part, by her avoidance of negative feelings and a sense of incompetency. As the therapist observed the dynamics (a sense of working rapport seemed to be emerging), he offered a clarification, "You seem scared and are running away." In his clarification, he was suggesting, indirectly, that this type of active avoidance of her baby was not in the patient's interest. The difference is sometimes only semantic between a clarification which indirectly suggests that a patient should do something and what may appear as direct advice—for example, as an illustration of the former: "You are avoiding being with your wife by working late"—the patient knows exactly what you are suggesting—or "You flit around from one relationship to another because you are frightened of the intimacy in a one-on-one relationship."

Here, too, the patient knows what you are telling him. In the case of the latter you tell a patient: "You should try a more intimate, long-term relationship," or "You should try to spend more time with your spouse." The patient readily senses the indirect message as well as the direct one. In some respects it is more forthright for the therapist to say both at once: "You are avoiding A and if you didn't avoid A, you would be able to try out B which you are scared of."

At all times, one must be respectful of the need for the patient to choose his or her own options, including disagreeing with your covert or overt message. One must also make sure one is sympathetic to the patient's reasons, including fears and anxieties, for choosing to avoid a difficult situation. At all times, the context for these clarifications must be to facilitate representational elaboration and differentiation. The context must not be values, moralizing, or a hidden desire to control the patient. The goal of increasing representational differentiation provides the patient with the freedom to choose.

After the patient's avoidance of her baby was explored, she understood that in spending more time with her baby she might be able to work out some of the anxieties and conflicts that she was having.

Here, the critical principal of short-term developmental dynamic psychotherapy was implemented. The patient got back into the situation that would provide opportunities for representational elaboration and differentiation. One cannot learn without being in the emotional milieu in which that learning will occur.

Short-term dynamic psychotherapy requires one be involved in those experiences which will help one elaborate (abstract the affective states of relevance) and differentiate those states in terms of understanding their relationship to the rest of one's personality. In her experiences with her baby, the patient could experience fleeting feelings of depression and discomfort, not later in the day, as was her pattern, but right at that time. As she spent more time with her baby and was more aware of her own feelings, she also experienced, for the first time, anger at her baby. She had an image of wanting to show off her baby to other women, as well as her own mother. Her mother, in the fantasy, would look critically at her, as though to say, "I didn't have a premature baby and you did." As the patient clarified this competitive dynamic between her and her mother, her desire for the baby to be a "showpiece" to outdo her mother (a new dimension of her representational experience) was elaborated. She connected this wish to "show off" to the competitive relationship with her mother (their intellectual games and tennis). She also connected it to the anxiety she had about her awareness that her mother was not secure about her marriage. She, in this sense, was not only elaborating a new dimension of experience (wanting to "show off"), but also was differentiating and integrating it (i.e., connecting it to other current and historical patterns). She understood that her own anger at her baby was in part related to her competitiveness with her mother, and saw this pattern alongside her worry, depression, and self-blame. She was also differentiating further the experiences of competition, loss, and guilt, yet she was still reluctant to spend much time with her mother for fear her mother would now gloat over her with a sense of victory.

Another element in the short-term dynamic psychotherapy became clear: to help this patient not avoid her mother so that she could try to tolerate the affects experienced. Tolerating these affects would foster further representational elaboration and differentiation. The avoidance was pointed out to the patient, the affects she was scared of feeling with her mother were empathetically reviewed, and, through clarification, she decided to "bite the bullet" and spend extra time with her mother to deal with these issues.

Because of her flexible, intact ego structure, she could experience mother's little grin, and could see how she interpreted mother's off-handed comments as "put-downs." At the same time, however, she saw that her mother was also deeply worried and concerned about the new baby and in part identified with her in wanting the best for the baby. The competitive side was only one aspect of the relationship and certainly not the entire relationship. The patient further saw that mother tended to make her put-downs, such as, "Gee, so-and-so's baby is already walking," at times after the patient ignored mother and paid more attention either to father or to a friend. Mother was being sensitive to being ignored and responded with a competitive jab back. The patient's observation of her relationship with her mother (i.e., picking up on how mother reacted to her) facilitated representational differentiation. She understood a dynamic connection between herself and mother. She could focus on her own behavior and notice that sometimes she tended to ignore her mother partly because of her own competitive goals. If she was feeling unsure of herself she might choose to make a phone call while her mother was visiting, knowing that this offended her mother. As she explored her own desires to offend her mother, she began seeing their relationship dynamically (e.g., competitive flux). She began seeing her mother's comments about the baby as simply the latest derivative of this competitive flux.

She ceased having to avoid mother because she understood mother's comments about the new baby as part of their overall competition. With her greater understanding of what stirred mother's competitiveness (her own ignoring of mother), she was able to feel more in charge of what occurred. She was also able to talk with mother about how they nurtured and supported one another and how they tended to make each other feel uneasy. Mother could be responsive to a discussion of nurturing and support, but could not hear much about how they competed with each other. The patient was able to feel better about nurturing her new baby. The depressive affect slowly gave way to positive pride in her baby's accomplishments. Her guilt about her own prenatal activity and diet began to be viewed in a more realistic perspective.

This short-term work took eight months, once every other week. The bulk of the work took place in daily life with the patient's active scrutiny of her relationship with her baby, her mother, and her motherlike friends. The therapist served as a consultant and helped her stay in the thematic–affective areas she was avoiding; helped her engage in new affective–thematic areas she was frightened of (such as a closer relationship with her mother); and helped her to make her own formulations about what was going on. The therapist–patient relationship was a warm, mutually respectful one. Only occasionally would the patient get irritated with the therapist for "pushing me too far." The transference relationship was never fully explored. The quality of engagement and the consulting attitude of the therapist was used by the patient to work on her own. This approach is only possible in a patient with a relatively intact ego structure where the current concerns reverberate with unresolved past issues and the past issues have to do only with a narrow dynamic band of representational elaboration and differentiation.

In this model for short-term developmental dynamic psychotherapy, step one involves the therapist relating to the patient's already intact capacity for engagement and prerepresentational intentional communication. This establishes rapport and an immediate collaborative foundation. In step two, the therapist and patient try to use their collaborative skills and the patient's considerable ability for representational elaboration and differentiation to understand the nature of the current challenge and its dynamic relevance. In step three, the therapist, as a consultant, helps the patient become involved in the avoided areas of representational elaboration and differentiation, the affective–thematic domains, which may be restricting or constricting the full flexibility of the patient's ego. In this case, it had to do with competitive issues. In another case, it may have to do with issues of dependency, intimacy, or pleasurable excitement. In step four, the therapist helps the patient elaborate and differentiate representationally the new affective themes she is experiencing (e.g., competition). The disequilibrium stirred by the new challenge is eventually dealt with and new adaptive patterns emerge.

With the successful short-term dynamic treatment, not only is a new challenge addressed, but an area of relatively vulnerability, an area where representational elaboration and differentiation that was not solidly developed, becomes further developed. In this sense, the challenge becomes an opportunity for new ego growth in a narrow band of the personality related to the new challenge. New challenges, such as having children, illness, job change, moves, loss of a friendship can all become growth-producing experiences. Similarly, life changes associated with stages in the life cycle—the shifts and challenges in going from adolescence to adulthood to middle age to aging—can also become vehicles for stimulating ego growth if the individual, either on his own or with a therapist as a consultant, further elaborates and differentiates aspects of his representational system.

One more example will amplify this conceptualization. A young man came in somewhat anxious and worried about his marriage because, "I have to fake sexual enjoyment. If I tell my wife the truth, I'm afraid she will not want to stay married to me." He then described a pattern where he adjusted entirely to his wife's sexual rhythms, preferred positions, and practices for achieving orgasm. He felt he sacrificed his own pleasure. He believed that she had an underlying insecurity about her sexual competency and he, therefore, had to "go along with her" or else "suffer the consequences." Interestingly, this man claimed to have a highly successful marriage in all other ways. They experienced a great deal of pleasure and joy together, could argue and fight, and enjoyed competition with one another. This man was doing well at work, experienced a wide range of feelings, had positive self-esteem (except to feel anxious and annoyed for a few hours after they made love). The consultation was hastened by the fact that this man was enjoying a flirtation with a colleague at work and, while not completely conscious of it, he was concerned that he might be tempted to have an affair with her. He thought it better first to try to discover if he could improve his sexual relationship with his wife. His history suggested intact differentiated ego functioning.

Following the model outlined above, we first engaged in understanding his history and current functioning and, in the context of his own associations, the nature of his current situation. Although this man, did not assert himself in the sexual relationship, he was comfortable asserting himself in other areas of life. But from the time he was a teenager, beginning with masturbation, he was somewhat concerned with the fact that if he was too satisfied and too excited he would lose a relationship he depended on. When he started masturbating he was afraid it would separate him from his parents. With his first girl friend, at age seventeen, he felt that if he got too excited, she would find him unattractive. This fleeting concern didn't impede him from partially enjoying himself and being capable of an orgasm.

As we reviewed his life with regard to the issue of intensity of experience and intense pleasure, it became clear that his mother did not strongly condone intense, excited experience. She was a controlling person who liked order. While she was warm and engaging, she did not enjoy the "horsing around" or playfulness that he enjoyed with his father. His father could "let go." As the patient talked, it became clear that his wife, too, was a person who tended to be controlling, though far less so than his mother. She could "let go" sometimes, but not as much as he would like. In talking about "letting go," an interesting fantasy emerged. He imagined his wife completely out of control. He was sadistically and pleasurably enjoying her being out of control. He was teasing her sexually to such a degree that she couldn't "contain herself." As he became aware of the competitive and sadistic side of his pleasure, he was struck by the fact that he would want to see her so out of control. Associations followed relating to when, as a child, he would tease his mother by not going along with her desire to have him dress a certain way or to "behave himself" when they had company. He would tease her and try to "get a rise out of her." He wanted to "drive her crazy," that is, "out of control."

He could see a dynamic relationship between his own fear of getting too excited and his desire to drive someone out of control. He became aware of the fact that he was avoiding experiencing this conflict with his wife. The consultant–

therapist and the patient outlined all the areas in which this dynamic occurred (e.g., with his wife and other key individuals in his life). He saw the many situations where he avoided "letting go" even when it would be appropriate to do so. This was conflict not only in the sexual arena, but in other aspects of "peak pleasure," as he put it. He elaborated these areas and with the support of the consultant–therapist relationship he engaged in rather than avoided "intense experiences." He worked to gain an awareness of what he was feeling and what the other person was feeling. He focused on his own sadistic wishes to make the other person go out of control, as well as his wishes for pleasure. His pleasure could range from verbal forms (telling jokes) to the sexual relationship with his wife.

He became more aware of his own sadistic wishes to drive people "crazy" and the fleeting feelings while making love to his wife to do the same to her. He realized that his motive was not simply to protect his wife and preserve the relationship. He had two motives while making love: one to "let go" himself and make the sexual pattern more collaborative, and the other to "drive his wife crazy," in a sadistic as well as pleasurable way. His capacity to elaborate these affective themes was in part related to his ability to now "jump in the water" and engage his wife more fully. (He had pulled away from having sex with his wife and had reduced the frequency to once every other week. Earlier in their relationship, they had enjoyed a pattern of three times a week.) He reestablished a pattern of having sex once a week and at times twice a week.

He learned to elaborate representationally the full range of his themes, sadistic wishes, desires for sexual pleasure, and to differentiate them (as he understood the relationship between his pleasurable and sadistic inclinations). He gradually saw that his wife was a more flexible person than he imagined. She had many ways she could experience pleasure as they made love together. As he became comfortable exploring these, he could representationally elaborate her pleasure. He could separate or differentiate his picture of her pleasure from his own sadistic wishes to "drive her crazy." Eventually, he could elaborate the pleasurable side, the sadistic side, the competitive side, and the fearful side of his relationship with his wife and others. Interestingly, he also saw these patterns at a more subtle level in visits with his mother.

The patient's short-term dynamic therapy lasted nine months and took place at a once-a-week level. The major part of the work occurred through the patient's active understanding of the full range of themes at the level of representational elaboration. He used his own newly developing differentiating capacity to comprehend this narrow area of experience having to do with peak excitement, sadism, and pleasure. As the patient elaborated and differentiated this narrow band of experience as it related to his wife, mother, and other relationships, he developed greater ego flexibility.

We have discussed two cases where the short-term approach to treatment involved the patient doing a great deal of the work on his or her own using the analyst as a consultant, not as a transference figure. The intensity of experience was in the relationship with the baby on the one hand, and with the wife on the other. The therapist's role as consultant was to constantly help the patient engage in the experiences that would likely lead to new capacities for representational elaboration and differentiation. The therapist becomes the consultant for self-observing skills. He helps the patient to "jump in the water" to deal with those areas of experience that require greater representational elaboration and differentiation.

The therapist must be aware that he must go at the patient's speed and according to his readiness. As a consultant, he is collaborating with the patient and patient's readiness to engage in new areas of experience, elaborate these representationally, and find differentiating bridges to connect up the different aspects of experience.

In this model the positive elements of the transference are harnessed. Negative elements are interpreted. The patient is helped to make a developmental progression, to take narrow areas of experience that either have lacked representational elaboration and differentiation, or that have lacked only representational differentiation, and engage in, represent, and differentiate these experiences.

In figuring out where the patient nccds work it is necessary to have both a developmental and cross-sectional model in mind. The developmental model involves the four levels mentioned earlier. Here, the therapist is looking to see which experiences are elaborated, but not differentiated, or which are not fully elaborated. The therapist is also looking cross sectionally at the different types of experience of the patient, including dependency, pleasure, assertiveness, curiosity, competition, anger, empathy, more mature forms of love, and self-limit-setting (and the opposites of these experiences), as a way of profiling the breadth of the patient's capacity for representational elaboration and differentiation.

Chapter 8

Developmental Perspectives on Couple, Family, and Group Processes: Implications for Therapy

Traditionally, couples, family, and group therapy has rested in part on dynamic and systems understanding of "contents" boundaries, structures, and organizations. For example, in couples therapy there is interest in the mechanism of projective identification. One member of the couple projects certain contents of their own onto their spouse. The spouse unconsciously carries out these projected expectations which may also be unconscious in the mind of the originator. The mechanism of projective identification has also been postulated to operate in families where, for example, an adolescent may be carrying out the unconscious wishes of a parent, much to the parent's chagrin (Greenspan and Mannino, 1974; Shapiro and Zinner, 1975).

Intrapsychic collaborations among the different members of the group, including mechanisms such as pairing and fight–flight, have been postulated (Bion, 1961) to account for the dynamics of groups of eight to ten people. Developmental

241

concepts are well integrated into many of the different approaches to couples, families, and groups, (e.g., Level of differentiation).

The developmental approach to be discussed below will not offer an alternative to traditional conceptualizations of group process. Rather, it will try to offer a complimentary perspective which will explore levels of development in group processes.

The developmental perspective is based on a number of principles. The first principle, well established in many approaches, is that group patterns are an entity in their own right, whether it be a couple, a family, or small group. Different people are component parts of a larger whole. Participants—family members, group members, or spouses—are the elements in a larger structure.

Consider a family where the male child appears to be "hyper" and is coming for a consultation for a problem with "being destructive." His older sister seems quiet and reserved. She has excellent concentration and is called a "model child." Mother tends to be overprotective and "hovers over" her children in an infantilizing manner. At other times, however, mother is overstimulating and intrusive. Father is an "aloof workaholic" who becomes intensely involved in hyperstimulating the family when he is home. He is often away, however, and even when he is home, when not overstimulating his family, is unavailable, shut away in his study. This is not an atypical family constellation. Each member of the family has a unique character. Even with their unique characteristics, all members of this family had difficulty with one common characteristic—negotiating closeness or dependency. The "hyperactive destructive one" was very uneasy with being too close. In fact, it was at times that he either wanted closeness or closeness was offered to him that he became the most hyper. His older sister had given up on closeness and had withdrawn into a self-contained shell. She only felt close to her books and was too fearful to reach out to be close to people. Mother tried to be close by her overprotectiveness, but was constantly frustrated and feeling "empty" and that "nobody cared." Father had a lifelong difficulty with being close to other people, using a style similar to that of his older daughter— avoidance. He created an artificial sense of security and dependency around his work. Each family member, in their own way, was struggling with closeness, each, however, was marching to a different drummer and had different symptoms or complaints.

Once it became possible to see that they were dealing with a common theme, closeness (even though each one had other themes, they were concerned with as well), it was possible to look at a number of parameters of this family's functioning.

One parameter we looked at was the one just stated: What was the theme that they were all concerned about? In this case, it was dependency. Then we asked a number of related questions that follow from our developmental approach to ego functioning.

First, at what developmental level was this family functioning in its common concern? Once we understand that they are interested in something together, we want to know how they are negotiating this issue. Are they negotiating it at a level suggestive of prerepresentational patterns, even preengagement patterns? Where are they as a group on our developmental scheme? Are they engaged? Are they involved in intentional behavioral interactions? Have they made it to the representational level? If so, are they elaborating the different interrelated emotional themes around dependency and closeness or are they representationally constricted? Have they made it to the level of representational differentiation? If so, are they elaborating different themes at a differentiated level?

In this family, they were all engaged to some degree, even the more reserved ones that used aloofness and detachment. They were all purposeful in their behavior, except for the "hyper" one who sometimes regressed to a preintentional chaotic pattern. More often than not even his aggressive behavior was purposeful and targeted. When it came to abstracting affective patterns around dependency and closeness, however, including the anxieties, fears, and coping strategies associated with dependency, the family only had a limited ability to representationally elaborate their concerns (i.e., put feelings into words, complex gestures, rituals, or even playful games). At best, they were marginally at the level of representational elaboration when it came to dealing with dependency. They seemed to be somewhere between an intentional behavioral level and an early representational level. For example, only on rare occasions would mother talk about feeling loving or lonely or gesture father for closeness. More often she followed her pattern of trying to overprotect and overdo for him. This made him feel suffocated; in turn, he avoided her. This pattern was never discussed but it was played out at the behavioral level.

We also observed that at the level of intentional behavior and representational elaboration, this family was quite constricted. They were not able to negotiate, even at the behavioral level range of themes. Their ability to negotiate curiosity, excitement, pleasure, and anger and aggression was quite limited. For example, anger would often lead to loss of an attained developmental level. The youngest child would start to behave chaotically and regress to a preintentional level. Mother, when she would get furious, would withdraw, in spite of her overprotective style, regressing to a preengagement level. When angry, father would do the same.

We saw a family that was quite constricted in terms of their representational and prerepresentational range, and which at best, made it up into the late stage of intentional behavior and early stages of representational elaboration. The family members had no capacity for discussing dependency issues in a highly differentiated way, where feelings would be abstracted, verbalized, and examined in terms of their relationships to each other. We have a family who, at best, operated in a constricted way at the level of behavioral and beginning representational elaboration.

The challenge for this family is clear: To progress to the point where they can represent more broadly patterns at the level of representational elaboration and then progress to the level of representational differentiation.

As we think about how to help such a family, we should be clear that this family had regressive potential back to preintentional and preengagement levels of ego development. At the same time, we should also be clear that individually each one of the members of this family may have been capable of a higher level of adaptation in terms of their individual psychological functioning. When one talked to father alone (not in the family setting), he would appear to have a capacity for representational elaboration and differentiation as he reflected about himself, his parents, his relationships with siblings, and key relationships at work. At work he was able to be assertive and often compassionate with people who worked for him. He even reflected on his relationship with his own father and mother in a highly elaborative and differentiated way. However, in the family sessions he operated like a different person, aloof or competitively attacking and overstimulating other family members. Other family members showed similar profiles. Individually they were capable of a higher level of functioning than they were in the family group.

The family becomes a unique entity. It has its own developmental level which is in part independent from the individual dynamics of each member. The group constitutes a whole in its own right.

There are a number of principles that can be applied to the family group. The group is an entity in its own right: it organizes around a common theme or set of themes. This theme (or set of themes) is organized at a developmental level (engagement, intentionality, representational elaboration, representational differentiation). At the developmental level there is a thematic and affective range that the family is capable of. The range may be constricted or broad and flexible. Each family can be described (or even profiled and diagrammed) in terms of the predominant themes and the developmental level and thematic–affective range.

Consider a larger group, such as a therapy group of seven

to nine members. They have been meeting for a year. As the group members get to know one another, one sees how they deal with different themes. Inevitably, early on competition and rivalry emerge as a major issue between group members. Each member tries to flex his or her muscles and show that he or she is smarter than the other one. Themes of dependency and caring also emerge, particularly as one member or another becomes upset and reveals a depressed or sad side. During crises, members will often try to rally around one another. At other times one is surprised that just as a member seems most vulnerable, other members will attack and become very competitive. Themes of separation and loss emerge, particularly at vacation time. Pleasure and sexual curiosity emerge rather readily, particularly in groups with both men and women, although homoerotic feelings will emerge in groups of same-sexed individuals.

One observes all the themes in the life of the group that one observes in individuals. The life of the group is enhanced by the many vectors between individual members. Each member has a different agenda. Just as in a family group, the larger group organizes itself around certain themes. Different sessions will tend to focus on either pleasure and excitement, mystery and curiosity, assertiveness and competition, dependency and caring, anger, separation, and the like. As the group gels, one looks not only at how individual members participate in the group and how their own individual psychologies become part of the larger whole, but the composition of this larger whole. What are the predominant themes of this group? Some groups are more competitive initially, and may become concerned with dependency later on. For others the reverse may be true.

Consider one group as an example. It was made up of nine individuals, a mixture of men and women between ages twenty and forty. They had a variety of different diagnoses, ranging from neurotic patterns and character disorders to borderline and severe borderline conditions. The group sessions would usually start with individual members talking about what had happened to them during the week. This would then lead to some members beginning to criticize others about why they were "so neurotic," or why they weren't "changing their patterns." One attractive young lady who always rejected men and then felt isolated and alone was severely criticized by the other women in the group for once again being "cold" to a new young suitor. She shouldn't complain because she had scared him off with her coldness. It was her own fault that she was lonely and "depressed" again. Another young woman, who was promiscuous, countered with her own pattern of having two or three men all the time. She claimed this was far better than being anxious, cold, and rejecting. While the women talked about dating, the one married man in the group often engaged two other men in the group with discussions about work and bosses and how unfair it was that other people were getting the credit for his work. The other men quickly criticized him saying that it was his own fault. He was so passive and that he didn't know how to assert himself and get proper credit for his efforts.

After a quick catching-up with each other, this competitive mutual bobbing characterized the second element of most group sessions. The group would fluctuate back and forth between a member of the group further elaborating aspects of his or her week, competitive interactions, and fleeting attempts at support and expressions of warmth for one another. No sooner would a group member try to be warm and empathize with another group member's sadness, fearfulness, or frustration at work, than some other member of the group would come in and start attacking and criticizing either the supportive member for being "too hand-holding," or the member with the problem for not having used the group's insights of the week before.

When a group member would come in with a real crisis— severe depression or disorganized thinking—the group would rally and became very warm and supportive. The members of the group would ask the disorganized members what had happened and offer concrete yet positive and empathetic suggestions. There was a cohesiveness around the member with the crisis. All other members of the group would spend as much as thirty to forty-five minutes listening and talking to the upset person.

The group leader would try different comments: for example, he would comment on the way the group supported one another in times of crisis. The group could abstract the concept that they were caring and had close feelings for one another. The group even went so far as to abstract the notion, that as a whole group, even when they criticized one another it was more out of love and caring than out of a desire to hurt one another. They "cared so much."

Around the theme of caring and closeness in crises, the group seemed to have some capacity for intentional behavior. They organized their focus around the group member in crisis. They also had a capacity for abstracting a feeling state. A stage of representational elaboration had been reached. That they might be defending their critical attitude by calling it "caring" further suggests their capacity to elevate their dialogue to the representational realms.

In comparison to the themes of closeness in crisis, the group leader pointed out that group members felt very competitive with each other. That one of the reasons why they always criticized one another and couldn't be more supportive to one another, except in crises, was because of the competition amongst the men, and the competition amongst the women, and sometimes even between the men and women. In response to this comment, the group would become somewhat aloof and disengaged from one another. Each member would talk in an isolated way about his or her own week. There would be very few comments to other members. They disengaged from one another. Some of the more disorganized members of the group would become chaotic. They would talk or behave in a nonpurposeful way, talking diffusely and unrealistically about feelings of sadness or anger. They would also begin horsing around with teasing and joking, including getting off their chairs and lying on the floor. At times they would throw coffee cups or crumbs from cookies that they were eating at each other. In response to an attempt to see if they could abstract a feeling state having to do with competition, anger, and closeness toward one another, patterns of isolation, disengagement, and nonpurposeful behavior emerged. Initially, there was no evidence of representational capacity to abstract these themes.

The highest level in this group was at a stage of purposeful behavior and some representational elaboration with limited capacity for representational differentiation around themes of caring and being close to other people during a crisis. However, when it came to competitiveness and assertiveness in the context of closeness within the group (each member could talk about competitiveness and closeness in their individual lives at a level of representational elaboration and differentiation), prerepresentational levels predominated.

We see an interesting pattern characterizing a group. We have a series of individuals, all of whom in their own lives can operate at representational or differentiated representational levels. In a group of nine people, however, they are capable of operating within certain thematic areas at representational levels, but in other areas only at prerepresentational levels. The major theme of the group, early on, was around competition, which is the way they organized about eighty percent of their behavior, even though one could argue that the underlying theme was how to be close and warm and take care of one another. The more problematic theme, and the one they evidenced, was the competitive issue. The dominant theme of the group, as it was organizing itself, was at a prerepresentational, intentional behavioral level with regressive potential back to prebehavioral intentional patterns and even preengagement patterns.

At the level of intentional behavioral patterns, the group was capable of dealing with both dependency as well as competition. At higher levels, they were only capable of dealing with more superficial aspects of dependency and closeness having to do with taking care of people in crises (interestingly, an area in which many of the group members had a lot of practice and experience).

In work with couples, the same principles apply. In one couple, the wife operated at a somewhat undifferentiated representational level. Meanings become confused. She could abstract feeling states and talk about competition, dependency, caring, excitement, and like, but got confused as to whether it was her own or somebody else's content. Projection and incorporation were rampant at a representational level. The husband tended to be concrete, but organized. He operated at an intentional behavioral level. He believed in the principle of "behavior in action," and had a limited capacity for abstracting feeling states.

As a couple their characteristic patterns were at a level of either disorganized behavior or nonengagement. At home, there were long periods where they did not engage with or talk to each other. When they did talk, they often talked past one another. Neither responded to the other's behavioral or representational cues. In sessions they appeared to be very disorganized, yelling at one another, accusing each other of things that neither one had said or done. They were unable to respond to each other in an organized purposeful manner. Their joint (couple's) behavior was one or two notches below each one's individual capability. The one theme that organized them was competition for who was the worst individual of the couple (i.e., the worst parent or the worst spouse). As each one accused the other and tried to get the other to "'fess up" there was intentional communication. Quickly, there was a regression to preintentional patterns. The wife projected her wishes onto the husband and used the mechanisms of projective identification. The husband used massive avoidance, vacillating between avoidance and intrusive, critical behavior. We have a projecting, incorporating wife (at the representational level) and an intrusive, avoidant angry husband at the behavioral level. It was not surprising that when they came together the overall pattern was a notch below each one's developmental level. There was very little capacity for organizing each other at a common level. They regressed to a level of preintentional, disorganized behavior and preengagement patterns.

A principle is that the characteristic developmental level organizing the behavior, feelings, thoughts, or wishes of the family, large group, or couple is often less than what each individual member is capable of. One may wonder why the group, family, or couple pattern is often at a lower developmental level and a more constrictive thematic range than each individual person comprising the group or couple.

Within the group a new definition, sense of common ground, or identity must be sought. Perhaps in any social structure there is an attempt to find an organizing principle, a way the elements can relate to one another. In this model, even disharmony or lack of relating would be considered a level, although it would be a low level of organization—the preengagement level. In our developmental model, middle levels would perhaps be characterized by disorganized behavior patterns but with engagement between the elements. The next level would be organized behavioral patterns. The next after that would be abstracted patterns such as shared meanings. Within this framework, every social organization would have some level. Where each element is marching to its own drummer (each person was operating in isolation) an early level would be indicated. Where there was no physical proximity between the elements, one might argue that no organization existed at all. Where there is some proximity among the elements, one could argue that there is an organization which can be characterized by one or another developmental level.

Why does the group level always seem to be less than the level each element may be capable of? Perhaps, in seeking a unifying theme, an organization to characterize a new structure, the elements find a common ground. The elements may have two ways of finding this common ground. One is to go higher and the other is to go lower. Social organizations can go higher and find some abstracted unifying theme, such as a high ideal or principle (the United States constitutional theme of balance of power in government would be an example; the Ten Commandments, the expression of a religious ideal, would be another). At the same time, unification could be found by going lower.

When an abstracted theme cannot be found, a more concrete theme or rhythm may hold the elements together. Even when each element is beating to its own drummer, they may still have something in common that is concrete. For example, a group of individuals that were trying to find something in common might find that none of their thoughts are in common (precluding the representational level) or that none of their intentional behaviors or inclinations are in common (precluding the intentional, organized behavior level). They might find that all they have in common is that they all eat and all go to the bathroom. The theme that would tie them together would be a very concrete theme about bodily needs— eating and elimination. Concrete, bodily derived rituals might organize the group.

At a slightly higher level, a group may find that they all have in common a need for some engagement with one another, a sense of relatedness, a social hunger. If this is all they have in common (their individual interests, behavioral inclinations, and thoughts are at cross-purposes with one another), the only level that they might be able to organize around is this level of engagement. At every other level there is no unifying theme. An example of primary engagement might be blind obedience to an "engaging person," a demagogue, or charismatic leader.

At a still slightly higher level, intentional behavior expressed through common rituals may link a group together. A group may vacillate between engagement and intentional behavior at a lower level type organization. At these prerepresentational lower levels, a person or a concrete ritual is the link, rather than values, ideals, or ideas.

As the group organizes around lower developmental levels, they may also organize around certain concrete themes, such as dependency, anger, or excitement. At the lower levels, they do not organize around higher level themes, such as empathy, love, higher level forms of competition (which involve being aware that you can be competitive with your opponent on the one hand and still have a loving, caring relationship on the other hand). Nor do they organize around higher forms of love (which would suggest that you can care for and love someone on the one hand and still be angry and competitive with them on the other hand). Higher-level feeling states tend to deal with multiple levels of emotion in some relationship to each other. Lower-level themes tend to reflect polarized emotional states, such as rage, global undifferentiated love, and so forth.

The group can try to organize itself by going lower to find some common theme or link, or higher to find some highly abstracted feeling state or ideal. It is interesting to note that many organizations which try to unite people, such as religious organizations, often find a seemingly high-level and low-level structure simultaneously. For example, a religion may emphasize higher-level love which accepts anger and sins. It may value traits such as empathy, sharing, and concern for others. Yet at the same time the same religion will have concrete rituals that appear to exist at the prerepresentational, behavioral, and/or engagement levels. There are do's and don't's or there is blind obedience to an authority, neither of which requires judgment or abstracting. Rituals that tie people to the religious organization (e.g., certain religious practices having to do with prayer and ways of dealing with your fellow man), may often operate at the intentional behavioral level. Others operate at the level of engagement. There is a sense of unity between the individual and the religious organization. We simultaneously see levels that are low in the developmental sequence (concrete rituals and images) and at the same time high, seemingly abstracted feeling and ideational states.

Seemingly "high" abstracted values may not be at the highest or most complex level in the developmental continuum. "High" level values are often portrayed as quite abstract when, in fact, their developmental level may be much lower; there is an illusion of complexity. Consider the doctrine of "forgiveness." It can be perceived as a concrete doctrine. Love does not integrate anger, resentment, and competition; it simply ignores them. Evil or aggression simply disappears in the face of love. This ideology may rest on a notion of "splitting." Feeling states are polarized and split from one another and love wins out. "Splitting" is part of the level of behavioral intentionality and indicates only the very beginning of representational capacities.

A more abstract, complex view of love is one in which love can tolerate and integrate anger. Thus, one can sense that within a loving relationship one can have competitive and angry feelings, and this is quite different from the polarized view that love is all that is needed. In this more abstract view, love doesn't undo the anger, it coexists with it and tries to organize it toward some higher goals.

To take this discussion one step further, let us look at the values that organize nations. Values may exist in a highly integrated way or may be portrayed in terms of concrete images, with little flexibility. People may misinterpret the values of a country into dichotomous, concrete images. For example, countries which are organized along the lines of race, skin color, or ethnic origin may tend toward concrete images.

A group identity may be formed at various developmental levels. What may constitute more flexible large group identities and more concrete prerepresentational identities? It might appear that higher-level integrations are fostered by experiences of a country in continually reintegrating new elements into a larger structure. If the organizing ideals of that country exhibit some flexibility and if the political structure of that country exhibits adaptability and flexibility, then the constant reintroduction of new elements into that structure may facilitate further invigoration of that flexibility. On the other hand, there may be countries where there is no challenge for higher-level integrations. There is no influx of new elements or values, but simply the repetition of certain patterns (in terms of the ethnic stock and cultural patterns). If at the same time the historical values and ideals of that country are rather concrete in the first place, you may get a continuing further concretization of the country's values and ideals.

For a country that has constantly changing values, ideals,

and new challenges, if the original organizing patterns or values are concrete, the introduction of new elements may lead to regressive polarizations rather than new levels of integration.

Returning back to the issue of the family, couples, and eight-to-ten-person groups, we can see how even in small groups there is a need to form a link between the elements. These can exist at different developmental levels. Unfortunately, even though there is the option of finding a higher level, the group starts off with finding some concrete pattern. Group structure itself does not seem to have the integrating principles to abstract higher themes. In other words, you can either find similarities among people in a very concrete way (we all have skin, we all eat, we all go to the bathroom), or at a higher level, we all require love, competition, and anger in some mix with each other. We have to learn how to integrate these.

THERAPEUTIC IMPLICATIONS

The following discussion will focus on how to use these observations of group processes for therapeutic purposes. The therapeutic goal may be stated as follows: To shift the equilibrium of the group from a lower level found naturally by the group because of a lack of integrating and differentiating structures in that group (be it couples, family, or a larger group) to a higher level. Some social organizations may do this naturally. (Perhaps these are the types of social organizations we should advocate as being therapeutic in their own right.)

But first, let us consider how we do this therapeutically. In the group, be it a couple, family, or group, the role of the therapist is to facilitate the shift upward in both structure and broadening of themes (that could be differentiated and integrated at any given structural level). The therapist is constantly trying to get the behavioral and prebehavioral issues into the representational level by abstracting central affective states. In a couple, family, or group, the therapist might comment, "In spite of all the competitive rhetoric in this family, where you criticize one another, you all seem to be struggling with how to be close to one another." Each member may then review his difficulties with closeness in his own history, as well as in the family. Nonetheless, family members might quickly lapse into back-biting critiques of one another.

As the therapist keeps his eye on the difficulty this family has in dealing with dependency, he may continually return to it until the family can abstract a feeling state having to do with dependency. He will point out all the ways the family defends against, avoids, or regresses from this issue as a way of helping them see the interrelationships between the main theme and their other behaviors. Over time, they see that what, for them, were seemingly random states of mind are part of a larger pattern. Each individual's styles are part of this larger pattern. The group is seen as a theme and a series of interrelated ways of dealing with, avoiding, or otherwise defending against this theme.

The overall goal is to switch from the lower level to the higher level. To abstract the feeling states, the couple, family, or group must see which feeling states they are having difficulty with. If, for example, in the family the situation is closeness, the family may nonetheless perceive the difficulty they are having as "we fight too much." Then the therapist's job is to keep abstracting the difficulties with closeness out of each interaction. The family may be involved in behavioral interactions where they attack one another. Around each attack, the therapist sees frustrated dependency longings. At some point after observing this, the therapist may offer a comment such as, "Gee, when mommy attacks daddy or daddy attacks junior, each time it seems to be because the other one wasn't paying enough attention to the first one and wasn't taking care of that person enough. Junior seemed to want mommy to give him a verbal hug, so to speak, and daddy seemed to want something similar from daughter. Each time you folks get angry, there always seems to be some related issue having to do with how can we be close to one another." The family may respond to this initially with anxiety and a further intensification of their behavioral patterns. But over time, they will begin to abstract and represent something about the family's needs. As closeness and dependency is elevated to the representational level, the family can find a higher equilibrium, a way of meeting each other's needs and conceptualizing the family in a different way. The family goes from being "a fighting family" to a family that is struggling to find a way to meet each other's needs. (This is a very different equilibrium and orientation, particularly when this shift is from a behavioral intentional action level.) They may eventually reach a level where feelings are abstracted, experienced, and discussed.

Similarly, within the therapy group of eight to ten, where the theme of competition was being acted out, the therapist repeatedly pointed out how the men and women were competitive with each other. As the group dealt with this organized theme, they began abstracting a feeling state. When one member would come in and talk about their woes of the week, instead of acting out the attack on that member with verbal abuse, each person, individually and collectively, would sense the desire to outdo one another by undermining him or her. This capacity evolved in an interesting way. When one or two members attacked each other, other members of the group (the chorus in the back, so to speak) would point out what the therapist had pointed out earlier, the members were being competitive with one another. Over time, members of the group could feel this competition. The group, as a whole, seemed to evidence a feeling state having to do with competitive rivalry. Any member of the group, after a period of time, could make the comment about competition. When the group reached a representational level (because of repeated abstractions of their behavioral tendencies), any one member's comment, if it was on the mark, would be responded to by a shift in the group's equilibrium. This wouldn't mean that everyone in the group said, "That's right, we're competitive," but one would see the associations in the group shift from attacks to a discussion about competition and rivalry (in work relationships, family relationships historically, etc.). The theme of competition was abstracted and elevated to the level of ideas. The process of the group would then become more collaborative and new associations about the danger of closeness would emerge.

Within a couple's relationship, this pattern works quickly and dramatically. The couple observes that together they function at a much lower level than either one functions at individually. As they begin exploring how they negotiate dependency, competition, aggression, or other elements, the therapist helps them abstract those feeling states which exist at prerepresentational levels. As they become aware of the way they are behaving toward each other, and as they become aware of those feelings that they can only deal with in a concrete way, they begin learning to abstract those feeling states (whether it has to do with sharing, or competition, or closeness and dependency, or anger, or sexuality, etc.). As they learn to represent these feeling states that had formerly been acted out in intentional behavior or disorganized behavior, or in levels of engagement or in preengagement patterns, they progress up the developmental ladder.

The group can often only take members so far. When in a couple situation, for example, the group relationship reaches the highest level that one of the members of the couple is capable of individually, the therapeutic relationship in the couple work may not be enough to help one member of the couple break new ground. Sometimes individual therapy is needed at this point to help such a member advance developmentally. What is needed at such a point depends on the intensity of the couple's pattern with the therapist and the nature of the deficit in one or another member of the couple's relationship. For example, if one member has a very severe character disorder where certain aspects of representational elaboration and differentiation have never been experienced, the group experience may not be able to help the person develop the security to advance. Not infrequently, however, the group pattern can be sufficiently intense and secure (a couple, family, or larger group) so that new development may occur in an individual. It will occur in the way we discussed earlier—with the security of an engagement with the therapist, with the security of intentional communication, and with work on creating new representational abstracted understandings and meanings for affects and behaviors.

As one is progressing to higher developmental levels, inevitably one reaches the level of representational differentiation. As one reaches this state of representational differentiation, one helps the group understand its own process.

There are many steps that must go on before the traditional therapeutic level of examining meanings is achieved. Many therapists assume the couple, family, or group is already at this level. Much verbalization goes for naught because the group is really struggling with issues of engagement and purposeful intentional behavioral communication. They are not yet ready to see relationships among affect states, and when the therapist is two levels higher than the patient, they continue to be disorganized at their prerepresentational or early representational levels.

The therapeutic goal is to help the group progress from a lower level of equilibrium to a higher level of equilibrium. In doing this, the therapist makes use of understanding the group's dynamics by helping them abstract their feeling states. He also creates a milieu following the general principles that we talked about earlier. He is engaged and mobilizes each member to be engaged to the entire group. He sets up a structure for intentional, purposeful communication within the group. He communicates a value system (that the group organizes around) which is that abstracted representational communications will help group members understand earlier patterns of communication and that representational differentiation is to be strived for as a goal. Within this context and with the relationship with the therapist facilitating developmental momentum, over time the group uses the security afforded by constant engagement and purposeful communication and a focus on abstracting feeling states as a vehicle for moving into the representational levels. Once there, the therapist helps the group elaborate the representational levels into themes they were incapable of representing earlier and then move into more differentiated patterns. There is a shifting back and forth between engaging the group in its fantasies and pointing out the limits of realistic thinking.

In addition, the therapist in the couples, family, and larger group provides other functions. The therapist creates a sense of safety and security by focusing on verbalizing rather than acting. He fosters engagement between members, pointing out when one member is isolating himself or disengaging, and helping him reengage (he fosters engagement between the group members just as he fosters it between himself and the group). Similarly, he is always fostering purposeful communication. Disorganized behaviors are always reorganized in the context of group intentions. When a member behaves chaotically, he helps that member communicate what he wants to say more purposefully or helps the group see the unpurposeful communication in a purposeful manner. The person who is lying on the floor comes to see that they are asking for discipline or asking for closeness or trying to be provocative. Lying on the floor now becomes a purposeful behavior for the individual and for the group. The individual side and the group side operate synergistically.

In some respects the group has the opportunity to create an even greater sense of security at the level of engagement and prerepresentational reality testing than individual therapy. The multiple members of the group create multiple connections and engagements. The sense of security can be enormous. Similarly, the ability to negotiate in an organized, purposeful way the many nonverbal gestures of the group, the prerepresentational intentions of the group, also provides an enormous sense of security, in part related to the ever-present possibility of chaos.

In the family, the ability for engagement and purposeful communication can often reinstitute a structure that has been dangerously undermined by miscommunications. Sometimes one is putting into place a system that has never been present in the family. To the degree the new family "structure" continues outside the therapy sessions, there is now a new sense of security through engagement and differentiated behavioral communications. The family now has prerepresentational reality testing, the predictability and understanding of each other's gestures, and constant engagement with one another. Earlier, there may have been unpredictable, frightening gestures, overwhelming confusion, withdrawal, and avoidance. We often overlook the importance of establishing the baseline experience of engagement and the interactional logical communication most take for granted.

Similarly, with couples, instituting engagement and the purposeful communication provides a cohesive structure and foundation for that couple. Against this background, it is not surprising that families, couples, and groups experience relief and can begin engaging in representational elaboration and differentiation.

It must be remembered, that people only exist in relative terms in the context of the various groups in which they participate; we exist as part of a nuclear family and an on-going set of relationships, including new families, larger groups in work and play, and various societal structures. One's experiences in the therapeutic group have profound influences not only on that group's level of adaptation, but one's own way of finding equilibrium points in one's natural groups (and vice versa), in day-to-day life. Group relationships, in part, define one's self just as individual psychodynamics do.

One final note. Something that makes group life somewhat different from individual life is that in a group the different members are operating not just in some verbal and behavioral connectedness to one another, they are also in spatial relationships to one another. The visual–spatial domain is another aspect of one's psychic economy (how one operates in interpersonal space), particularly when different affective proclivities and meanings are associated with interpersonal space.

We commonly think of individuals in a group in terms of meanings, particularly when we talk about developmental level and thematic–affective range. Similarly, we need to think about how people operate in visual–spatial domains. For example, some children operate very well in two-person systems. When you put them in a group of seven or eight children, however, they freeze and/or become very disorganized. There is something about trying to deal with seven or eight people in various spatial configurations ("Who is behind me? Who is beside me?"). What are these multiple acting, behaving, feeling, and thinking people doing to one another? One only has to be impressed with mob psychology and the contagion effect to realize that the sense of self in interpersonal space has remarkable impact. The various projective and introjective tendencies that occur because of permeable boundaries in large groups have been described (Turquet, 1975).

At the same time, each individual has his own ability for visual–spatial abstraction, integration, and differentiation. Just as we all come into the world with different abilities to abstract verbal meanings (some people read quicker, talk sooner, and intuitively understand meanings more easily than others), similarly, on a maturational basis, different people have different abilities for abstracting and understanding relationships in space. The person who becomes a great architect or theoretical physicist may have an enormously gifted ability in this area in comparison to the great novelist.

Two capacities relate to the group experience. One has to do with the ability to abstract themes, verbal meanings. This is on a continuum with abstracting affect tendencies. The other has to do with the visual–spatial domain; relationships (behavioral and eventually affective) in the context of the spatial domain rather than the auditory–verbal domain. When a sound or word hits your ear, you abstract a meaning. When you see someone in space, you abstract something about their spatial relationship to you. For example, if someone says, "I hate you," but looks smiling and makes no gestures you might assume they are just joking. On the other hand, someone who says, "I love you," but grimaces and makes aggressive gestures to you, you may assume they are mad and trying to fool you. If that person is twenty feet away, you may not be too concerned.

If they are two feet away, you might well be alarmed. If you have a deficit in your ability to judge interpersonal space (people who are twenty feet away appear to two feet from you), you may get confused and anxious whenever there are three or four people surrounding you, and you may regress and disorganize as a function of spatial meanings, not verbal meanings.

In summary, a group can be described according to its developmental level, its thematic–affective range. Experiences that facilitate individual ego development, when applied to the unique features that characterize groups, also facilitate the collective ego development of the group as a whole.

Chapter 9

A Developmental Approach To Psychopathology: Implications for Treatment

Critical ego functions are developed at certain ages. If there are deficits in that same ego function in a type of adult psychopathology, one may surmise that the developmental perspective will shed some light on the nature of the adult psychopathology.

There are double relationships between a set of functions, the developmental relationship, how this function comes into being or is compromised during development, and the role of that function in the adult psychopathology. It is always tempting to jump to causal relationships. Because there are so many factors that contribute to adult psychopathology, one should not make such a leap. For example, a type of adult psychopathology may stem from a compromise in adulthood which leads to the loss of a well-established function. The fact that this lost function is the same function that developed at age two and a half would not necessarily imply a casual relationship between the two. In understanding the dynamics of this lost function in

265

adulthood, one's detective work would be advanced if one understood how this function evolved in early childhood. In other instances, however, a developmental deficit may, in fact, have etiological significance. In this discussion, we will not deal with this issue. We will only show how the developmental perspective aids in our understanding of certain types of psychopathology.

To use the developmental perspective for understanding adult psychopathology it is useful to create four broad categories in the early organization of experiences. The framework of these four levels of organization, which were described earlier in the chapter on the therapeutic process, will also enable us to look at psychopathology in developmental terms. The developmental perspective will offer a way of looking at psychopathology that is dynamic, rather than static, and in keeping with the way in which certain functions come into being. It will allow us to create new subtypes of many of the types of dysfunctions. These subtypes will be useful in generating better operational definitions of psychopathology, as well as new hypotheses about the factors that influence either the genesis or course and natural history of psychopathology. We will begin with a brief review of the four categories of experience.

1. *The Level of Engagement.* The ability to engage is, in part, originally learned in the negotiation of the first two stages in ego development, the achievement of homeostasis and the achievement of an attachment. These stages dealt with going from a world self–object, where the animate and inanimate worlds are undifferentiated, to a part self–object seeking stage, where self and object are not clearly differentiated (but the animate is clearly differentiated from the inanimate world). This stage, which characterizes the development of the first four to six months of life, can be summarized in terms of the infant's ability to engage with the human world. As was discussed, this capacity for engagement has to do with both physical capacities of the infant, such as the ability to modulate and process sensory experience (including visual, auditory, tactile, olfactory, vestibular, propioceptive). Equally important

are the infant's ability for motor coordination and planning; the ability to distinguish affective from nonaffective stimuli; and interpersonal capacities such as the ability to engage in mutually satisfying experiences with the affective world.

The ability to engage can be compromised by difficulties in sensory modulation or processing, such as the baby who is sensitive to touch or high-pitched sounds and avoids or withdraws from the human world. Other difficulties that compromise the ability to engage include problems with motor tone, coordination, and planning, such as an infant who cannot signal interest in the world generally, and in the affective world in particular. Caregivers who do not respond, or respond inconsistently can also compromise engagement. Then there are compromises in the affective world, even when the infant's perceptual and motor equipment is fine, such as a caregiver failing to draw a baby into a relationship (e.g., a caregiver who is exceedingly depressed or who is so self-absorbed that there is no "wooing" of the new infant). Physical characteristics of the baby, as well as interactive characteristics stemming from deficits in the environment, or combinations of both, can play a significant role in the baby's capacity for engagement. Variations in the capacity for engagement is central to different types of psychopathology in later childhood and adulthood.

2. *The Level of Intentional, Interactive, Organized Behavior and Affects*. This level includes the stages of somatopsychological differentiation (intentional communication) and behavioral organization—the formation of a complex sense of self. This level, which encompasses the periods from about five months up to about eighteen months, characterizes the baby's ability to become increasingly more intentional, complex, and organized (in terms of drive affect dispositions). Organized behavioral and affective domains broaden to include dependency, pleasure, assertiveness, aggression, and, eventually, even self-limit-setting. From the point of view of ego development, we see the infant go from part differentiated self–object patterns (e.g., the eight-month-old baby who can reach out to be picked up and then smile gratifyingly when his wishes are met), to whole

behavioral self–object patterns. The eighteen-month-old baby can experience the parent as a full human being, not just as a smiling face or a reaching arm. He can put together the "angry mommy" and the "nice mommy," the "playful, rough daddy" and the "soft, cuddly daddy." This level is still a behavioral level of whole self–object differentiation because the toddler has not yet evolved to the point where he can represent his behavioral and affective world.

During this stage of more intentional organized approaches to the human interaction, we observe the ever-increasing importance of interactive signaling. The eight-month-old can gesture for dependency with reaching out to be picked up, can clench his fists and look angry, and even bang on the table to show his anger. Assertiveness, curiosity, anger, dependency, and pleasure are all intentional and organized. By fifteen to eighteen months, we see the signaling system become even more organized. The toddler also communicates across space. He can be playing building a tower on one side of the room, look over and see if mother is nodding at him approvingly from the other side, and if she is offering nods with vocalizations, he can decode the rhythm of her sounds, understand a few of her words, understand her gestures, and go on building his tower without having to go back and cling or sit in her lap. He can feel like he is in her lap through her nodding approvals, much like two adults feeling warm through their accepting gestures and supportive vocalizations. He can also gesture about anger and even gesture about self-limit-setting, such as hitting himself on the hand or holding one hand with the other when there is something he shouldn't do. At the same time, our sophisticated toddler is learning how to go from the stage of ego splitting to more integrated states (e.g., he learns that the angry mommy and the nice mommy is one person). At thirteen months, it doesn't appear he can do this, but, as indicated earlier, by eighteen months he has a sense of a whole operational person.

We have a level of intentional organized behavioral and affective patterns. This level, which involves complex preverbal gesturing, allows the toddler to engage with his world in a new way. The toddler is part of a two-way communication system. He is capable, through his sensory (perceptual) and motor systems of receiving and giving information. He can now use his capacities for ongoing gestural communication. He is continually abstracting what his parents and others are signaling and, in turn, providing them with information. Information exchanges of a complex nature are now possible. What of emotional value is communicated through this gestural system? Safety versus danger, acceptance versus rejection, approval versus disapproval, love versus hate, respect for "me" versus impersonal expectations, and a reciprocal empathetic definition of "me," it is suggested, is prerepresentationally communicated through this gesture system (just as an adult decides on a new person's safeness or danger before he even speaks). The main emotional messages of life are organized at this second level.

The first two stages are the stage of engagement, where the critical issue involves forming a relationship, and the stage of intentional organized behavior where the toddler is able to communicate and signal ever more intentionally across a wide range of behaviors, affects, and drive–affect dispositions.

3. *The Level of Representational Elaboration.* Earlier, we described how the child elevates behaviors, affects, and drive–affect dispositions to the level of representation. The child can now create images which can be manipulated, as evidenced through his pretend play and his functional use of language. The child broadens this symbolization of behavior, affect, and drive–affect patterns to include all the relevant affective thematic domains, dependency, pleasure, assertiveness, anger, and self-limit-setting. During this stage, the youngster is developing representational self–objects, first undifferentiated and then

gradually differentiated. These representational self–objects first undergo drive–affect elaboration and then undergo a second level of differentiation.

We have a third level in the infant's developmental sequence— the ability of label drive–affect patterns and elaborate them across many thematic domains.

4. *The Level of Representational Differentiation.* Self–object representations which have been elaborated, and continue to be elaborated, simultaneously undergo differentiation. The self and the object representations become organized along dimensions of affect proclivity, time and space, and self and nonself. Experience is categorized in functionally relevant patterns. The young child can now shift between fantasy and reality, understand his impact on others, and separate different drive–affect patterns involving dependency, assertiveness, pleasure, sexuality, and so forth.

Basic ego functions emerge, including reality testing, impulse control, a stable mood, and the ability to concentrate and anticipate.

We have suggested four levels of organization, those of

1. Engagement
2. Intentional Organized Behavior and Affect
3. Representational (Symbolic) Elaboration
4. Representational (Symbolic) Differentiation

These four levels will aid in our understanding of types of psychopathology, including operationalizing and subtyping them. The following discussion will not challenge traditional descriptions of these types of psychopathology, rather, it offers another perspective, a developmental one. We will not go into the clinical characteristics of these psychopathologies, but will assume a fairly well-versed reader. We will attempt to add to the existing psychodynamic and clinical understandings of these disorders.

We will consider four types of psychopathologies: psychotic patterns, borderline phenomena, character disorders, and neurotic behavior and symptoms.

PSYCHOTIC BEHAVIOR

When considering psychotic phenomena, what often strikes the observer is the lack of ability in the patient to differentiate, at the symbolic or representational level, different thoughts or ideas and affective states. The psychotic individual seems either flooded with a series of ideas that have no logical relationship to each other, or is overwhelmed with seemingly organized ideas, but which are inadequately categorized into subjective and objective, self and nonself, or reality and fantasy. Also, at times the psychotic individual may lack the capacity to integrate ideas and affects. At times, also, the mood of the psychotic individual appears to be labile rather than stable or inconsistent with reality demands. Behavior, too, can be inconsistent with reality.

These difficulties can be looked at from the point of view of a deficit in representational differentiation. Representational differentiation underlines basic ego functions and includes the capacity to differentiate along the dimensions of self/nonself, time and space, and affective–thematic proclivity. Self–nonself differentiation relates to poor reality testing. Differentiating experience along dimensions of affect and connecting dimensions of affect to thought underlies the integration of affect and thought (inappropriate affect or flattening of affect often represents a compromise in this capacity). The ability to organize a stable mood involves organizing many seperate affective inclinations into larger patterns—this normally occurs between the ages of two and a half and four. Impulse control requires an ability to differentiate self and nonself in a casual and temporal context; that is, anticipate the consequences of one's actions on others and on one's self later. In different states of psychosis, one or another of the capacities for representational differentiation is compromised.

With this background discussion, let us now look at the stage of representational elaboration that precedes representational differentiation. We can subtype psychotic experiences, not just in terms of the deficits in differentiation, but also in terms of deficits in representational elaboration. This capacity is originally evidenced in children through their ability to communicate using words and pretend play. It is the ability to symbolize wishes and affects. The psychotic individual is often limited in representational elaboration; for example, consider such themes as closeness, bodily pleasure, anger, curiosity, or concern with limits. These themes can be scrutinized for the degree to which they are at a symbolic level, however disorganized, or not at a symbolic level. Psychotic phenomena may be quite different depending on whether or not symbolic capacities are part of the psychotic experience. The seemingly symbiotic person may, in fact, not be able to symbolize closeness (e.g., the patterns of neediness and clinging are acted out and only verbalized in behavioral disruptions, "You must be close to me." Feeling states of sadness or loss are not experienced). The angry paranoid may be quite limited in his ability to symbolize anger. For example, the suspicion that the FBI is following him or people are talking about him are at the level of behavioral disruption. One does not frequently hear "The FBI is really *mad* at me, " or "The people talking about me are so *excited* with me." *Mad* feelings or *excited* feelings are more representational. "Following me" is more behavioral. In fact, in both instances the behavioral and gestural level around certain core affects (closeness, anger) may predominate. The symbolic level is more of an illusion in some of these cases. Interestingly in some developmentally advanced affective disorders, we hear of projected abstracted affect states (e.g., "They hate me").

One can go one step further and look for the degree to which behavior and communication is intentional and organized. This capacity for organized intentional communication is separate from the degree to which behavior and experience is symbolized. Many psychotic individuals, for example, will talk in quite a "crazy" fashion. They appear undifferentiated; however, at the same time they behave in an intentional and organized manner. They come into the psychiatrist's office on time, even if they are in a hospital, they sit down, make good eye contact, they may light up a cigarette, gesture for a match or an ashtray, make appropriate smiles, and gesture their desire to start a conversation. In short, they intentionally use nonverbal cues and gestures and adjust their behavior to the nonverbal expectations of their environment, even though they are flooded with frightening thoughts, are frightened by their delusions, and overwhelmed by the extremes of their affect. An individual may be relatively undifferentiated, in terms of his capacity to symbolize affective experience, and even have compromises in representational elaboration, but this same person may be highly intentional, that is, highly organized at the level of behavioral organization.

On the other hand, we may have a person who appears organized at the level of representational elaboration, but is quite disorganized at the level of nonverbal gestures, in terms of the ability to organize behavior in accord with reality. For example, this individual may lose sight of the appointment time with their psychiatrist. They may stare at their clinician rather than offer an opening smile, and be unable to make various hand gestures suggesting that they would like to talk. Such an individual looks through or past the clinician, or misreads his cues (when the clinician makes a hand gesture to come, the person stiffens up as though the clinician has attacked him). Yet this person may talk about what he had for lunch or how the nurse wouldn't give him a cigarette, and deny delusions or hallucinations. A person whose preverbal cuing system is off, may be compared to the person whose preverbal cuing system is working. The system of intentional, organized behavior and affect is therefore another way to categorize psychotic behavior.

At the third level we can subdivide experience into dependency, pleasure, assertiveness, curiosity, anger, and self-limit-setting, and see how the preverbal, intentional behavior system is organized or disorganized for each affective thematic area. Some individuals may be quite comfortable around dependency and have an organized system of gestures that have to do with being close to people, but become rigid and stare off into space (having no ways of communicating behaviorally or gesturally) when it comes to anger. Others may be the opposite. They are very good around manipulating grievances, but are disorganized at the preverbal level when it comes to dependency and closeness.

The fourth level, developmentally the earliest one, is the level of engagement. At this level, we also may be able to see a variety of differences among individuals experiencing psychotic phenomena. A compromise in this basic ability for engagement is evidenced in a lack of relatedness to the human world; some of these individuals may be characterized as aloof, distant, "marching to their own drummer," or autisticlike. Other psychotic individuals can make the examiner feel very close to them. They have a great deal of "wooing" power. The clinician can feel either symbiotically involved, heavily relied upon, or excited. The dimension of involvement can exist somewhat independent of how the psychotic individual operates on the other dimensions. A very engaged person may be gesturally disorganized, representationally constricted, and undifferentiated. An aloof person may be quite intentional and, in limited ways, quite logical. One can also look at the quality of engagement in terms of its stability; how well it tolerates stress (what it takes before the person disengages and becomes aloof and distant), in terms of types of stress the person is sensitive to (e.g., loud noises). The qualities of the engagement will also vary (e.g., mechanical, labile, needy, etc.).

One can look at psychotic phenomena from the point of view of four levels of experience. Is the person engaged or nonengaged, and in what way? Does the person communicate through behavior, gesture, and affect intentionally at a behavioral presymbolic (preverbal) level? Does the person begin to organize affective experience symbolically, even in undifferentiated ways? Is the person differentiated in areas of experience alongside obvious undifferentiated areas that have warranted a diagnosis of psychotic phenomena?

Categorizing individuals along dimensions of engagement, intentional behavioral patterns, representational elaboration, and representational differentiation allows one to subgroup psychotic phenomena in potentially new ways. It will also, as it will be discussed later, suggest new treatment approaches. For example, one would be hard pressed to work with a person predominantly around affective meanings when there is a fundamental deficit in the capacity for engagement or preverbal intentional communication. One may have to concentrate on shoring these up, either in collaboration with the representational work, or as an earlier foundation-building step. In considering prognoses, one might assume that even a person who is quite disorganized, but who has solid presymbolic signaling and gesturing capacities may have a better prognosis than a less delusional person who has compromises in intentional behavioral communication. As one looks for biological contributions to psychotic phenomena, one may look at the degree to which there are differences in various biological patterns as they relate to these four areas of functioning. One may find that this subdivision offers new ways to categorize clinical phenomena and that it will be easier to find biological corollaries with the categories suggested by developmental perspectives rather than traditional descriptions. Similarly, when looking for family patterns and environmental corollaries, this type of a subdivision may prove useful. This issue will be discussed later.

BORDERLINE PHENOMENA

We observe borderline phenomena in individuals who are sometimes capable of appearing engaged, intentional, organized, representational, and even highly differentiated. At other times, however, we notice difficulties in their ability to know what is real from unreal or to regulate mood and behavior. The tendency to shift gears from a higher to a lower level of functioning is characteristic of this diagnostic group. Whether the difficulty is in affect regulation or organizing thinking, it is the transient nature of the more primitive-appearing phenomena that often leads us to consider this diagnosis.

In considering borderline phenomena, it may also prove useful to look at the four levels of organization discussed earlier. Typically, the first three levels are often partially mastered. A borderline individual engages well, seems to want relationships with other people, interacts intentionally, in terms of preverbal communications, and is capable of symbolizing in an undifferentiated way different drive–affect proclivities and behaviors (i.e., they can verbalize about dependency, assertiveness, anger, etc.). Most borderline individuals evidence their major problems in the area of representational differentiation. There is often not a complete deficit, but a lack of stability in the differentiation of self/nonself. At times of stress, for example, there is confusion as to what is their feeling and what is someone else's feeling. There may be disruptions in the capacity for impulse control, the sense of a "me" acting on a "you" becomes temporarily confused as part of an intense feeling state involving passion, rage, severe separation anxiety, or loss. One may also see labile mood states where the ability to integrate different emotions into larger patterns becomes compromised, especially under extreme stress (e.g., states of calm, panic, rage, and despondency all vacillate rather quickly). The ability for concentration and attending may also be fleetingly compromised as the person feels: "I can't get my thoughts together. My mind is blank. My thoughts are rushing in so many different directions at once that I can't concentrate." The borderline state may take on more of an obsessive quality (the person who tries to be supercontrolled, but has fleeting paranoid feelings) or more of an hysteroid–depressive quality (mood states seem to be more vulnerable than the organization of thinking). Constitutional, as well as certain early environmental patterns, as discussed earlier, may determine which pattern is in evidence. Nevertheless, the major challenge for the borderline seems to be with the stage of representational differentiation.

In the context of the stage of representational differentiation, it may prove very useful to subgroup borderline phenomena along two parallel dimensions:

1. the different types of ego functions that can be compromised;
2. the different areas of thematic drive–affect experience that can become undifferentiated.

First, let us consider basic ego function based on the ability to categorize experience according to self, nonself, time, space, and affective–thematic domains. One difficulty is with organizing experience according to verbal-thematic symbols. Such a person may attend and engage well, and cue and interact purposefully, but have a lot of undifferentiated thoughts. He is never sure whether other people are talking about him, whether he is angry or the other person is angry, whether he is needy or the other person is needy, whether he desires to manipulate or wishes to be manipulated, and so forth. Another area is where affect regulation is extremely vulnerable. The person feels panicked because of the intensity of affect storms or rapid swings. He then may tend to disorganize his thinking or relationships. Even preverbal cuing and intentional behaviors can be secondarily disorganized. The person who goes into a rage and loses his capacity for preverbal signaling and gesturing, as well as for engagement, would be an example. Impulse control (the person who functions well most of the time but under stress manages to hit people or shout inappropriately), attention, and concentration (blanking out—"I have no thoughts") may also be intermittently compromised.

Another way of organizing borderline phenomena that is less conventional and potentially quite useful is to divide up the thematic–affective domains of the borderline. These include dependency, pleasure, assertiveness, curiosity, anger, self-limit-setting, empathy, and consistent types of love. These different thematic–affective domains are described only in the positive, but the positive side also suggests the negative corollaries (e.g., dependency includes separation anxiety, etc.). For each affective–thematic domain, one can look at the degree to which there is differentiation. For example, some individuals can behave in a highly differentiated way when it comes to compet-

itiveness, anger, and assertiveness. At work, where these
themes dominate, they perform admirably well. They compete
effectively with other people, feel organized during states of
competition, and have no difficulty at these times in sensing
who they are and who other people are. When they come
home, however, and deal with dependency, sexuality, and
pleasure, they may have a sense of "losing my boundaries."
They are frequently unsure of what they are thinking and what
the other person is thinking. They easily fell rejected and hurt.
They go into reactive rages secondary to problems around
dependency and pleasure. One thematic area is highly differentiated and another area is quite undifferentiated. To be sure,
many individuals who are undifferentiated in one area are only
partially differentiated in another. But some individuals surprise us with the degree to which they can organize themselves
around some thematic–affective domains and not around others.

It can therefore be useful to subcategorize borderline
phenomena, not just in terms of the self/nonself differentiation, but in terms of different affective–thematic domains. For
each affective–thematic domain, the level of development
would be described (e.g., engagement, purposeful organized
communication, representational elaboration, and representational differentiation). With borderline phenomena, the focus
would be on the degree and stability of representational
differentiation in each thematic–affective area. This approach
may provide a way not only of organizing one's therapeutic
efforts and monitoring progress, but also a way of further
understanding where early development went awry. We have
observed that for many young children their families are highly
differentiated in certain areas, in terms of responding to
symbolic elaborations. For example, a family that is comfortable
with competition and assertiveness may be highly responsive to
the youngster's communication of assertiveness in a supportive
and constructive way. However, when it comes to dependency,
pleasure, and closeness, the same family may be constantly
misreading the youngster's signals leading to confusion, anxi-

ety, and regressive phenomena. In other families, we may see the reverse. Therefore, the accurate reading of representational cues so important to representational differentiation (one can only differentiate from an interactive human relationship), is usually not global, but occurs in certain areas and not in others.

The early levels of development may also help us further categorize borderline phenomena. Even in a transient borderline state, as indicated earlier, the stages of representational elaboration, intentional organized behavioral and affective communication, and engagement can be secondarily compromised. Affect storms can lead one to totally disengage and lose one's ability for preverbal communication. Disorganized thought patterns can do the same. Suspiciousness can lead to a pulling away from relationships.

Two parameters of importance are the tendency for regressive phenomena to occur and the ease to which regression occurs; that is, the ability of the borderline to lose the capacity for representational elaboration, intentional communication and engagement. The degree to which the borderline already has difficulties at prerepresentational differentiation stages (they coexist with a more clear-cut difficulty for representational differentiation) will determine the likelihood of temporary disruptions in the early stages of ego organization.

At the stage of representational elaboration, many borderline patients will already show the signs of having some areas of experience which are going to be relatively well differentiated and some which are going to be relatively poorly differentiated. Sometimes the difficulty starts in the area of representational elaboration. A family that has difficulty in dealing with competition and anger is less likely to respond to these themes, even in the stage of representational elaboration. When little Johnny is playing out themes of competition in pretend play, or actively competing with his mother, if mother is not comfortable with these themes, she is likely to deal with them in concrete presymbolic ways rather than symbolic ways. For example, in pretend play when Johnny starts the car race, mother is likely to ignore the race and say, "Uh oh, the dolly must be hungry. Let's feed the dolly," or "You must have to go to the bathroom. Let's go to the bathroom now." Two-year-old Johnny does not receive practice in elevating assertiveness or aggression to a symbolic form. Instead, these themes tend to remain at a presymbolic level. Consider another example. Johnny is practicing using language and says that he can do something better than daddy. Instead of playfully engaging Johnny in a little competitive drama, father switches it to a dependency drama and decides that Johnny must be unhappy and therefore they had better read him a story or give him something extra to eat.

One can therefore look at borderline phenomena, in terms of the different thematic–affective domains described above, and see which themes have access in representational life. In comparison to the overtly psychotic person, one would expect more areas to have undergone some representational elaboration in the borderline.

In going back one more step to the stage of intentional behavioral organization, one can observe to what degree the functions of this stage were well established. In the borderline person, this stage was usually mastered, for the most part (in comparison to the psychotic individual who may experience fragmentation in terms of behavioral whole-objects). While the borderline person may have behavioral whole-objects, he may not yet have symbolic or representational integrated whole self–objects. The borderline, however, may also evidence subtle deficits in the ability to communicate across space and integrate affective polarities. For example, the ability to go from the thirteen-month state, where the angry father and the nice father are two separate people, to an integrated state where they are one person, may not be completely achieved by the borderline (even though they are generally intentional and organized in their communication). Similarly, the ability to communicate across space and feel close to the object (e.g., the ability to be in another room and feel secure from hearing mother's voice or to look over and interpret someone's gestures without misreading their cues) may not be wholly accomplished in the borderline. It may not be that there is a total deficit, but it may be that under states of stress or anxiety there is confusion in the interpretation of the person's signals across space. In comparison with the psychotic phenomenon, invariably these subtle issues in behavioral organization would be severely compromised. Often there is not integrative, whole, behavioral self–objects or the ability to presymbolically communicate effectively across space without distortion.

With borderline phenomena, many of the intentional communication patterns (e.g., signaling for dependency, assertiveness, or curiosity) would have taken place appropriately, but there is some tendency toward misreading along specific thematic–affective domains (e.g., sexuality and excitement). It is these areas that will later fail to achieve representational differentiation. In other words, we may see an earlier state of prerepresentational undifferentiation at the part to whole behavioral object stage.

In addition, the psychotic may have two deficits in reality testing—a deficit in the stage of prerepresentational part-object differentiation (a behavioral lack of reality testing characterizing maladaptive four- to ten-month-old behavior) and a lack of differentiation at the symbolic level. The borderline, in comparison, may have accomplished behavioral reality testing at the four-to ten-month-old stage and have vulnerabilities mostly at the later prerepresentational and representational stages.

In terms of the stage of engagement, we would expect most borderlines to be well engaged, except for those that may use schizoid-type withdrawal (but these may not be borderline in the true sense of the word). We might, however, expect some subtle compromise in the ability to reengage after stress or we might see a tendency toward dysphoria around minor threats to engagement. Because of parental responses to the baby or the baby's own constitutional tendencies, one may also see some difficulties in the stability of engagement. The stability has to do with the ability to maintain engagement and recover after mild to moderate stresses, including separation, angry protests, and short illnesses.

CHARACTER DISORDERS

Character disorders usually involve fixed, inflexible, maladaptive, pervasive, and repetitive patterns of thought, feeling, and/or behavior in relationship to internal drive–affect patterns, feeling states, conflicts, and external relationships. Obsessive and hysterical patterns, passive–aggressive patterns, passive–dependent patterns, depressive patterns, narcissistic patterns, antisocial patterns, and mild schizoid patterns are all examples.

From the point of view of the stages of ego development, character disorders involve the individual's tendency to "wall off" certain areas of experience. For example, rather than thinking of the obsessive as using isolation of affect, one might think of the obsessive as walling off certain domains of affect. Metaphorically, one might think of character disorders in terms of a balloon. The healthy person's balloon is blown up on all sides. The fully blown-up balloon engages in all the affective–thematic domains of life in highly differentiated ways; that is, dependency, pleasure, assertiveness, curiosity, empathy, love. The character disorder walls off certain of these areas. There may be no stretching of the balloon or no air in the part that would normally concern assertiveness or aggression or, in another person, dependency or closeness, or in another, sexuality and pleasure.

Character disorders may be usefully categorized in terms of the two levels of representation–representational differentiation and representational elaboration. In character disorders, it appears as though the person has little access in terms of representational life to certain broad patterns of drive–affects and behavior. The person has either not fully differentiated his experimental world or has not fully elaborated his experiential world in terms of representational patterns in one or another broad thematic area. One might juxtapose the traditional diagnostic categories of the character disorders alongside the developmental approach which focuses on the ability of the person to (1) representationally elaborate, and (2) representationally differentiate certain areas of experience. How well does the person representationally comprehend and categorize experience in terms of pleasure, dependency, assertiveness, curiosity, anger, empathy, love, and limit-setting?

A broad pattern of avoidance of a whole area of affect, thought, and/or behavior would occur when it does not even have access to representational elaboration. A youngster who is not able to elaborate competitive and aggressive themes, would tend to have competitive inclinations organized at concrete prerepresentational levels (behavioral levels). Such a child would tend to either inhibit the behavioral level or exaggerate it and become a behavioral "actor-outer." In either case, he would have little representational access to themes around competition and aggression. Such a pattern would constitute a rather broad and moderate to severe piece of character pathology. On the other hand, where the person had pretty good representational elaboration, but lacked aspects of representational differentiation, the pathology might be of a slightly different and more moderate nature. In such a case, we might also see a walling off, but for a more complicated reason. In this case, our prototypical child is engaged in competition and anger, but this engagement does not include the ability for symbolic cause-and-affect interactions around these themes. The child's parents' ability to bring his aggression into temporal and spatial, self/nonself, and comparative juxtaposition (with other affective domains) is not well established at the level of representational differentiation. Anger and competition have access to representational life, but not in a differentiated form. As a relatively undifferentiated state, these feelings tend to operate in more global and unrealistic ways. To the degree that this same youngster is highly differentiated in terms of fears, anxieties, and prohibitions, he would naturally be quite cautious about this undifferentiated part of his personality. His aggressive feelings would be perceived as dangerous and easily uncontrollable. After all, they are imbued with qualities of magical thinking. Therefore, he might have to completely avoid these themes in his life because of their lack of differentiation. The person appears to be supercontrolled, passive, and avoids aggressive competition at the level of thought, feeling, and behavior. He avoids these themes because they are a threat to the integrity of his otherwise differentiated ego structure. He maintains differentiation by walling off the undifferentiated "dangerous" feelings.

The person who does not have representational access at all to these different thematic domains, will find it hard to even verbalize confusing feelings. As noted in an earlier chapter, when you say, "What comes to mind?" and "How did you feel in this situation?" he will only describe behavioral patterns—"I hit him," not "I wanted to hit him." With the husband who acts out the aggression, or the husband who is very passive and withdraws from his wife (who has never developed representational access), when you say, "How did that feel?" he will also describe behaviors. "I sat still," says the passive one; "I hit her," says the aggressive one. You do not hear "I *felt* like this or that." The therapist often has a tendency to put these words into the patient's mouth, particularly the patient who frustrates the therapist by not having representational access. For example, when the therapist says, "You must have felt so and so," the person may say, "Yes, I suppose so." But, spontaneously, the person will rarely volunteer a complex affective state. The person only volunteers descriptions of behaviors. Only behaviors are described because the person has not reached the level of representational elaboration, where affective states are abstracted out of the behavioral realms into the symbolic realm. On the other hand, the person who has reached representational elaboration and has a problem with representational differentiation will verbalize confusing, undifferentiated representational states. By discussing his anxiety concomitant with these states, together with a transference give-and-take around representational differentiation, he can be helped, for the first time, to undergo differentiation.

Therefore, at the stage of representational elaboration and differentiation, we can see character disorder as involving a lack of differentiation of certain thematic–affective states and/or a lack of representational elaboration of certain thematic–affective states. If both occur, the implications for pathology will be slightly different than if the deficit is just at the stage of representational differentiation. The difference between the lack of representational elaboration or differentiation in character disorders and borderline pathology is that in character disorders the overall capacity for representational elaboration and differentiation continues. The problematic area is walled off. In borderline states, the problematic area is not walled off, it manifests itself fully in its primitive form. Broader areas tend to be involved, and the basic overall capacities for elaboration or differentiation are often compromised as well.

Even with the character disorders, where the early engagement and the early intentional communication system is usually well established, we may see some contributions from early development that would be useful in subgrouping some of these disorders. In some severe character disorders, the preverbal behavioral negotiation of certain thematic–affective domains will have also been compromised. But the compromise is not to such a degree that overall developmental progression is limited in terms of the broad stages outlined earlier. At the stage of intentional communication, consider a person who also has difficulty in the area of competition and anger. Whenever assertiveness and anger is evidenced behaviorally, it is not responded to in an intentional organized manner. The reasons may include anxiety on the parents' side and constitutional vulnerabilities on the youngster's side (e.g., the youngster's ability to signal that affective–thematic domain in terms of motor gestures or other interactive signals may be compromised, due to problems in processing information, problems in motor planning, or motor coordination). Consider an earlier situation, that of the eight-month-old who is slightly disorganized in his aggression. Instead of seeing it as healthy assertiveness, his parents see it as a pattern of helpless disorganization and treat it either with overprotectiveness, indulgence, or sadistic counterattacks. At this stage, part-object behavioral differentiation may be compromised. If this type of early pattern becomes part of a character disorder, it would involve a narrow sector of behavior, as compared to the broader sectors involved in borderline and psychotic phenomena. Ego development will continue, but with a vulnerability in behavioral differentiation will be less pervasive. Problems in presymbolic intentional behavior may be revealed through the nonverbal gestures and behavioral focus and organization of the adult patient.

Maturational tendencies in the person's style of engagement may suggest another early contribution (though not causative agent) for some character pathologies. For example, consider a very demanding engaging baby who, at four months, looks at mother and smiles robustly, as though to control and demand her attention. If she tries to disengage, he vocalizes loudly, makes boisterous arm gestures, and goes from a smile to a yell until she reengages. He evidences a sense of control even at this earliest stage of engagement. This infant's intensity and ability to control his mother may be built on a constitutional tendency involving sensitivity to sensory stimuli, precocious sensory– affective processing, and organized and coordinated motor planning capacities. The youngster is sensitive to his environment and can take in and pursue what he wants rather easily. If this same youngster tends to be emotionally labile, feels displeasure easily, and relies on his mother to comfort him, we may have a type of early "executive" or "tyrant," depending on how his parent responds. The infant's pattern of control can, even at this early stage of engagement, lead a parent to feel intimidated and passive. The parent may, because of her underlying anger and sense of intimidation, not engage the infant fully around competition, anger, and limit-setting. She avoids setting limits, passively complies, and deals with her mounting anger by not engaging in assertive, joyful activities. Both parents are always trying to "escape" from their infant's demandingness. The infant does not experience real engagement around his own assertiveness. A false sense of expectations, as well as a lack of full differentiation of anger and "bossiness," may then serve as a contribution to later character pathology.

Throughout this discussion, we have not dealt with the issue of conflict in generating character patterns. When an area of thought, feeling, or behavior is walled off, there is invariably conflict associated with the lack of representational differentiation, lack of representational elaboration, or difficulties with intentional communication or engagement. As indicated in earlier discussions, when a child experiences a lack of support for a natural tendency, it generates frustration and anger. In turn, fear, inhibition, or behavioral intensification may occur. To the degree representational differentiation does not occur, the original tendency and the reaction to its nonsupport creates unbridled conflict of a primitive nature.

NEUROTIC BEHAVIOR

In neurotic behavior, the stages of organization of the ego, progress through the levels of engagement, intentional communication, and representational elaboration. The ego organizes drive–affect proclivities, behavioral tendencies, and interactive patterns. At the level of representational differentiation, conflicts between different tendencies, wishes, and internalized prohibitions lead to various symptoms, characterologic compromises, and/or behavioral patterns.

In terms of the organization of the ego, we can postulate that neurotic behavior occurs when there is the juxtaposition of a relatively undifferentiated stage of experience together with more differentiated states of experience. The undifferentiated states are the ones likely to be caught up in conflict. As discussed earlier, the less differentiated states have, in a relative sense, restricted access to the differentiated states because of the way in which state-dependent learning occurs. One doesn't tend to have access to all states of mind at once. Less differentiated states are repressed in a structural sense, even though they may be additionally repressed on dynamic grounds.

Consider an example: Assume that anger, and its behavioral and drive–affect derivatives, has not undergone differentiation at the stage of representational differentiation. Assume that the anger in question is a very narrow band of anger relating to family dynamics. In this case, the area that does not undergo differentiation is not a broad area, as in the character pathologies, but an area that is defined and contoured by certain narrowly defined dynamic meanings. In character pathology what does not undergo differentiation may be the tendency for anger in general (against women, men, future employers, friends, etc.). However, in the neurotic configuration, the lack of differentiation of derivatives of feelings of anger will only be in a narrow thematic band; such as, for example, competition with an authority figure or with one's own father and his subsequent derivatives. Similarly, if the neurotic pattern has to do with pleasure, it may only be with sexualized pleasure with women who are thematically and dynamically related to mother. As this plays out in adulthood, we might see difficulties in bosses who remind the patient of father. The difficulties may be in certain specifics of the competitive relationship that were based on the competitive relationship in childhood or certain specifics of the erotic relationship based on those in childhood. In other words, the person is not globally constricted and often can be competitive and assertive or sexually joyful. Only in the narrow band that is dynamically relevant (related to the historical relationship which plays itself out in the present) is the person limited in his flexibility.

Consider the example of a child (Johnny) who has problems with competition with authority figures. Father enjoys rough-and-tumble play (horsey, space cadet). He gets on the floor with the action figures supporting "pretend" play, and participates in games such as checkers. Father is even comfortable with Johnny manipulating the rules to win some of the time. Broad areas of assertiveness are elaborated in representational terms. There is enough cause-and-effect/give-and-take and negotiation around the dimensions of self/nonself, time and space, and in the different thematic–affective areas to facilitate representational differentiation. Whenever little Johnny begins to compete with his father around the relationship with mother, however (e.g., Johnny gets a big smile on his face when he cuddles mother and looks at father as though to say, "See, now I have her"), a different picture emerges. Father comes home from work and mother is sitting with little Johnny reading him a book. Johnny gives father that little "See, I 've got her" grin. Father becomes somewhat anxious and withdraws from Johnny for fifteen to twenty minutes. After reengaging and being Johnny's horse, he manages to knock Johnny off his back a couple of times. Johnny gets to feeling a little scared (father's "getting carried away"). After this retaliation, father returns to his normal pattern of support toward Johnny's healthy competitiveness. Over time, though, Johnny pieces together, not in a highly intellectual fashion but in an intuitive fashion, that his feelings toward his mother are associated with being scared over liking to "beat Dad." Johnny feels anxious around the theme of competition for mother. As indicated in earlier chapters, anxiety tends to make the ego less differentiated. Johnny's ego structure, in relationship to this theme, remains relatively less differentiated because he doesn't get a clear response from his father (as he does around checkers or the typical action figure play) with regard to competition over mother. In this area, Johnny sees that he gets either no feedback or overwhelmingly aggressive feedback, leading to less capacity for discrimination in this thematic area. In addition the increased anxiety also leads to a lack of differentiation. There is, therefore, a lack of differentiation in a narrow thematic area. This narrow, dynamically relevant band provides the seeding for neurotic behavior.

In this case, Johnny's interest in competing around mother remains in the stage of representational elaboration and does not progress to the stage of representational differentiation. Therefore, it does not undergo the normal amount of reality testing, impulse control learning, or mood stabilization. It does not undergo the differentiation that helps Johnny put his experience into the context of self/nonself, time, space, and affective–thematic compartmentalization. Undifferentiated, these experiences are available to states of magical thinking and defenses that operate during the predifferentiated stage of ego development. Mechanisms of condensation, projection, and displacement are more likely to operate during predifferentiated stages such as representational elaboration and behavioral intentionality and organization.

To the degree that undifferentiated states exist alongside highly differentiated states, the undifferentiated ones not only tend to be structurally repressed, but they tend to generate conflict. Conflict is generated because other aspects of the personality continue to develop, including fears and prohibitions. Fears and prohibitions will have undergone differentiation. At the same time there may be undifferentiated earlier fears that correspond to the narrow band of undifferentiated inclinations. The encapsulated undifferentiated states pose a threat to the integrity of the overall organization of the ego, particularly in the light of differentiated fears and prohibitions. This threat serves as another reason for conflict, the formation of secondary defenses (maintaining the original repression), and states of anxiety or other dysphoric affects (that accompany the relatively undifferentiated state).

We have a situation where patterns of behavior evidenced in a narrow band may stay relatively undifferentiated compared to more differentiated capacities in other areas. This dichotomy characterizes neurotic behavior. We may also see contributions at the stage of representational elaboration and, at the earlier stages of intentional communication and engagement. For example, father may evidence jealousy around the early engagement patterns. This tendency will be sufficiently encapsulated so that it does not offset the overall progression of the ego. Nonetheless, an interactive pattern is set up that ultimately finds access to representation and becomes the basis for internalized conflict.

THE THERAPEUTIC PROCESS AS IT RELATES TO DIFFERENT DIAGNOSTIC ENTITIES

In the foregoing, we have described how the patient is involved in four developmental levels at once. The patient progresses both upward and outward at the same time. The broadening of the thematic–affective range helps the patient abstract patterns which, in turn, facilitates movement to the next developmental level. Next the therapeutic process for different diagnostic entities will be considered.

With psychotic phenomena, one is often working at all four levels at the same time. In the most regressed psychotic states, there are often severe disruptions in the presymbolic states of purposeful communication and engagement. One will often spend long periods of time reestablishing engagement and simple types of purposeful communication. At times, this requires extreme attention to the components of the engagement process in terms of the patient's sensory reactivity and ability to process sensory information, including abstracting simple gestural, vocal–verbal, or visual–spatial meanings.

The goal is to establish an intentional, interactive behavior on a solid foundation of engagement. Hyperarousal in each sensory modality has to be overcome so the patient can attend to and pursue sensory input, form an engagement with another human being, and use the engagement as a vehicle for an on-going sense of relatedness, which, in turn, becomes a vehicle for organized intentional communications with another human being. As these early stages are established, the psychotic individual then begins to try to reorganize whatever representational ability existed in their premorbid state. It is important to note, in the therapeutic process, that the early stages of ego development serve as a foundation for the later ones. Even while exchanging verbal information one must pay attention to the quality of attending, engagement, and purposeful organized communication which underlies a reconstruction of the world of meanings.

In considering borderline phenomena, the work may focus

on all four levels as well. Although one would assume that there is stability of engagement and purposeful communication, they are open to regressive shifts. While keeping an eye on all levels, the main focus may well be at the level of representational elaboration and differentiation. There are major sectors of the personality which remain undifferentiated and when touched upon by new challenges, such as intimacy or loss undergo disorganizing affective states. The initial phase of the work often will relate to helping the patient maintain a level of representational elaboration in the face of intense affect. This involves establishing engagement and purposeful communication as a vehicle for representational elaboration. The long-term therapeutic work will often involve helping the patient construct patterns of representational differentiation in areas that were never differentiated in the first place. The person's life-style history, and functioning in clinical interviews will provide clues as to which areas remain relatively undifferentiated. It is not unusual for an individual to be highly differentiated when it comes to assertiveness but relatively undifferentiated when it comes to intimacy. Around intimacy and longings, projective and incorporative mechanisms predominate. The effort will be on using the quality of engagement, purposeful communication, and representational elaboration to patiently engage in the thematic–affective areas that have been undifferentiated, and empathetically look for relationships between different thematic–affective domains. Building bridges will allow the patient to begin compartmentalizing experiences in ways that permit both engagement in a full range of experiences and categorization of experience along the dimensions of self-nonself, time and space, and the thematic–affective domain.

The simple ability of the borderline patient to engage verbally in emotional expression may not be a signal that they are mastering the differentiating work. In fact, at times expressions of only one feeling can be a way of avoiding the differentiating work. The ability to elaborate strong feelings is indeed one aspect of the work. The ability to then look at the relationships between feelings is the more difficult part for the verbally articulate patient. At times the refusal to see connections will be related to the stubborn desire to retain an undifferentiated state as a fantasy of early childhood gratification. One child was quite explicit about his "mixed up" feelings as a way to make his parents "stupid" and to get them to "do everything." One will need to systematically identify the avoidance of shifting between subjective and objective as part of a facile ability to only elaborate certain fantasies at the level of representational elaboration. The spontaneous ability to shift back and forth between the reality-oriented concerns and the more subjective concerns, signifies the stage of representational differentiation.

Moderate to severe character disorders have a significant degree of representational elaborative and differentiating capacity. What seems to be missing here is the thematic–affective range. Range of experience is given up for stability of experience. Hence, we get the repetitive behavioral patterns where certain areas of experience are avoided to evade disruptive anxiety. The avoided areas may not exist in representational life at all or may exist as part of fragments of representational elaboration.

The work often involves helping the person move into the thematic–affective areas that are being avoided. A first step is pointing out the fact that these areas are avoided. Then it is important to understand some of the disorganizing feelings associated with the pattern. The patient gradually begins to put one toe in the water at a time and engages in some of the walled-off areas. They do this in two ways at once: They do it thematically in the hours as one hears more associations about the formerly walled-off area. They do it in daily life as they begin flirting with some of the areas that they were scared of in the past.

In character disorders, it is important to also consider fear of progressing into developmentally more advanced and thematically broader areas. Often, one mistakenly focuses only on anxieties associated with conflicts and regressive positions. The fact that the regressive positions have their own conflicts and anxieties, and that a circular, never-ending process can be continued is missed. For example, the patient who wishes for passive longings to be gratified but is fearful of being controlled, and at a representational elaboration level, of being engulfed, may endlessly play out this regressive drama. There is an assumption that once the reasons for the character pathology are understood, the patient will spontaneously move into the formerly walled-off areas of life. For some patients, this is the case, but for many others, the active recognition of the fear of forward progress is a required focus of the therapeutic work. It is necessary to facilitate the representational elaboration of the walled-off areas to increase awareness of what is avoided. It is further necessary to facilitate representational differentiation to bring these walled-off areas into a differential verbal and visual–spatial symbolic mode. The representational differentiation phase involves understanding of the walled-off areas, in terms of their meanings, their relationship to other areas of the patient's life, and their integration with a reality adaptation. So, the ability, for example, to shift between the reality aspects of intimacy or aggression and the subjective aspects, coupled with the ability to use new patterns in daily life is part of the successful differentiation of these functions. The differentiation may be thought of as involving both the differentiation of subjective and objective intratherapeutic and extratherapeutic daily life (reality-oriented) work.

The patient who gets lost in regressive conflicts over longings, fear of control, and fear of engulfment may ultimately need to become aware of the fact that the challenge that lies in front of him relates to being more independent. Furthermore, he may need to see that his enormous longings and separation anxiety relate to an inability to feel "loss." He may discover that he has never mourned anyone in his life. Potential loss was always defended against with separation anxiety, helplessness, and regressive conflicts over longings and being controlled. The "walled off" feelings of "loss" may have been seen as dangerous because of their association with greater assertiveness and competition (i.e., oedipal dynamics). However, only a focus on the fear of moving forward and an awareness of "new" feelings such as loss that are avoided will reveal the hurdles blocking progress.

In working with the character pathologies, as with psychotic and borderline conditions, it is the engagement and qualities of purposeful communication that create the foundation for working through new abilities. Engagement and purposeful communication solidify the early stages of ego development. They create the sense of security needed to now engage in the representational elaborative and differentiating activities of these new thematic–affective areas. There is no reason why a patient will "jump into the water" that they have been scared of earlier unless they sense that the anxieties they have had in the past are no longer operable in the present. They sense this fact through greater awareness of their anxieties. In representational forms, they can reason out their formerly irrational fears. But greater awareness alone is not sufficient. The qualities of engagement and purposeful communication which define the active neutrality of the therapist in the current situation, is, one hopes, drastically different from the parental responses of the past. Through this different foundation, the patient has the courage to elaborate and then differentiate these new areas of experience.

NEUROTIC EXPERIENCE

With neurotic phenomena, there are reasonably intact levels of functioning at the level of engagement, organized intentional communication, and representational elaboration. The neurotic's problem is encapsulated. He has difficulty in a dynamically relevant narrow thematic band. A young man has problems only with authority figures who are possibly controlling like his father. The young man otherwise differentiates experiences. There is a narrow band of undifferentiated experience (assertiveness toward fatherlike authority figures) in an otherwise differentiated ego structure. It is this juxtaposition of an undifferentiated domain, in comparison to otherwise differentiated domains, that leads to the relative repression of one area and the relative access this one area has to primitive modes of transformation, including primitive defenses. There is a neurotic encapsulation in an otherwise differentiated personality structure.

The therapeutic work involves using the differentiated parts of the personality to help the person representationally further elaborate and differentiate the encapsulated area. The free-associative process of psychoanalysis or the "free-talking" processes of many explorative psychotherapies serves this purpose well. The qualities of engagement, organized preverbal intentional communication, and representational elaboration serve the purpose of fostering differentiation in the formerly undifferentiated area. To the degree that the undifferentiated areas are associated with transformations of experience as part of the defensive alterations, understanding the defenses becomes a vehicle for building transformational bridges between the already-existing differentiated part of the ego and the undifferentiated nuclei. The work is similar to the work with character disorders, only here, instead of trying to elaborate and differentiate major sectors of the personality, one is attempting to elaborate and differentiate narrow, dynamically relevant bands of the personality in the context of the person's unique history. The patient has the goal of understanding the fears and anxieties associated originally with differentiating the now encapsulated area of experience.

In addition to differentiation, another aspect of ego structure requiring attention is integration. Different components of the ego are not only differentiated, but they are also integrated with one another. There are major splits, as seen in borderline conditions, and subtle splits, as seen in the defense isolation of affect as part of neurotic conditions. Fostering integration of these splits involves elaborating thematic–affective areas, looking for connections between them, and fostering more integrating bridges. The security of ongoing engagement and purposeful communication are essential. Strong effects will not be tolerated, and certainly not integrated, without this foundation. The analogy is a relationship that a baby or young child has with his parents. The security of engagement and the early signaling system (which makes the world understandable and logical) creates the basis for mastering subsequent psychological hurdles. Without these early levels, there is no security for the toddler, for example, to deal with the anxiety associated with putting together into one image extreme anger and love. There is no ability to integrate desires to be independent and, at the same time, close and dependent. The integration of affective polarities, as well as the ability later to "represent" strong affects, depends on the security of early relationship patterns. An important component of this security is limit setting, which eventually becomes internalized. A youngster who has secured his early relationship and is secure in the reality that he can communicate his needs, that they will be responded to, and that he can preverbally (through gestures) figure out if his world is safe or unsafe, approving or disapproving, or accepting or rejecting, and where necessary limiting is going to find later challenges much less frightening than the youngster who hasn't acquired these early capacities. The therapeutic relationship must, in many respects, pay attention to these early capacities, as well as to the representational elaborative and differentiating ones.

In this chapter the development deficits, constrictions, and encapsulations characteristic of a selected group of disorders have been discussed. Developmental formulations suggest psychotherapeutic approaches that deal with both structure building and conflict resolutions.

Chapter 10

Developmental Considerations in Diagnosis, Psychopathology, and Psychotherapy with Children

This chapter will apply to developmental perspective, and in particular the concept of four levels of experience, to work with children. Let us consider first the level of shared attention and of engagement: As a three and a half to four-year-old child comes into the room, you first focus on how he attends to you. Are you ignored or is the child responding to your words and looking at you? Can the child sustain attention, or, do you suspect that there are difficulties in processing information through vision, hearing, smell, touch, and/or movement patterns?

The first goal is the assessment of sensory, motor, and aspects of receptive language functioning, in terms of the way the youngster is attending and processing information. Next, look at the evolving relationship and quality of engagement. What is its affective tone? Is there pleasure or trust? What is the quality of the child's mood. By age four, you are expecting a reasonably stable mood because by this age a child should be able to pull together different affective polarities into an organized pattern (in a two-year-old, you would expect a more labile mood). Three critical functions are assessed as part of the quality of engagement, attention and sensory processing, relationship capacity, and mood.

The second level involves intentional signaling or gesturing. Before one pays attention to what the child is saying, look at the child's nonverbal behavioral–affective inclinations; what is the child trying to tell you through his gestures and signals. Is he signaling, "Let's sit down and play," by pointing to the toys and looking at you with an "Is it okay to play?" expression? Or is he telling you, "Get away from me," by sitting quietly in a corner and turning away when you come near? Or is he telling you he wants to be close, by sitting almost on top of you and looking longingly? Without using any words, the child is showing behavioral inclinations and letting you know that he can communicate intentionally (intentional and organized or chaotic, random, and disorganized). The child is also telling you something about his behavioral–affective range. In the first half-hour, are these gestures having to do with warmth and closeness, exploration and assertiveness, and anger (e.g., if the child wants something you don't want to give him). Does the child show a full range, or is he only passive and obsequious or diffusely aggressive, showing only one polarity? An impression of focus and intentionality, major inclinations, and range of inclinations is gained before verbal content is considered.

The child will also tell you about his response to anxiety, as part of the level of gestural signaling. The child begins playing with a toy around a theme (e.g., aggression, dependency, or pleasure and sexuality). Then he looks anxious or concerned. What kind of response does the child have to his concern? Does he become fragmented? Withdraw? Does he attack and become disorganized, or increase his motor level? Does he become compliant, or does he freeze for a second, pause, and then try to play out what he has been anxious about? These patterns, which are based on preverbal organization, tell you a great deal about the child's ego development.

At the representational (symbolic) level or level of meanings, we finally look for the content. But even at the representational level, we first look for the existence of the child's ability to symbolize behavior and feeling through pretend play or functional use of language. Then we look for the breadth and depth of the child's thematic–affective representational inclinations, for what the child is concerned about. If he has reached two and a half to three and is able to use pretend play, words, or both, look at his themes. Is he concerned about bathroom scenes, the mother and father dolls fighting, monsters hurting children, soldiers fighting? Are these themes part of a full range or are they part of a narrow focus where, for example, only separation predominates (mother and father leaving, or animals leaving)?

Thematic sequence will also be revealing. What goes before what and what comes after what? Does anger come first and then fearfulness (the animals get angry and then the animals all become scared and fall down)? Or do the animals get angry and heads and arms are cut off? Or is there closeness and right after closeness diffuse aggression (closeness is always followed by fragmentation and anger)? Paying attention to the sequence of themes provides a picture of how a child begins organizing his internal world.

At the next level, the level of representational differentiation or the level of categorization of meanings, one asks "How well does this child organize his themes?" Consider a four-year-old: He comes and says, "Toy box," and then takes out the toy and looks at one of the robots, starts playing with the robot, has it hit another doll, and when you say, "What's going on?" he says, "Oh, this robot is mad." Then the child quickly loses interest in that theme and goes to the other side of the room and picks up a piece of paper and starts scribbling. He says, "I like to draw." Then after two minutes, he goes to another side of the room and picks up a box and starts building a little fort and says, "Gonna build a fort."

This pattern of one fragmented theme here and one there is different from the pattern of the youngster who develops bridges from one play activity to another. As the child leaves the robots, he takes one with him and says, "Now we are going to take the robot and we are going to build a fort to protect ourselves from the bad guys." The child who builds these bridges obviously has a way of organizing and tying together his different contents. The first child is a little more fragmented.

The capacity to differentiate, means to categorize and organize different contents. By four years of age, a child should be able to build bridges between different contents. Building bridges shows there is an infrastructure holding the child's different themes together (the four-year-old who is acting more like a three-year-old operates in little islands of content or concern). With a developmental map in one's mind, one can, after a few minutes, obtain a sense of whether this child is more like a four-year-old or a three-year-old when it comes to organizing his internal life. This capacity for thematic organization is not unlike an adult's capacity to organize thinking.

By looking at the sequence of themes and the organization of themes, we can also begin obtaining a picture of the child's organizing fantasies. For example, one child tends to have themes of closeness, followed by provocativeness. The provocativeness leads to fighting. The fighting leads to a theme of, "You owe me more toys, more money, more of everything. You took my toy, so you owe me." The child elaborates that her parents owe her also. An organizing fantasy is emerging. Closeness leads to hurting and provocativeness and fighting. This leads to "being owed" because "what you give is not enough." "Closeness is scary because of fighting. You lose things, things are owed, and you never get enough."

The level of representational differentiation also reveals the degree to which the child has established basic personality functions (including reality testing, impulse control, a stable mood, concentration, and self–other differentiation).

At the end of the evaluation session, one asks two basic questions: How well is this child established at his expected developmental level? For example, how well has a four-year-old, developed the capacity for representational differentiation, and mastered shared attention and engagement, intentional signaling, and representational elaboration. If the child is not at his expected developmental level, is he a four-year-old who is operating more like a two-year-old, just barely using mental images in terms of pretend? Is he a seven-year-old who is really like a three-year-old? In addition to considering symptoms, it is useful to think in terms of developmental level. Where is the child in comparison to his age? Age versus developmental level is useful in talking to parents, because parents already think about Johnny reading at a second- or third-grade level, even though he is in the fourth grade. If you say "his relationship patterns are more like a two-year-old and his ability to organize his ideas are more like a three-year-old, but he's four years, therefore we have some work to do," parents readily understand. If you say "he is neurotic" or "has character pathology" or is "borderline," they are likely to feel confused and frightened.

The second question is: What is the thematic and affective range at his developmental level? What areas of human endeavor (dependency, pleasure, assertiveness, aggression, and so forth) is the child comfortable with and/or unable to engage in at his age-expected developmental level. If he is uncomfortable with or avoidant of or disorganized or regressive with certain thematic domains, such as closeness or aggression, a related question is why? Are there conflicts, developmental lags, and so on? What are the family patterns, original (and now represented) and ongoing, and the relationship between constitutional–maturational patterns and family patterns in the context of the early stage of ego development and related aspects of drive and affect development.

An especially interesting part of a developmental model is its application to psychotherapy with children. Consider two components of treatment. One component may be considered a structure-building part of psychotherapy; another a conflict resolution part. Many are familiar with the conflict resolution part, but I would like to suggest it is important to focus equally on the structure-building part. The latter takes place often without either the therapist or the patient thinking about it. The structure-building part helps the child build the sequence of ego structures he needs to deal with expectable and challenging experiences. Every child needs the ability to attend to and engage in the human world. Simply by engaging the child, finding a way to pull that child into a relationship (e.g., not permitting a child to spend three months' of sessions standing in the corner looking away), trying to develop visual and vocal contact and attention, and ultimately engagement, one is building structure around relating and engaging.

A second component relates to developing intentional, nonverbal gestural signaling, and communication. The child comes in, you make a hand gesture showing him where to sit, a facial gesture suggesting warmth and acceptance. You are animated and involved. If you are not too preoccupied and thinking about the child who just left or your own family or friends, you will be in a pattern of intentional nonverbal relatedness (in a thousand different ways). You are automatically creating an opportunity for this child to learn about a nonverbal signaling system. But some children do not have this system and do not participate in it at the intuitive level. For them, basic nonverbal communication of safety, security, acceptance, approval, definition of self, and personal uniqueness is missing. Understandably, they have to spend enormous energy and preoccupation in trying to figure out these basic issues at a more symbolic or conscious level. Here, the therapist has a special challenge—to strengthen the nonverbal intentional communication level. One has to concentrate on one's own gestures and motor activities and try to help the child into a mutually intentional system of communication.

At the representational level, simply helping the child play out the most simple pretend sequences (the trucks are moving back and forth and then they crash), solidifies the representational level. One four-year-old came in because his teachers complained that he was only capable of parallel play with his peers. He was a verbal and bright youngster, but became aggressively diffusive and pinched and bit. He dealt with his frustration by behavior discharge at the seventeen- to eighteen-month-old level. When I saw him, there was no pretend play; he engaged in spatial block play and was able to talk to me a little bit about nonemotional issues (e.g., the toys in my office). His parents said he never engaged in pretend play. For this child to roll the cars back and forth, have them crash, show delight, and say, "The cars are angry at each other," would constitute having helped him reach the third level of structure to represent emotional experience. A child, however bright, may, in part, be biting and kicking other children because he has no "ideational life" to deal with emotional issues, even though he can use ideas in an impersonal, cognitive sense. There is a difference between the impersonal, cognitive use of ideas and the emotional labeling and comprehending of ideas. The simplest kind of representational elaboration is essential for this type of child.

More complicated but constricted representational elaboration is seen in a four-year-old who is very verbal and organizes complicated dramas. He plays out themes around separation and dependency. The mother doll comes with him to school. Then there is a dream about losing animals and people and "feeling alone." This child, however, never elaborates dramas dealing with aggression; there are no soldiers fighting, and the dolls are never angry at other dolls and are always frightened and clinging to mother. At the third level, representational elaboration, one might simply wonder out loud with such a child, "Gee, this doll is always scared. This doll never, never gets mad at anybody." This would help the child, perhaps over a period of months, to explore themes of anger. The anger doesn't have to emerge with either mother or therapist. It could emerge between the pretend figures. At this third level, one provides the child with an opportunity to apply his representational capacities to a new domain. Representational elaboration is an important structure-building step. Even though at this level one is already working with conflicts, helping the child elaborate a broader range of representational themes is a structure-building exercise as well. At this stage understanding fears and conflicts, is not only important in its own right, it facilitates structure building through increasing the breadty of themes represented and eventually differentiated.

The fourth level of structure building is representational differentiation. Here, you may help a child in critical ways that are often overlooked. For example, consider our four-year-old. He is playing out themes. You are supportive, following his lead, and saying what he is doing: "Oh boy, the soldiers are hitting each other. Now the doctor is coming and making them feel better. Now they are going and eating and feeling even better. Now they are hugging because they feel so good about each other." You are helping the child articulate and represent his feelings. You are helping the child also further elaborate his feelings. But, you are still not helping the child "differentiate." At this point, in terms of structure building, you must pay attention to another issue—the degree to which the child representationally elaborates as part of a real two-person system. In practice this means he uses and follows up on what you say. *Are you closing circles?* In other words, when you say something, does the child ignore you or respond to you as a causative agent in his ideational world? Is there a "you" and a "him" talking or is the child marching to his own drummer? (Circle closing involves the following: The child says or does something, then you say something, and the child uses what you say and says something back. He is cuing off from you.) Within the fantasy or play drama the child is developing, there are the opportunities to build a logical infrastructure. Closing circles helps build this infrastructure. Often in therapy youngsters and therapists are marching to different drummers. The same thing happens with parents and children. The circles are not being closed. One can have phantasmagorical play—the He-Man and She-Ra dolls are going off in to space in all kinds of rockets. But within this drama there can be a logical discussion about how the rockets work and why this character is mad or scared. Within the infrastructure of the discussion the therapist and the child can talk logically to one another. They can have a dialogue. If the therapist and child are marching to different drummers, one may be helping elaboration, but not differentiation.

Some children have difficulty with circle closing because they have receptive language problems. Unbeknownst to the therapist, the child doesn't have the vaguest idea of what the therapist is saying. He is a very imaginative child and comes with exciting fantasies. The therapist thinks that's terrific. The child communicates well at the nonverbal level. He senses enthusiasm, and is therefore receiving structure building from the quality of engagement, the nonverbal intentional cuing; support for his pretending, and labeling feelings for representational elaboration. Assume he cannot figure out what you are saying, because he can only understand a two-word sequence and you are using four- and five-word sequences, or because his attention is fleeting and he favors movement in space. If he is not using your information to further elaborate his own ideas, then representational differentiation is not occurring. Under such circumstances, you must bring the child back and explore how he ignored you or didn't understand you. If the child looks confused, you may try a simpler word or offer him cues. He may hook on to your simpler word and respond. If the child is negative and deliberately ignoring you, you still must pull him in for a response. You cannot go on to something else until there is at least acknowledgement of your input, including the child saying, "*Shut up!* I don't want to talk about that!" The child who says "Quiet!" or "Shut up!" while being impolite is still closing the circle. Circle closing or a self–other dialogue is necessary for differentiation.

In addition to closing circles, representational differentiation is also fostered by responding to limits (using ideas), shifting back and forth from fantasy to reality, experiencing temporally and spatially appropriate feedback (symbolic) for different thematic affective inclinations, and by having reality-based logical conversations (e.g., about school or friends or bedtime, toilet training, discipline, problems, gripes, birthday presents, and so forth). It is also encouraged by using rules in

games or activities and tolerating, recovering from, and remaining engaged during strong feelings, such as anger. These
types of experiences must be present both within the therapeutic sessions, at home with family, and in school or related
settings.

Consider an example of a six-year-old child. The child
comes in and just rolls cars back and forth for the whole session.
You feel, "Gee, how can I just sit on the floor for forty-five
minutes rolling the car back and forth." Ask yourself, "What's
really happening? We've been working on engagement as we
focus on each other's rolling movements and enjoy each other's
empathy and regard. We've been working on nonverbal intentional cuing as we nod approvingly to each other, point, and
motion to determine who will get the car when it goes under the
couch and look at each other in a surprised, curious, annoyed,
fascinated, or excited way (in an intentional, reciprocal manner). We have established a preverbal reality-based logical
structure for communication which, at a minimum, conveys a
sense of safety, security, and approval, and at a maximum also
conveys a sense of self-definition and respect for personal
uniqueness. We've been working on representational elaboration as we describe the activity of the cars and see how we can
elaborate a drama. We've even been working on elements of
representational differentiation. As the car goes back and
forth, we have a logical dialogue around whether the car is fast
or slow, or whether it is heavy or light, or whether the blue or
gray car is faster. We closed twenty circles around discussing
the cars. We may even get into why the cars like to crash.

As can be seen, a great deal of structure building can take
place around a simple activity, even if not much conflict
resolution is occurring. We will not discuss the resolution of
conflict here except to emphasize that the structure-building
aspect of treatment leads to the capacities to elaborate (representational elaboration) and resolve (representational differentiation) conflicts. The elaboration of wishes and feelings
(thematic–affective domains) allows one to see if certain themes

are opposing or in conflict, such as curiosity about bodies and also, at the same time being scared of bodies getting hurt.

As indicated, parents can also facilitate structure building. Through "floor time" with their child, a half-hour or more, where they are engaging and following their child's lead in interaction or pretend play. The engaged, attentive parent supports the child's attentiveness, engagement, purposeful-ness, in thematic elaboration and facilitates the closing of the circles. The parent is not being a therapist, but simply is having a chit-chat with their ten-year-old, or playtime with their four-year-old. Some parents have a difficult time gaining their child's attention, engaging and following their child's lead. Inattentive, negative, and/or aloof or withdrawn children are especially challenging. Small gains, going from one minute to two, have to be appreciated. Parents with anxieties and conflicts of their own may get overly bossy or controlling or become aloof and tune out, or confused and disorganized or overly literal or concrete. The inability to implement this simple task often reveals family difficulties and helps develop a working alliance. One parent said, "It's the darndest thing. It's sounds so easy and yet when I'm down on the floor I get anxious." He wanted help in figuring out why it was hard. One is trying to help parents do what many intuitive, gifted parents do auto-matically. Parents can provide structure-building experiences every day. In addition to "floor time," reality-based logical conversations (for children over three and a half), limit-setting, closing circles, and respecting assertiveness are types of expe-riences and attitudes parents can be helped to work on as part of their daily routine and daily provision of the four levels of experience described earlier (see Greenspan and Greenspan [1989] for a description of the types of experiences parents can provide).

In summary, the developmental sequence of ego structures reveals the types of experiences children require to build an adaptive psychological structure. By focusing on the structure building aspects of therapy, the intuitive and nonspecific ther-apeutic elements can become both specific and systematic. Two brief case illustrations with further discussion will amplify these points.

CASE ILLUSTRATIONS AND DISCUSSION

Consider a seven-year-old who has not reached the representational level in terms of emotional life. Even if he is getting A's at school, and is precocious in math, he may not have elevated his emotional life to the representational level. This youngster has a behavior and impulse control problem. Because he never developed his representational capacities, he has no way of labeling his feelings. Without "emotional ideas" he has no way of symbolically knowing whether he is angry, sad, jealous, curious, or fearful. He has no internal signaling system. He feels sensations in his body; he feels motor or behavioral tendencies. But he has no way of knowing what he is feeling or telling anyone else what he is feeling. When he hits another kid, he says, "I just did it," as though his arm acted on its own. We will frequently say to such a youngster, "You must have felt angry." We would say this to an adult, too; for example, a spouse abuser. "You must have been angry." "Yeah, I hit her three times." "You must have been furious." "I also kicked her in the stomach." "Boy, you must have really been furious." "And then I threw her down." "Oh, you must have been enraged." "Yes, and then I kicked her again." In this sequence, only behaviors are described. (This suggests a developmental level of eighteen months, where organized intentional patterns of behavior predominate.) We often assume that because they can describe organized patterns of behavior they also can abstract behavioral patterns into a central affective state. Abstracting behavior into a central affective state is part of going from the stage of behavioral organization at eighteen months old to the twenty-four to thirty-six-month-old stage where one learns to abstract central affective states through abstracting the common denominator of a group of behaviors into a category like anger (i.e., the representational level). Adults and children often "act out" because their body feels uncomfortable and then their body seems to want to hurt someone. They claim the hurting relieves the discomfort. They seem angry. But they don't experience anger the way others do.

If we assume they are already at the representational level, we do not make headway. "Gee, you must have felt angry." "Yes, I hit and kicked her." "Why do you do it?" "I don't know. My hand wanted to do it." "Come on. You're not taking responsibility."

Frustrated with the person's inability to take responsibility, one may turn to a behavior modification program—time-outs for bad behavior, M&Ms for good behavior. If the behavior modification is firm enough, it may change the behavior. Every child is fearful and every child wants candy. But it will change the behavior at the level of an eighteen-month-old. You can get an eighteen-month-old to stop biting and kicking with rewards and punishments alone. But you are still leaving the child with a basic defect in ego functioning, even though his behavior may come under greater control. That child is not learning to elaborate and label feelings as a basis for reasoning about the consequences of his behavior. Understanding at the symbolic level is required for reasoned impulse control.

Our goal is to facilitate representational elaboration and differentiation. We try to help the impulsive child elaborate emotional themes in terms of symbols or ideas and then differentiate the different categories of experience. We help the child learn to differentiate "me" from "you" and across different thematic–affective domains. You are asking, "Is the eight-year-old child with impulse problems representational? Can he, in pretend play or discussions engage in different themes? Do I see dependency, aggression, assertiveness, curiosity, and competition?" One further asks, "How well does the child differentiate these different areas from one another?" For example, some children will represent dependency and closeness by having the dolls hug each other. But then the hug becomes a "choke" and the doll is "dead." In addition, with direct and intense anger, they are still behavior-discharge oriented. There is either no play with the dolls fighting, or if there is play with the dolls fighting it is discharge type of play. The dolls are torn apart and the child has to be restrained. The aggressive drama is not organized and lacks depth.

To help our impulsive child further, we want to see if he has a logical structure to the subplots of his drama. For example, the child who is two and a half switches rather randomly from dolls hugging to dolls fighting. But by four years of age, the child should evidence representational differentiation in terms of a plot line and subplots developing. The dolls are hugging, but then a wolf comes to attack them. They get angry at the attacking wolf and a fight starts. This plot line shows you that there is a differentiation, a bridge, between the theme of dependency and the theme of aggression. The aggression does not emerge randomly.

Many children who present for therapy have not fully made it into the stage of representational differentiation in at least some areas such as aggression, sexuality, or dependency (even though they may be differentiated in other emotional areas). One can see this just in the spontaneous play. As you engage in play and say: "Oh gee! The soldiers were fighting and now they are hugging. How did they get from fighting to hugging?", the child does not have even to acknowledge the question. But in the next play sequence he can answer your question. If he does, he is building bridges. The child who becomes more random shows you he has difficulty building bridges.

To help our impulsive child, we work on helping him elaborate dramas and see the relationship between his themes or plots (building bridges). At the same time, his parents must help him with limits and with engagement, purposeful signaling, and verbal elaboration and differentiation of his themes and feelings.

Consider another example: This child comes in, not, as the first child, with behavior discharge problems (he never learned to represent his emotional world), but with clinging behavior. Her mother says, "She is waking up at night, won't go to school without her mommy and I am a nervous wreck because I thought finally she would be independent from me and she (Sally) won't leave me alone." You bring Sally into the play-room. She is very related. Her attention span is excellent. She is intentional in terms of the preverbal communication and seems to abstract preverbal patterns of interaction. She also can tease gently, be cooperative, and play out (in make-believe) very rich and varied fantasies. She has abilities from all the stages. As you observe more, you see that while she plays out the doll scene, there are tea parties, hugging, and doctors taking care of sick babies, there are no spontaneous themes of anger or assertiveness. After three sessions, you are perplexed. You want to see Sally in the context of mother's description of the problem. To be sure, mother is ambivalent and has her anxieties, and father is a workaholic, and you can create a rationale for why Sally has a problem. But there are a lot of children with this family pattern who don't have this exact problem. How does Sally organize the "problem areas" in her mind? As Sally plays some more, after feeling a little more secure with you, she takes a chance. She has one of the dolls get mad at the other doll. The play gets kind of chaotic. You lose sight of whether it's the mommy doll or the baby doll who is angry at the other. Then the play gets more fragmented and random, as opposed to the nice elaborate, organized dramas she developed earlier. You say to yourself, "Gee, I'm losing track," and you try to clarify things, but it doesn't help. You are still not sure if it's the "mommy" or "Sally" doll who is angry. She seems more like a three-year-old and the self/nonself differen-tiation is a little muddied around themes of anger. You see this repeated a number of times (when she is tired and when she is not tired). She is having trouble differentiating, in terms of the representational level, the theme around assertiveness and anger. You also see some hints that curiosity relating to mommy and daddy behind closed doors also leads to some undifferen-tiated play. Themes having to do with assertiveness, aggression, and curiosity are less differentiated for her. As you try to integrate these observations with the family history, you learn from mother that she is a very passive woman who is anxious with aggression. She always dealt with her anger by being overprotective toward Sally. You learn that Sally, as a baby, was sensitive to touch and was easily overwhelmed. Mother got used to overprotecting her. But mother also often felt rejected. When mother tried to overprotect her, Sally would often push her away because of her sensitivity to touch. Mother's ambivalence was heightened by the interaction set up in part by Sally's constitutional pattern.

In the area of representing and differentiating aggression, Sally did not get enough practice. Your focus in the therapy begins to make sense. What you are doing in the playroom at the same time helps you advise the parents about strategies at home. Mother, for example, feels entirely different as she understands that Sally needs more "space" and control over her world than a less tactily sensitive child, and that part of the clinging is Sally's way to gain control over her neediness, her anger, and her desire to be in charge on her own terms.

In these examples, we see a developmental perspective can aid in understanding the genesis of difficulties. In addition to symptoms and phenomenological categories, the developmental perspective helps you ask, "What really went awry developmentally? Where did this child go off the track?" It also supports specific ways of intervening. For example, with the first case, the child with behavioral discharge problems who has never learned to represent feelings, it was important to help him represent his feelings. As one is playing with him and he is behaving aggressively, one is working with him on labeling and expanding his themes. At the same time one is working on setting limits and his parents are working on setting limits. For example, to help him label and elaborate, one is not going to assume that he knows he is angry. One is going to say to him, "When you do that, what do you feel like?" "I feel numb inside. Nothing," he says. Then he describes vague sensations of discomfort, mostly physical. One will say, "Well, what would relieve this discomfort?" (He likes to watch wrestling.) He says that when he gets this numb feeling and vague sense of discomfort and disorganization and a little gastrointestinal distress, that watching wrestling makes him feel better. Sometimes when he wrestles with his friends he also feels better. He says, "Gee. Maybe I'm angry when I feel numb." But he still doesn't feel angry. One does not push him and say, "Well, it doesn't sound like you really feel angry," but one says how "numbness" seems very uncomfortable. He says, "I have to get rid of it. That's why I fight." The focus on the feeling of numbness, gradually leads to the abstraction of a feeling state having to do with being "furious" at someone who had humiliated him. The "someone" was his father, who was in fact intrusive, undermining, and humiliating. It is a slow, painstaking task to abstract a feeling state out of a physical, often physiologic, sensation. The anger had to come up spontaneously in relationship to "being humiliated." The "numbness and anger" could both be felt as he left one feeling and become aware of the other. Eventually he talked about how "out of control" he felt with his father.

With the little girl, the work focused on letting her engage, feel secure, and then experiment with the anger, first behaviorally and then symbolically. Whereas her mother, while Sally was growing up, would get frightened and overprotective at the anger, the therapist says, "Boy, that doll is hitting that other doll hard." As this little girl elaborates her anger, her natural ability enables her to represent it and differentiate it. The therapist, with clarifying and interpretive comments, helps her partition the anger from dependency: "I got lost. What's going on here? We went from hugging to hitting. How did that happen?" Often there are underlying conflicts and the child is fearful. This little girl was clinging to her mother because she was fearful that if she put the anger into words, her mother would leave her. She was scared that mother would leave her not just because of the notion that a thought can lead to someone leaving you, but in her mind thought and behavior (around anger) was equated. She said, "If I think it, I'll do it," at one point. She was convinced that there was no difference between the thinking and the doing. A person who is still, in part, living as an eighteen-month-old believes that the fleeting thought, the fleeting idea, is tied to the behavior. Thinking is doing at eighteen months of age. Even some adults say, "I can't talk about that because it will happen." It's a magical belief on the one hand, but also evidence of a lack of full abstraction of an idea and feeling state as separate from the behavior. It is also evidence of a developmental lag or regression. A child may need to learn for the first time, how to abstract a feeling state and separate the idea from the behavior. It will not help to say, "Oh, you can tell me how you feel. You can talk about anything in here." Such a statement doesn't do much because the child will not believe you. The child believes, "If I say it I do it. My body will do it. I know it will." Over time in her relationship with you, the child becomes secure enough because of the engagement and the preverbal intentional communication, to abstract representational states. You create the infrastructure of a working alliance. This alliance need not be a vague concept. It is a concept having to do with engagement, preverbal communication, and preverbal abstracting of intentions.

Against this background, the child becomes brave. With bravery she tries the words. She learns that feelings and thoughts can be safely elaborated. Your interpretations may put her experiences into a verbal framework. Your interpretations of her fears and anxieties ("frightened that she was going to hurt you"), together with the new opportunities to practice age-appropriate representational experiences, gives her a chance to represent and differentiate her anger. Sally's anxiety and clingyness abated somewhat as she began verbalizing how "mad" she felt when mother tried to be the boss. "I want to be the boss." Saying it helped her need to be it a little less.

COMMENTS ON CHILDHOOD PSYCHOPATHOLOGY

Concepts of early ego development and essential early developmental processes suggest different ways of viewing childhood psychopathology. Entities which now might be considered an organizational disorder, in this view, would be considered as perhaps a final common pathway of a variety of different developmental problems. This view would also have implications for treatment. The goal of treatment would be to deal with the contributing developmental problems in order to help the child regain an adaptive developmental progression.

Consider, for example, pervasive developmental disorder and autism. At present, children (usually between eighteen months and four years of age) receive a diagnosis of pervasive developmental disorder or communication disorder with autistic features or, if severe enough, childhood autism, when they evidence a severe disturbance in interpersonal relating, communication, and overall adaptation. Most of the children I have seen with this pattern have significant developmental problems at each of the early stages of ego development. They often, for example, have a severe difficulty with auditory processing and, later, receptive language. They may also have various types of sensory hyperreactivity (e.g., tactile sensitivities) and subtle irregularities in motor tone and planning. These constitutional maturational patterns are often sufficient to throw off the early negotiation of shared attention, engagement, intentional reciprocal gesturing, and early representational capacities. Even reasonably stable, supportive, and empathetic families often do not have the intuitive skills to help their child successfully negotiate these early challenges. Not infrequently, a combination of two events seems to significantly derail the child's forward momentum between sixteen and twenty-four months. One of these appears to be the child's own emerging capacities for higher level presymbolic and symbolic functioning. Overloaded with new information about the world (because new information is being processed a vulnerable and shaky foundation such as poor behavioral causality), he begins regressing in terms of behavioral organization, regulation, interpersonal patterns, and emerging motor control and language. In many cases, careful history often reveals environmental stresses around this time, such as the loss of a nanny, a parent going back to work, preoccupation of a parent with the birth of a sibling, and so forth. For children who already have a tenuous hold on their interpersonal relationships and emerging functional capacities, the combination of these two types of challenges is overwhelming (although for some even the former challenge alone seems sufficient).

Furthermore, the child usually succeeds in confusing his parents sufficiently that they stop offering him developmental support in terms of the four processes outlined earlier (shared attention and engagement, reciprocal intentional gesturing, representational elaboration, and representational differentiation). Having disengaged, in part because of their confusion and anxiety and in part because of the challenging nature of the child's behavior, a number of parents report growing feelings of alienation, anger, and loss, and unintentionally behave with increasing ambivalence. The child, as he loses his engagement and intentional interactive relatedness to his key caregivers, seems to spin more and more idiosyncratically out of control. For children who are prerepresentational, this may manifest itself by greater motor and behavior randomness and lack of intentionality. For children who have achieved some degree of representational capacity, their use of ideas and words become more personalized and fragmented. The lack of an intentional and organizing human relationship mediates this disorganization.

In the cases where it has been possible to catch this process early, an intense effort has been made to reestablish a quality of shared attention, engagement, and preverbal, gestural, and reciprocal intentionality. Parents and children are worked with together to reestablish these processes. For example, one child would only look away from his father and turn the screw on a chair. Father, whose initial reaction was to feel frustrated and angry that his son wouldn't respond to his words, was helped to take great pride in gaining simply a few seconds of shared attention while holding the screw his son was turning. Soon, this shared attention led to a flicker of a few smiles and some reciprocal gestures as father would turn the screw one way and his son would turn it the other. The same child enjoyed perseverating by opening and closing the door in my office. Here, too, as mother and father learned to harness their child's inclinations by getting on the other side of the door and creating an interpersonal game with it, perseveration became interaction. To be sure, these efforts have to be carefully graded and the child's anger and frustration, including tantrums, have to become part of his or her learning about how to reestablish comfort, security, and relating. Interestingly, as child and parent become more intentional at the behavioral level in the context of shared attention and engagement, islands of representational activity, including the use of words, gradually become more reality-based. This latter step is, in part, dependent on the degree of receptive or expressive language difficulties. Even in cases where the language difficulty seems severe, the child may be able to improve significantly in a short period of time in terms of relatedness, intentionality, self-comforting skills, and peer interactions. The child's language and/or motor problems may then be more clearly seen in their own right. It should also be mentioned that as part of this approach to reestablishing critical developmental processes (engagement, etc.), there often needs to be highly specialized collaborative work with occupational or physical therapists, speech pathologists, and early childhood special educators to remediate specific motor, language and speech, and/or cognitive difficulties.

Some children diagnosed as borderline or psychotic often evidence only highly personalized unreality-based thought processes. One such child, a six-year-old, who had some capacity for engagement and intentional use of gestures, after about ten minutes of talking about "how good I am in math," said, "I really have much more special powers, but you have to keep it secret from my parents." He then went on to tell me about his private communication with powerful sea creatures from another planet. His delusional system was quite elaborate and sophisticated. Interestingly, he had a mild, undetected receptive language problem and from about age three and a half to six seemed to be constructing his dialogues more and more only with himself. As he cut himself off from interpersonal relationships, he also had cut himself off from an important ingredient in learning to balance reality and fantasy. The external object serves as a bridge to reality because in relating to someone else one must put one's own thoughts into the perspective of a "me" and a "you." The process of representational differentiation normally depends on shared representational experiences between a child and a significant other. As this child experienced confusion and difficulty in taking in information from other people, he gradually found it was easier to communicate only with himself. His parents were of the kind described in chapter 2—they tended to confuse meanings and also overwhelm him with confusing affects. Their ambivalence led them to deny and ignore his difficulties with peers and his greater and greater degree of isolated play. Because he was so bright and precocious in math and because his play was creative and sophisticated they rationalized that he was just a little too advanced for his friends.

Although they will not be discussed here, needless to say, there were important psychodynamic issues in this family. The point to be emphasized is that in a number of children who have not developed an appropriate balance between fantasy and reality, an important contribution may be a relative difficulty with receptive language between ages three and five which is then accentuated by certain family patterns. These two factors together conspire to undermine the stable development of representational differentiation. Treatment which is sensitive not only to understanding the meaning of the youngster's idiosyncratic world, but also to reestablishing object-related symbolic communications, is often very helpful. In fact, the very success of the clinician in understanding and communicating with the child becomes a first step in reestablishing an interpersonal rather than an idiosyncratic dialogue.

Attention deficit disorders is another category that may represent a common pathway for a variety of different developmental difficulties. In some children, I have noticed that the major problem seems to be in sequencing auditory–verbal symbols. For example, with a number of children with this diagnosis I noticed that they "tuned me out" when I used complex sentences. As long as I kept my communication simple they were attentive. To confirm this impression, I played a "Simon says" game with them. When I said, "Simon Says put your hand on your knee" or "Simon Says put your hand on your head," the child was usually cooperative and attentive. If, however, I strung together three commands such as "Simon Says put your hands on your knee, then your hips, and then tie your shoes," the child would often begin pulling the books off my shelves and engage in other kinds of provocative behavior. If I quickly returned to a simpler command, I could regain his attention. For this group of children, while there was a tendency toward inattentive and provocative behavior, the behavior seemed partially precipitated by, and related to, a difficulty with holding in mind a sequence of auditory–verbal patterns.

In other children with these same behaviors, there have been difficulties with visual–spatial processing, a tendency toward fragmented, rather than cohesive, thinking, a tendency toward irritability and agitation, and a pattern of getting lost in the issue of the moment and not seeing the larger picture. Still other children, either alone or in combination with one or both patterns above, evidence overreactivity to such basic sensations as touch and high-pitched sounds. Motor planning problems or subtle motor tone difficulties and a general difficulty with controlling one's body in space is also not uncommon in, and contributory to, attentional difficulties.

In working with specific sensory processing, reactivity and/or, motor challenges, in the context of activities which support the four developmental levels outlined earlier, a number of children appear to make significant gains in their attentional capacities. For a subgroup of children, who also use their constitutional maturational vulnerability for defensive purposes, such as to get even when they are angry, to avoid competition, or to ambivalently gain dependency support the psychotherapeutic work must help them learn to compensate for, rather than accentuate, their constitutional maturational patterns.

Another group of children who might be described as

conduct disorders recently provided an interesting insight. A number of bright, verbal two- to five-year-olds (with excellent motor and language abilities) had a common problem with either hitting peers or parents and/or unpredictable provocative behavior which was quite resistant to routine parental limits. In observing these children over a period of time, I noticed that neither they nor their parents used anticipatory gestural communication, including facial gestures, vocal gestures, affect gestures, motor gestures, and so forth. It occurred to me that perhaps these families, which seemed to evidence a high degree of "poker-faced" individuals, had failed to negotiate an important aspect of gestural communication in the second year of the child's life. During this time, it is likely that gestures serve a number of functions for the child with regard to self-limit-setting. Gestures may help the child identify his own feelings and intentions. Adults in part know their feelings through the feedback from their own facial expressions, clenched fists, or angry voices, and it seems as though affects are, in part, defined by their somatic manifestations. Furthermore, the parents' gestures, such as an angry look, a stern grimace, or a firm finger-pointing may help warn the child of his parents' reaction, before a parental sanction is necessary. Finally, the child's gestures may also help the parents anticipate what the child is about to do, allowing them to intervene in a warning way before the child misbehaves. This system of gestural communication, which seems so well developed in the animal kingdom (one only has to look at two animals posturing and gesturing to one another, seeing who will back down so they can avoid a fight) would appear to play a significant role in the safe handling of interpersonal aggression. It is not surprising that where, for a variety of reasons, psychosocial as well as constitutional, this system has not developed properly, one might see impulsive behavior.

This relatively recent observation is presented here as an illustration of the potential value of developmental observation to our understanding of the "pathways" to different difficulties.

Another observation pertains to children who are prone to

affective lability, depression, and anxiety states. They seem to have relative lags in their visual–spatial integrating ability (they have difficulty seeing the forest for the trees and tend to become overwhelmed by the experiences of the moment). This pattern was described in chapter 2. The childhood version of this pattern seems to manifest itself sometimes with symptoms of irritability, inconsolable temper tantrums, demandingness, perfectionism, and a general difficulty with perspective taking and balanced empathy. Environments characterized by lack of empathy and lack of limit-setting seem to intensify this pattern. Environments that can balance empathy and limit-setting in the context of supporting the developmental processes described earlier help children deal with the pattern. Developmentally based prevention and treatment approaches may therefore have unusual promise.

This section has outlined a few clinical impressions regarding the development of psychopathology and developmental approaches to treatment. These impressions are based on a limited number of case studies. It is hoped, however, that they provide useful hypotheses for more systematic study. Because of the propensity to complete development, children especially require approaches to diagnosis and treatment that harness their potential and build on their own natural developmental processes. It was shown how disruptions in critical developmental processes (e.g. engagement, purposeful communication) are an integral part of many types of disorders and how mobilizing these same critical processes may serve as a foundation for prevention and treatment.

Chapter 11

Emotional and Social Development in Infants and Young Children with Developmental Disabilities

Infants, like all human beings, do things, at least in part, to satisfy emotional and social needs and goals. As infants develop, they want to be close to another person, to experience pleasure and excitement, to be intentional by making things happen, to be assertive and curious, and to receive responses to and confirmation of their own inclinations. These basic emotional experiences are a foundation for motivation and mastery.

Most infants with developmental disorders or delays are capable of progressing through adaptive stages of emotional and social development, but research and clinical practice teach us that such progress cannot be taken for granted. To surmount the challenges to reaching their emotional potential and achieving robust relationships within the family and in the outside world, infants with disabilities or delays may need

This chapter was originally published in *Zero to Three*, September 1988.

special patterns of care. Many babies with special needs now
receive therapy designed to remediate motor delays, language
delays, cognitive lags, or sensory processing difficulties. But the
social and emotional aspects of development are at least partially ignored in such work. This chapter represents an effort to
help professionals who work with infants and toddlers with
disabilities and with their families attend to the stage-specific
emotional needs of these children along with their physical and
intellectual needs. Professionals and parents can then work
together to provide experiences that will promote adaptive
emotional patterns in the context not only of changing emotional needs, but of individual differences in infants and
families as well.

In this chapter we will discuss (1) adaptive and maladaptive
patterns of ego development in the first three years of life, with
special attention to the challenges presented by disabilities; (2)
domains of experience that will help all children achieve ego
growth; (3) pilot research findings comparing the emotional
interaction of handicapped and nonhandicapped infants and
their families; (4) clinical principles to guide an integrated
approach to sensory, motor, cognitive, and affective challenges
confronting infants and toddlers; and (5) implications for
effective alliance among the infant, the family, and the service
system.

OVERCOMING BARRIERS TO EMOTIONAL GROWTH:
PREVENTIVE THERAPEUTIC APPROACHES

In a number of publications for professional and general
audiences (Greenspan, 1981, 1987; Greenspan and Lieberman,
1980; Greenspan and Lourie, 1981; Greenspan and Porges,
1984; Greenspan and Greenspan, 1985, 1989), we have formulated the emotional stages of the first three to four years of life
and the related principles of preventive intervention. At each
of these stages a child's development may be adaptive, or
development may be compromised in varying degrees, result-

ing in diminished range, depth, and/or stability of emotional experience and expression or in a limited emergence of personal uniqueness. Various types of developmental delays or disabilities pose challenges to the attainment of specific emotional goals. Special patterns of care, however, may help the infant or young child surmount these obstacles to emotional growth. We will briefly consider each stage from the perspective of the challenges of disabilities.

REGULATION (HOMEOSTASIS)

Central nervous system immaturity may render infants over or undersensitive to the routine tactile, vestibular, auditory, or visual experiences that most babies enjoy. Caregivers need to find types of experience that will comfort sensitive infants and gain the interest of underreactive infants. For example, firm holding and pressure may be helpful for the infant who is overly sensitive to touch. On occasion, the use of large muscle groups in helping an infant pull from a sitting to a standing position in one's lap, combined with special patterns of visual and auditory experience, may enable the child to attend more effectively.

If motor coordination difficulties prevent an infant from getting his hand to his mouth or exercising the control over body position expected at his age, he will be less able to comfort himself. Integrating special patterns of holding and movement in space are therefore important to facilitate the infant's comfort, regulation, and interest in the world.

Feeding difficulties may be associated with either low muscle tone (e.g., difficulty swallowing) or high muscle tone (e.g., tongue thrust pushing fluid or food out of the mouth). Such problems interfere with an important early source of pleasure for most babies. They also interfere with patterns of regulation, and with the use of feeding as one element in a mutually satisfying relationship between infant and caregiver.

ATTACHMENT

A motorically delayed infant may lack some of the tools most babies use to express joy in the presence of a caregiver. The caregiver will need to look beyond poorly coordinated motor responses, lack of synchronous vocalizations, and difficulty in organizing even a smile, until she finds a special look or gesture of pleasure unique to her infant, and can respond. Otherwise, the infant is likely to become doubly frustrated when he cannot control his own body and, because of this, form joint patterns of joy with the people most important to him.

PURPOSEFUL COMMUNICATION (SOMAPSYCHOLOGICAL DIFFERENTIATION)

At this stage, as indicated earlier, the ability to integrate sensory experiences across the senses (e.g., auditory and visual); to connect sensory and motor experiences (e.g., looking and reaching); and to plan and implement motor activities in accord with adaptive goals (e.g., exploring mother's mouth), are all important elements to learning to communicate purposefully, to take the initiative, and to make things happen in the world.

Infants with compromised motor tone, motor planning, sensory discrimination, cross-sensory integration, or sensory motor coordination will require special help in mastering this crucial emotional and cognitive stage; otherwise, infants may confuse already anxious caregivers, and patterns of withdrawal, overcontrol and/or chaotic or disorganized interactions may replace purposeful ones. For example, the infant with low tone may enjoy being catered to and may elicit overprotective patterns and overcontrolling (and at times even overstimulation). The high energy, increased motor tone, distractible infant may find himself caught up in a confusing array of random responses from parents who are trying to keep up with this pace. In both of these circumstances parents require help in reading and responding to specific cues so that their infant learns to communicate in an organized and intentional manner. This is an especially important time to work with attention and focus. Finding the most appropriate pattern of calming and combining it with carefully modulated sensory-affective experiences (rhythmic vocalizations and facial expressions) can help the distractible baby or the seemingly inward-looking baby increase his attention span from one to two seconds to three seconds, then six seconds, and eventually a number of minutes. Helping an infant develop the first three- to six-seconds attention span can be a caregiver's hardest but most important task. Babies need to attend for this length of time at a minimum if they are to develop a *self-sustaining* interest in their environment.

COMPLEX SENSE OF SELF (BEHAVIORAL ORGANIZATION)

At a time when he is struggling to organize behavior, integrate a behavioral sense of self, and balance his needs for independence and dependence, the toddler who is motorically delayed may lack a sense of control over his own body and over space. Experimenting with the large muscle activity associated with assertiveness and aggression may prove frightening, leading to avoidance of these important domains of emotional life. Self-care activities, like dressing or bathing, may prove frustrating for both child and parent, as the child may learn to use arching, fisting, or stiffening of the extremities to avoid these challenging experiences. A toddler with sensory processing lags faces her own special challenges in experimenting with behavioral and organizational problems, and independence. If it is difficult to discriminate auditory and visual cues across space (e.g., staying in emotional touch with a parent from across the room, by decoding the parent's vocalizations and gestures), a child may need to rely on proximal forms of reassurance (e.g., being held), or may become frightened easily. The inability to negotiate space leads to fragmented rather then organized behavioral patterns.

Unique caregiving approaches that may help children with disabilities to organize and integrate behavioral and emotional patterns include working on increasing attention and focus, adding one more piece of behavior to an ever-growing complex pattern of interaction; supporting assertiveness through extreme patience in letting a toddler repeat motor gestures and acts for himself, providing only extra vocal and visual support; and working on communication across space by reading and responding to visual and auditory gestures.

CREATING IDEAS AND EMOTIONAL THINKING (REPRESENTATIONAL ELABORATION AND DIFFERENTIATION)

Adaptive development at this stage includes the ability to integrate across sensory, emotional, and motor experiences; to practice using ideas through "pretend play" and language; to distinguish the self from the nonself; and to express emotions intentionally in language (e.g., "I am mad). Compromised development is observable in the child with deficits in imaginative play and communication, reality testing, impulse control, or focused concentration, or in the child who withdraws from, or is chaotic or disorganized in relationships.

Motor delays or athetoid movement patterns may compromise a child's ability to engage in make-believe play, employ functional language, or regulate affect. Sensory processing integration or sensory-motor coordination lags also create special challenges for the child and her caregivers to find new ways to abstract experience in order to create and to practice using emotional ideas. For example, the preschooler with an auditory–verbal processing (receptive language) difficulty, if very creative, may begin marching to the beat of her own drummer because it is easier to communicate with herself than to figure out the sounds and words of someone else. In such a circumstance it is important to help the child take in and use the other person's information (e.g., "closing the circle").

DOMAINS OF EXPERIENCE THAT FOSTER EMOTIONAL DEVELOPMENT

As our discussion of the six emotional stages suggests, the process of emotional growth takes place, for all children, in the context of a caregiving environment. Four domains of critical developmental experience that can be extrapolated from the six stages and that cross age ranges and stages are especially important for infants and children with disabilities. While these four domains of experience have been described earlier, they will now be discussed with reference to infants with disabilities.

ATTENTION AND ENGAGEMENT

The first domain of experience is made up of attention and engagement, which means face-to-face contact, a sense of connectedness, and shared attention between the infant and another person, in a context of warm, pleasurable, or loving feelings. The developing infant elaborates a range of emotional inclinations, providing a context for attention and engagement. For example, an eight-month-old elaborating an inclination for dependency can gesture for closeness by reaching out to be picked up. She can also be assertive, using motor control to put her hand in Mommy's mouth or to squeeze Daddy's nose. She can already experiment with anger by knocking the food off the table if she doesn't like dinner, or she can make angry vocalizations. She can elaborate pleasure and excitement by touching her own body or by creating tactile contact with Mommy or Daddy.

The first question caregivers must ask is: Are we helping the child engage, and if so, are we helping the child to engage in the full human drama? How is the child letting us know about dependency, assertiveness, anger, pleasure, and excitement? Many parents are comfortable with one domain of engagement but not with others. Pleasure may be comfortable, but anger is not acceptable. Or assertiveness is encouraged, but too much closeness and dependency seem frightening. We must ask ourselves if we are helping a child to feel connected in terms of his *own* inner life. At the stage of emotional ideas, this will mean learning to elevate inner sensations to the level of emotional ideas, rather than simply to inhibit them. With the eight-month-old, we have the opportunity to engage behaviorally. With the three and a half-year-old, we have the opportunity to engage through words and pretend play.

Children with handicaps, for example, often have not been engaged around aggression. Later, as eight and nine-year-olds, they may be afraid of aggression because these sensations have never graduated from the "body" or behavioral level to the ideational level, where they can be reasoned about. Because such children lack the sense of security that emerges from an ability to reason out and control their anger, they are afraid of it: they may become passive, diffusely passive–aggressive, or diffusely aggressive.

INTENTIONAL, RECIPROCAL GESTURES, AND CUES

Essential for all children is the second domain of experience: Intentional, reciprocal gestures and cues. Even before words or other symbols become important or even useful to a child, he organizes his world and his sense of preverbal reality in the context of an organized gestural system of communication. As indicated earlier, the most basic emotional messages of life, dealing with safety versus danger, acceptance versus rejection, approval versus disapproval, respect versus disrespect for uniqueness, and support and pride in, versus undermining of, an evolving sense of self and its emotional inclinations, are communicated back and forth between the child and his caregiver. This communication takes place through movements and movement patterns, gesture, facial expression (including emotional expression), vocal tone and rhythm, and combinations of these. To the degree that there is an organized intentional give and take of information, the child "figures out" his preverbal, presymbolic world and has a secure foundation for moving ahead. When this gestural system is not mastered and later symbolic modes need to be used consciously to "figure out" issues of safety and acceptance, it is easy to imagine from one's own adult perspective how such preoccupation may leave little energy for new learning.

Communicating preverbally, with movements, will require special practice by young children experiencing motor difficulties. Visual, spatial, and/or auditory-vocal processing difficulties will pose challenges to infants trying to interpret the cues of others.

ELABORATION AND ABSTRACTION OF BEHAVIOR AND FEELINGS

Elaboration of behavior and feelings into higher forms, with a special focus on "ideas" or representations is a domain of experience between the young child and a caregiver that seems essential if the child is to become able to create ideas and engage in emotional thinking on his own. While the ability to create ideas appears to begin at eighteen to twenty-four months with language development, the ability to abstract and organize information at higher and higher levels is a gradual and continuing process. Between ages one and a half and two and a half, special pretend play times, or "floor time," often provides the context for these types of interactions. Such play times, where dolls or soldiers may carry forth the emotional theme, may demand a great deal from caregivers. As with the experience of attention and engagement, caregivers need to understand their own emotional reactions to the child's expressions of dependency, aggression, or grief. Especially challenging is the child who has difficulty communicating his ideas because of language or motor difficulties. Patient work to find ways to "share meanings" is essential if a child is not to remain concrete and behavior bound.

CATEGORIZATION OF EXPERIENCE

Differentiating experience along a number of dimensions (the most basic distinction being between the self and the nonself) forms the basis for a stable sense of reality, the ability to accept responsibility for one's actions and to control impulses, and the modulation and integration of thought and feeling. Children need experiences of responses from the environment that are logical and realistic, flexible, highly individualistic, and timely. The parent who can respond differentially and appropriately to subtle differences in the child's verbal, emotional, or facial expression that suggest playful teasing, serious teasing, a careless request, a serious demand, mild competition, serious competition, mild curiosity, and assertive curiosity, will encourage the differentiation and consolidation of the child's emerging categorization of experience. The child's ability to categorize both emotional and impersonal experience is the foundation of his basic personality functions. Because, a child with motor or communication difficulties may be confusing to his parents, they will need to learn how to read and respond to these higher level symbolic patterns.

In addition to these four domains of experience, children with disabilities have special challenges when it comes to other types of experience that promote emotional and social growth.

One such experience, described earlier, is the differentiated dialogue or "closing the circle." Consider a bright, creative three and a half-year-old with auditory–verbal processing difficulty. He is inattentive and marches to the beat of his own drummer. He may play out a nice pretend sequence in which he will have a rocketship going off in space. Mother will say, "Gee, it looks like your rocketship is going to the moon." The child will say, "Look at this horse here. The horse is going in the rocketship." And mother will say, "Oh, we're going to take the horse to the moon?" and he'll say, "Look at this cow here." And mother will say, "Oh, is the cow coming to the moon, too?" and then he will say, "Look at this truck." He is verbally creative, but he never takes in what mother says and builds on it. As one plays with a child like this, one realizes that the child is not closing the circle, building on what one says., The play is not really interactive, although it looks interactive. The child is relating warmly, but he is not using the other person's information. Even in conversations, there is lots of eye contact and warmth, but no real interactive elaboration or logic.

Helping children to close circles helps their differentiation. One way to do this is to respect what is said: for example, "I see the cow, but you're ignoring my moon. What about my poor moon here?" If the child says, "Shut up about your moon," he is still closing the circle, because he has responded to the other's information. Circles can also be closed at the level of gestures and behavior, where chains of behavioral interactions build on one another. The caregivers of a motorically delayed infant, for example, will need to be especially alert to even slight vocal or motor signals for interactions so that they can be quickly interpreted and responded to in a phase-appropriate manner. A seemingly disorganized slap on the nose during the "nuzzle dance" may provide the opportunity for Daddy to be a "honk honk" car, encouraging these touches to his nose with his novel and entertaining "honks." Here, Daddy is simultaneously providing movement, touch, head, shoulder, and trunk support, wooing (in a loving way), and cause-and-effect feedback for emerging motor patterns.

Another challenging area of experience concerns *limit setting*. Adults have a tendency to avoid setting limits with handicapped children. Limits should always be gestural or verbal, understandable, negotiated, and reinforced as needed with discipline. Without limits children do not feel safe vis-à-vis their own anger. The key is always to increase engagement, interaction, "floor time," and closing of circles together with limits. Too often, as we increase the limit setting, we disengage. Whenever we increase limits we must increase engagement and spontaneous communication, either through pretend play or through behavioral, social, and emotional interaction.

EMOTIONAL INTERACTIONS BETWEEN HANDICAPPED AND NONHANDICAPPED INFANTS AND THEIR PARENTS

We have described stages of emotional development during the first three years of life and some of the challenges confronted by infants and toddlers with various handicapping conditions. We have also described some of the interaction experiences that seem to be essential for all children in negotiating the tasks of emotional growth in the early years.

How do the emotional experiences of infants with handicaps compare with those of nonhandicapped babies? In a preliminary study to explore this question, G. Gordon Williamson, Shirley Zeitlin, Serena Wieder, Suzy Poisson, and I observed ten motorically handicapped infants and ten motorically competent infants in interaction with their parents. We matched the groups for motor age. For example, a fifteen-month-old infant who was functioning at a motoric level of seven months was compared emotionally to a seven-month-old baby without a motor handicap. A fifteen-month-old with a handicap would therefore only need to do as well in emotional interaction as a seven-month-old for there to be no difference in the rating between the two of them.

The results of the pilot study provide preliminary support for our clinical impressions. Presumed motorically competent babies were involved in social engagement with their parents 43 percent of the time observed. But parents and their handicapped infants were socially engaged only 18 percent of the time. Motorically competent babies and their parents were more contingent (they read each other's signals) than handicapped babies and their parents. Anticontingent (negative) responses were more frequent in the handicapped group. Overcontrolling, intrusive, or opposite-from-expected responses by parents were three times as frequent in the handicapped group as in the motorically competent group. We also saw more nonparticipating, noncontingent, or withdrawn responses in the parents of the handicapped infants. In addition, handicapped infants tended to be more negative to their parents.

It is important to note that the group of motorically handicapped infants were just as capable of sending emotional social signals as the motorically competent group. These children made opportunities to interact available to their parents just as the motorically competent babies did. However, they experienced more missed opportunities and more misreading of signals.

Perhaps these trends should not be surprising. Perhaps the expectable and even natural response of many parents to a baby who is not giving an easily read signal is either to shut down or withdraw. But infants will in turn become negative, disorganized, or withdrawn when their partners are not offering interactive opportunities.

The following principles may offer both professionals and parents guidelines for using their encounters with handicapped infants as opportunities to encourage emotional and social, as well as physical and cognitive growth.

CLINICAL PRINCIPALS OF AN INTEGRATED APPROACH TO SENSORY, MOTOR, COGNITIVE, AND AFFECTIVE CHALLENGES

At each stage of emotional development, specific sensory or motor challenges will create unique emotional challenges as well. Fortunately, there are many ways for an infant to learn to be regulated, to relate to others, to communicate intenionally, to form a complex self, and to use emotional ideas to guide behavior and feelings, and to categorize experience. The question then becomes: How do we turn each challenge into a unique learning opportunity? For example, how do we help the infant with increased motor tone to correct the motor difficulty and, at the same time, learn to use his motor system for "falling in love," cause-and-effect emotional signaling, emotional thinking, and so forth? In considering the objective of integrating the child's physical and emotional needs, a key guiding principle immediately suggests itself.

PRINCIPLE I:–Each activity aimed at improving sensory, motor, or cognitive capacities should also have, as its goal, facilitation of the relevant, age-expected emotional pattern.

For example, the traditional approach to working with an eight-month-old with motor lags and increased motor tone would involve the use of positioning and handling techniques to normalize tone and to facilitate normal patterns of movement (i.e., mobilization of trunk, rotation patterns, and use of weight shifts and weight bearing posture). One might position an eight-month-old infant with poor head control prone over a bolster so that the arms are in a forward position while rotating the trunk and shoulder girdle to mobilize the spine.

How does one at the same time create an opportunity for the emotional task of learning cause-and-effect emotional signaling? One might work toward teaching the infant to imitate simple movements of the hands (e.g., touching pictures or facial parts—"I do it. Now you do it"). One might help the infant learn an emotional, relevant, intentional gesture indicating dependency (e.g., reaching up to be held). To be sure, a complex motor gesture would be shaped through gradual approximations. But if each approximation, and eventually the complete pattern, was emotionally age-appropriate and relevant, and was responded to with a great deal of physical and emotion warmth ("That's great. I love you" and a big hug), the infant would be learning his own way to make things happen in the emotional world of closeness and dependency. He would learn "I can communicate my desire for closeness," rather than learning that closeness is random and the best he can do is remain passive or fragmented.

As this example indicates, there are two parts to learning: (1) helping the child organize emotionally and social relevant patterns, and (2) responding to each step in the sequence of the newly learned pattern in a pleasurable manner. Therefore, the next principle is:

PRINCIPLE II:—Each emotionally or socially relevant pattern, either in its incipient stages or in its complete form, should receive a timely, "phase-specific," pleasurable emotional response. This includes the caregiver's position (i.e., when possible, in front of the infant) and affective disposition (i.e., you can't fake pleasure).

The fact that the caregiver's response should be developmentally phase-appropriate is illustrated by the motorically delayed fifteen-month-old who manages to crawl away from his caregiver and looks back with a smile of accomplishment. Clapping and admiring the infant's accomplishment from afar with distal communication support (i.e., affective verbal and motor gestures) may at that moment be more phase-appropriate than a big hug and cuddle. This infant is learning to balance dependence and independence, and communicating across space with word and gesture. Distal communications modes, such as the use of words and gestures, support the infant's emerging ability to "be close" from across space. Because some motor exercises are carried out from behind the infant or child, to facilitate purposeful communication, innovative approaches will need to be developed to arrange for flexible enough positioning for appropriate, face-to-face emotional interactions.

A part of an infant's emerging communication capacities is his interest in self-control and initiative, leading to another principle.

PRINCIPLE III:—Each emotionally relevant interaction should facilitate self-initiative (in generating similar emotional patterns) and the generalization

(and abstraction) of these patterns to all
areas and contexts of functioning.

In facilitating phase-specific emotional patterns, one
should always ask, "Am I doing it *for* the child, or am I creating
a learning opportunity where he is learning to take initiative?"
The nine-month-old who hears a "toot toot" every time he
presses his hand near his father's face, is learning to take
initiative and make things happen. In contrast, the nine-
month-old who is only read to is learning to receive information
passively. The application of a new emotional skill to multiple
contexts (e.g., touching Daddy's face to make Daddy say "toot
toot"; pulling Mommy's finger to get her to stick out her
tongue; exploring the various ways the soldier doll can "destroy
the bad guys") facilitates the application of emotional–behavioral patterns and emotional–ideational patterns (through pretend play) to multiple contexts.

In addition to the challenge of learning to take initiative
and generalize new coping capacities, the infant or child with
developmental disabilities, as well as the infant or child with
cognitive lags or difficulties, faces another important challenge.
This challenge relates to the critical psychological task of
differentiating an emotional sense of self which is unique,
encompasses the full range of human emotions, and is clearly
separate from one's sense of others and nonself. Children with
difficulties in sensory processing often have difficulty in discriminating subtle aspects of sensory-affective experience (e.g.,
"Is she happy or sad?" "Does he intend to hold me or hurt me."
or "Am I angry or scared." "Is my wish to bite a part of me?").
The child with tactile defensiveness and motor planning problems who bumps into another child may yell, "Stop hurting me!
Watch where you are going!" While such emotional interpretations relate to one's experience, a basic difficulty in discriminating incoming information or information arising from
one's own body (e.g., somatic affective cues) because of discrimination problems would almost certainly make it particularly
difficult to interpret confusing experience. Cognitive lags,

involving limited ability to abstract, may contribute to a child's trouble with forming the difficult emotional aspects of one's self into an organized pattern. Similarly, motor planning or control difficulties would create an extra challenge in developing a secure sense of self in terms of body control, assertiveness, and handling aggression (e.g., "If I can't make my body do what I want it to, then what can I control, and where does my self-initiative and control end and someone else's begin?").

To facilitate a differentiated sense of self across the full range of human emotions in a child who has sensory affective discrimination, cognitive, motor planning, or control difficulties requires that special experiences be made available, leading to another principle.

PRINCIPLE IV:—To support and provide extra practice for self-differentiation. To accomplish this, provide extra opportunities for interpersonal interactions which have the elements of: (1) the infant or child elaborating the full range of human emotions and inclinations, including closeness or dependency, pleasure, assertiveness and curiosity, anger, protest, self-limit-setting, and, eventually, empathy and consistent love, and (2) caregiver responses which are clear and accurate in regard to the child's elaborations, including feedback which provides a sense of being understood and at the same time supports further self-initiated elaboration.

The caregiver will need to watch for any vocal or motor signals of pleasure from the baby in order to respond appropriately. A caregiver may encourage assertive exploration while a baby is secure in a bean bag chair, by making the adult's own body a multiresponsive human toy. The goal is to integrate the infant's need for increased motor tone and alertness with sensory interest in the world, a loving attachment, and cause-

and-effect emotional signaling. The preschooler may require extra practice in using "floor time" for pretend play and may also require extra patience to let him communicate themes of assertiveness and even anger alongside themes of dependency and closeness. The tendency to "do" and later play and talk and even "close circles" for the disabled child is enormous. Yet self-differentiation requires creating the empathetic and interactive context for the child to learn these on his own.

Understanding the milestone of emotional growth in the first years of life should facilitate, for both professionals and parents, attention to expectable, but nonetheless potentially undermining, interaction patterns, including resentment and overexpectation early on, and overprotectiveness and inability to let the infant take initiative when capable later in development. The phase-specific emotional needs of the infant provide a context for the professional and parent to reconsider their own attitudes and expectations in relationship to the infant's emotional requirements.

The guiding principles we have discussed and illustrated are designed to provide a base from which innovative therapists and parents can develop their own unique ways of working with an individual child's physical and emotional experience. For example:

- A speech and language therapist may use pretend play to practice vocalizations, and at the same time focus on the child's phase-specific interests and fantasies (e.g., a three and a half-year-old interested in how the different parts of the doll's body work).
- A parent may help her four-month-old, who is uninterested in being in the prone position, to roll over and tolerate the prone position by combining it with pleasurable, face-to-face interactions.
- A health professional helping a parent of an irritable and crying ten-week-old may suggest that special postures, holding, and touching patterns be combined with extra practice in using distal communication modes, including

looking, listening, and gesturing, to facilitate an "organizing" interest in the world.

Elaborating principles, of course, is far easier than implementing them, especially when the goal is to help the child catch up emotionally, as well as motorically, and when one is trying to work at all the levels described above. Consider, for example, the nine-month-old infant with a severe motor lag and hypotonicity. Assume that the child's alertness, interest in the world, pleasure in others (a warm attachment), and intentional communication are compromised. In such a case, one is working to help the child stabilize head, shoulders, and trunk, and at the same time provide enough tactile, vestibular, and other sensory input to facilitate increased tone, alertness, and interest in the world. Here, the first goal is to find ways to encourage and maintain alertness so that the child can eventually create by himself those movement patterns and sensory experiences that support increased tone and alertness. At the same time, one is attempting to "woo" the infant so that he finds the human world especially lovable. A game of vigorous dancing, nuzzling, and hugging may combine the beneficial effects of movement and touch with the warm, pleasurable emotions of being close.

THE INFANT, THE FAMILY, AND THE SERVICE SYSTEM

In order to help infant with disabilities attain important emotional milestones, professionals must understand the special challenges their families face. It is not unusual for a mother or father of an infant with a developmental disorder to go through a series of stages. Initially, parents may have a hard time accepting their infant ("he is not a part of me"). This may be followed quickly with a feeling of guilt and an overidentification ("he *is* me"). But if a parent feels negative about herself and her challenging infant, she may feel "he's a bad me." This stage also may last only a short time and be followed by a compensatory reaction in which the parent will resolve to make herself and her infant perfect ("he is going to be a perfect me"). These attitudes are often associated with characteristic interaction patterns between parents and infants with disabilities. Withdrawal and apathy may be related to the feeling that the infant is not part of the family. Critical, intrusive, and even punitive behavior may be related to the feeling that the infant is part of a "bad me." Overprotectiveness, overcontrolling, and undermining of autonomous behavior may go along with the "it will be a perfect me" attitude. A "perfect me" attitude may also mask only marginally a feeling that the infant is "inadequate without me" and lead to difficulties when the child tries to become more independent. As the child becomes more self-sufficient and competent, either abrupt withdrawal or depression and excessive fears about injury or illness befalling the child may, ironically, characterize caregiver behavior.

When parents' attitudes differ significantly from one another, marital conflict may result. Feelings about the challenging new infant may be so consuming that the parents have difficulty in being sensitive to each other's needs. In some instances, parents may feel so embarrassed about their "negative" private feelings that they may isolate themselves more and more from their spouse. Siblings (with worries about "Will this happen to me?" "Did my anger and jealousy do this to him?" "Can *I* get love and attention by being sick?") and extended family members are often involved in these patterns, as well. Not infrequently, the infant with a developmental problem becomes the focus of unresolved family issues centering on dependency, anger, damage, or loss. Lack of sleep, along with the expected physical and emotional stresses, may further compromise caregiver coping capacities.

It may be useful to view caregivers as faced with a number of general challenges, which include (1) providing physical protection and care; (2) recognizing basic signals of pleasure and displeasure in the context of providing an ongoing sense of acceptance and love; and (3) understanding and responding to the stage-specific, emotional, intellectual, and physical requirements of their infant, in the context of their infant's individual differences and unique abilities. For each stage of development, caregivers must understand their own emotional reactions in order to provide special experiences that are appropriate to the infant's unique characteristics. As we have described, infants and young children with disabilities may have difficulty returning their caregivers' "wooing" and may communicate emotionally in ways that are confusing rather than clear. Caregiver feelings of rejection, anger, or confusion are to be expected, and must by understood and responded to in order for them to remain engaged with and emotionally available to their children.

We must also recognize the special emotional challenges to service providers presented by infants and toddlers with disabilities and their families. Just as a caregiver may become "mechanical" with and emotionally distant from her chaotic and disorganized infant, the individual clinician or treatment team may become mechanical to avoid the intrusive, overanxious, disorganized caregiver or family. We have often observed a chain reaction in which the infant's special needs create a disequilibrium in the family (e.g., marital difficulties, alcoholism, or psychosomatic problems), whose members in turn communicate their stress to the service team. In this context, it is not unusual for the service team, with the best intentions, to themselves fall into a pattern of being covertly rejecting, critical, and punitive, or overcontrolling or infantilizing.

To remain helpful to a stressed family (and the infant involved), a service team must avoid reacting as one more link in the maladaptive chain. The following steps can help:

- Containing the emotional reaction of team members by extra empathy, support, and structure, including limits; this will often require opportunities for each team member to have one-on-one supervision or peer consultation.
- Working to understand the emotional patterns of infant and family.
- Using introspection to understand team members' own expectable emotional reactions to infant and family.

TABLE 11.1
Emotional Milestones, Family and Service System Patterns

Stage-Specific Tasks and Capacities	Infant Maladaptive	Family Maladaptive	Service System Maladaptive	Service System Adaptive
Homeostasis (0–3 mo) (Regulation and interest in the world)	Unregulated (e.g., hyperexcitable) or withdrawn (apathetic) behavior	Unavailable, chaotic dangerous, abusive; hypo- or hyperstimulating; dull	Critical and punitive	Supply support structure and extra nurturing
Attachment (2–7 mo) (Falling in love)	Total lack of or nonaffective, shallow, impersonal involvement in animate world	Emotionally distant, aloof, and/or impersonal (highly ambivalent)	Angry and impatient covered by mask of impersonal professionalism	"Woo" caregiver into a relationship; point out pleasurable aspects of baby
Somatopsychological differentiation (3–10 mo) (Purposeful communication)	Behavior and affects random and/or chaotic or narrow, rigid, and stereotyped	Ignores or misreads (e.g., projects) infant's communications (e.g., is overly intrusive, preoccupied, or depressed)	Vacillates between overcontrol and avoidance (of intrusive caregiver) or overprotectiveness (of depressed caregiver)	Combine empathy and limit setting with sensitivity to reading subtle emotional signals; help caregiver read infant's signals
Behavioral organization, initiative, and internalization (9–24 mo) (A complex sense of self)	Fragmented, stereotyped and polarized behavior and emotions (e.g., withdrawn, compliant, hyperaggressive, or disorganized behavior)	Overly intrusive, controlling; fragmented, fearful (especially of toddler's autonomy); abruptly and prematurely "separates"	Premature separation from or rejection of family rationalized by notion: "they are okay now"	Support family self-sufficiency, but with admiration and greater rather than less involvement
Representational capacity, differentiation and consolidation (1½–4 years) (Creating ideas and emotional thinking)	No representational (symbolic) elaboration; behavior and affect concrete, shallow, and polarized; sense of self and "other" fragmented, undifferentiated or narrow and rigid; reality testing, impulse regulation, mood stabilization compromised or vulnerable (e.g., borderline psychotic and severe character problems)	Fears or denies phase-appropriate needs; engages child only in concrete (nonsymbolic) modes generally or in certain realms (e.g., around pleasure) and/or misreads or responds noncontingently or unrealistically to emerging communications (i.e., undermines reality orientation); overly permissive or punitive	Infantilizing and concrete with family, providing instructions, but no explanations or real sense of partnership	Create atmosphere for working partnership; learn from caregivers and help them conceptualize their own approaches

- Using (rather than acting on) immediate feelings to understand how the family feels (e.g., "If the family makes us feel disorganized and aversive or overcontrolling, perhaps that is how they are feeling; perhaps we are feeling like them, or the opposite of them. Let's see how we can use our introspective understanding to be of assistance to them").
- Planning a corrective team and family emotional strategy to be integrated with the specific treatment plan.

Team members can help each other. Sometimes the team member closest to the family is the one who most reacts to, or overidentifies with, family distress. Others can take a step back and help the involved team member see the larger pattern. Table 11.1 outlines some common clinically-observed infant, caregiver, and service provider team patterns.

CONCLUSION

Recent understanding of infant and family emotional functioning now makes it possible to pinpoint emotional milestones and stages in ego development much like the neuromotor milestones. This "road map" may prove helpful in facilitating adaptive emotional growth in infants whose sensory, motor, intellectual, or physical differences set into motion unique family challenges.

We must always remember that there are many roads to Rome. Almost all infants and young children can learn—in different ways—to relate to others, to interact intentionally, to organize a sense of self, to learn to use ideas to guide behavior and label feelings to test reality, to modulate impulses and mood, to experience positive self-esteem, and to concentrate. Our challenge is to provide infants and young children with learning opportunities that are sensitive to their individual differences and to their unique potentials for physical, cognitive, social, and emotional development.

Conclusion

The ego develops from its somatic–sensory–affective foundation to embrace object relationships, to expand into a range of drive–affect–thematic domains, and to organize itself into self–object patterns and structures. It was postulated that the early growth of the ego can be characterized in terms of six levels of experiential organization. These levels include early stages of relatively undifferentiated somatic and behavioral self–object patterns and global reactivity, and later stages of differentiated representational experience and selective adaptive and defensive transformations of experience. Characterizing early ego development into six stages, it was suggested, would facilitate greater understanding of how the ego develops, as well as the contributions of unique biological and experiential patterns in adaptive and maladaptive development. In this context, it was postulated that each stage of ego development had, as part of its foundation, constitutional–maturational patterns related to sensory–affective processing and integration, as well as characteristic caregiver–infant and child interaction patterns. Specific hypotheses were suggested regarding the relationship between (1) auditory–verbal processing deficits and environments that confuse meanings and thought disorders and (2) visual– spatial processing deficits and environments that lack empathy and limit-setting and affective disorders. The contributions of specific constitutional tendencies and environmental proclivities to obsessive–compulsive, hysterical, and phobic patterns were also discussed.

The model of early ego development suggested a number of core developmental processes that are essential for healthy growth and development. These included the capacity for shared attention and engagement, intentional reciprocal gesturing (as part of a prerepresentational communication system), the elaboration and sharing of meanings, and the categorization of meanings. The relationship was considered between the stages in ego development, these core developmental processes, and aspects of psychoanalytic theory, the psychotherapeutic process, the psychoanalytic process, short-term psychotherapy, group and family processes, psychopathology, work with children, and emotional patterns of children with developmental disabilities. Developmental models of the psychotherapeutic process, and psychopathology were constructed.

Most importantly, the developmental perspective on the formation of the ego suggests principles of prevention. These principles, which have been discussed throughout the preceding chapters, may be visualized as a pyramid. At the base of the pyramid are essential experiences that all children require for survival, including food, housing, medical care, safety, and so forth. At the second level of the pyramid is another essential ingredient for every child: an on-going, relatively stable human relationship. At the third level are the phase-specific experiences that meet the child's changing developmental needs; for example, comfort, safety, and engagement beginning in the first months of life; intentional communication, including the empathetic reading of the infant's signals from the middle of the first year; and various types of gestural and then the different levels of representational interactions, described earlier to foster the organization, elaboration, symbolization, and differentiation of experience in the second, third, and fourth years. In addition, these phase-specific "experiential nutriments" which are so essential for growth-producing interaction patterns must also take into account the infant's emerging individual differences, including unique patterns of sensory reactivity, sensory processing, motor tone, motor planning, cognition, and affective and interpersonal style.

It was described, for example, in chapter 2, how specific pathogenic environments might accentuate constitutional vulnerabilities resulting in psychopathology and how especially tailored environments might help even the constitutionally vulnerable infant successfully negotiate his early stages in ego development. The relative success of prevention, both on an individual as well as group–community basis, will be directly proportional to our deepening understanding of the developmental pathways (including the relative contributions of biological and environmental variables) associated with adaptive and maladaptive development, and our ability to harness the resources necessary to enable each family to engage their children in the specific types of developmental experiences they require for healthy emotional growth.

References

Ainsworth, M., Bell, S. M., & Stayton, D. (1974), Infant–mother attachment and social development: Socialization as a product of reciprocal responsiveness to signals. In: *The Integration of the Child into a Social World*, ed. M. Richards. Cambridge, England: Cambridge University Press, pp. 99–135.

Ayres, A. J. (1964), Tactile functions: Their relation to hyperactive and perceptual motor behavior. *Amer. J. Occupational Therapy*, 18(1):6–11.

Backwin, H. (1942), Loneliness in infants. *Amer. J. Dis. Child.*, 63:30–42.

Bell, S. (1970), The development of the concept of object as related to infant-mother attachment. *Child Develop.*, 41:219–311.

Bergman, P., & Escalona, S. (1949), Unusual sensitivities in very young children. *The Psychoanalytic Study of the Child*, 3 & 4:333–352. New York: International Universities Press.

Bernfeld, S. (1929), *The Psychology of the Infant*. New York: Brentano.

Bion, W. (1961), *Experiences in Groups*. London: Tavistock.

Bower, G. (1981), Mood and memory. *Amer. Psycholog.*, 36:129–148.

Bowlby, J. (1952), *Maternal Care and Mental Health*. WHO Monograph Series No. 2. Geneva: World Health Organization.

———(1969), *Attachment and Loss*, Vol. 1. New York: Basic Books.

Box, G. E. P., & Jenkins, G. M. (1976), *Time-series Analysis. Forecasting and Control*. San Francisco: Holden-Day.

Brazelton, T., Koslowski, B., & Main, N. (1974), The origins of reciprocity: The early mother–infant interaction. In: *The Effect of the Infant on its Caregiver*, ed. M. Lewis & L. Rosenblum. New York: John Wiley, pp. 49–76.

Bruch, H. (1973), *Eating Disorders: Obesity, Anorexia Nervosa, and the Person Within*. New York: Basic Books.

Burlingham, D., & Freud, A. (1942), *Young Children in Wartime*. London: Allen & Unwin.

Cameron, H. S. (1919), *The Nervous Child*. London: Oxford Medical Publications.

Campbell, D. T., & Stanley, J. C. (1966), *Experimental and Quasi-Experimental Designs for Research*. Chicago: Rand McNally.

Caron, A. J., & Caron, R. F. (1982), Cognitive development in early infancy. In: *Review of Human Development*, ed. T. Fields, A. Huston, H. Quay, L. Troll, & G. Finley. New York: John Wiley, pp. 107–147.

Charlesworth, W. R. (1969), The role of surprise in cognitive development. In: *Studies in Cognitive Development: Essays in Honor of Jean Piaget*, ed. E. Elkind & J. H. Flavell. London: Oxford University Press, pp. 257–314.

Cravioto, J., & Delicardie, E. (1973), Environmental correlates of severe clinical malnutrition and language development in survivors from kwashiorkor or marasmus. In: *Nutrition, the Nervous System and Behavior*. Washington, DC, PAHO Scientific Publication No. 251.

Despland, P. A., & Galambos, R. (1980), The auditory brainstem response (ABR) is a useful diagnostic tool in the intensive care nursery. *Pediat. Res.*, 14:154–158.

Ekman, P. (1972), Universals and cultural differences in facial expressions of emotion. *Nebraska Symposium on Motivation*. Lincoln: University of Nebraska Press.

Emde, R. N., Gaensbauer, T. J., & Harmon, R. J. (1976), Emotional Expression in Infancy: A Biobehavioral Study. *Psychological Issues*, Monograph No. 37. New York: International Universities Press.

Erikson, E. H. (1959), Identity and the Life Cycle. *Psychological Issues*, Monograph Series No. 1. New York: International Universities Press.

Escalona, S. (1968), *The Roots of Individuality*. Chicago: Aldine.

Fish, B., & Hagin, R. (1973), Visual-motor disorders in infants at risk for schizophrenia. *Arch. Gen. Psychiat.*, 28:900–904.

——Shapiro, T., Halpern, F., & Wile, R. (1965), The prediction of schizophrenia in infancy: III. A ten-year follow-up report of neurological and psychological development. *Amer. J. Psychiat.*, 121:768–775.

Fox, N., & Porges, S. (1983), Prediction of developmental outcome from autonomic patterns measured in infancy. *Psychophysiol.*, 12:440 (Abstract).

Fraiberg, S. (1979), Treatment modalities in an infant mental health program. Presentation at the training institute on "Clinical Approaches to Infants and Their Families" sponsored by the National Center for Clinical Infant Programs, Washington, DC.

Freud, A. (1965), Normality and pathology in childhood. In: *The Writings of Anna Freud*, Vol. 6. New York: International Universities Press.

———Burlingham, D., (1945), *Infants Without Families*. New York: International Universities Press.

——— ———(1965), *War and Children*. New York: International Universities Press.

Freud, S. (1900), The Interpretation of Dreams. *Standard Edition*, 4 & 5. London: Hogarth Press, 1953.

———(1905), Three essays on the theory of sexuality. *Standard Edition*, 7:135–242. London: Hogarth Press, 1953.

———(1911), Formulations on the two principles of mental functioning. *Standard Edition*, 12:218–226. London: Hogarth Press, 1958.

———(1915), Instincts and their vicissitudes. *Standard Edition*, 14:109–140. London: Hogarth Press, 1957.

———(1920), Beyond the pleasure principle. *Standard Edition*, 18:7–64. London: Hogarth Press, 1955.

Gewirz, J. L. (1961), A learning analysis of the effects of normal stimulation, privation and deprivation on the acquisition of social motivation and attachment. *Determinants of Infant Behavior*, Vol 1., ed, B. M. Foss, London: Methuen.

———(1965), The course of infant smiling in four child rearing environments in Israel. In: *Determinants of Infant's Behavior*, Vol. 3, ed. B. M. Foss. London: Methuen, pp. 205–260.

———(1969), Levels of conceptual analysis in environment–infant interaction research. *Merrill-Palmer Quart.* 15:9–47.

Gouin-Decarie, T. (1965), *Intelligence and Affectivity in Early Childhood: An Experimental Study of Jean Piaget's Object Concept and Object Relations*. New York: International Universities Press.

Greenspan, S. I. (1975), A Consideration of Some Learning Variables in the Context of Psychoanalytic Theory. *Psychological Issues*, Monogr. 33. New York: International Universities Press.

———(1979), Intelligence and Adaptation: An Integration of Psychoanalytic and Piagetian Developmental Psychology. *Psychological*

Issues, Monograph 47/48. New York: International Universities Press.

————(1981), *Psychopathology and Adaptation in Infancy and Early Childhood: Principles of Clinical Diagnosis and Preventive Intervention*. New York: International Universities Press.

————(1982), Three levels of learning. *Psychoanalytic Inquiry*, 1(4):659–694.

————(1983), Clinical global ratings of the GLOS; Rules of interpretation. Working paper, Clinical Infant Development Program, National Institute of Mental Health.

————(1987), A model for comprehensive preventive intervention services for infants young children and their families. In: *Infants in Multirisk Families; Case Studies of Preventive Intervention*, No. 1, eds. S. Wieder, A. F. Lieberman, R. A. Nover, R. S. Lourie, & M. Robinson. New York: International Universities Press.

————Greenspan, N. T. (1985), *First Feelings; Milestones in the Emotional Development of Your Baby and Child from Birth to Age 4*. New York: Viking Press.

———— ————(1989), *The Essential Partnership*. New York: Viking Press.

————Lieberman, A. F. (1980), Infants, mothers, and their interaction: A quantitative clinical approach to developmental assessment. In: *The Course of Life: Psychoanalytic Contributions Toward Understanding Personality Development*, Vol. 1, *Infancy and Early Childhood*, eds. S. I. Greenspan & G. H. Pollock. DHHS Publication No. [ADM] 80–786. Washington, DC: U.S. Government Printing Office.

————Lourie, R. S. (1981), Developmental structuralist approach to the classification of adaptive and pathologic personality organization: Application to infancy and early childhood. *Amer. J. Psychiat.*, 138:725–736.

———— ————Nover, R. A. (1979), A developmental approach to the approach to the classification of psychopathology in infancy and early childhood. In: *The Basic Handbook of Child Psychiatry*, Vol. 2, ed. J. Noshpitz. New York: Basic Books, pp. 157–164.

————Mannino, F. V. (1974). A model for brief intervention with couples based on projective identification. *Amer. J. Psychiat.* 13:1103–1106.

————Porges, S. W. (1984), Psychopathology in infancy and early childhood: Clinical perspectives on the organization of sensory and affective–thematic experience. *Child Develop.*, 55/1:49–70.

————Wieder, S. I. (1984), Dimensions and levels of the therapeutic process. *Psychother.*, 21/1:5–23.

———— ————Lieberman, A., Nover, R., Lourie, R., & Robinson, M., eds (1987), Infants in Multirisk Families: Case Studies in Preventive Intervention. *Clinical Infant Reports*, No. 3. New York: International Universities Press.

Hartmann, H. (1939), *Ego Psychology and the Problem of Adaptation*. New York: International Universities Press.

Hobson, R. P. (1986), The autistic child's appraisal of expressions of emotion. *J. Child Psychol. Psychiat.*, 27/3:321–343.

Hofheimer, J. A., Lieberman, A. F., Strauss, M. E., & Greenspan, S. I. (1983), Short-term temporal stability of mother–infant interactions in the first year of life. Presented at the 93nd Meeting of American Psychological Association, Los Angeles.

Hofheimer, J. A., Strauss, M. E., Poisson, S. S. & Greenspan, S. I. (1981), The reliability, validity and generalizability of assessments of transactions between infants and their caregivers: A multi-center design. Working Paper, Clinical Infant Development Program, National Institute of Mental Health.

Hunt, J. M. (1941), Infants in an orphanage. *J. Abnorm. & Soc. Psychol.*, 36:338.

Izard, C. (1978), On the development of emotions and emotion–cognition relationships in infancy. In: *The Development of Affect*, eds. M. Lewis & L. Rosenblum. New York: Plenum Press.

Kernberg, O. F. (1975), *Borderline Conditions and Pathological Narcissism*. New York: Jason Aronson.

Jackson, D. D. (1960), *Etiology of Schizophrenia*. New York: Basic Books.

Klaus, M., & Kennell, J. (1976), *Maternal–Infant Bonding: The Impact of Early Separation or Loss on Family Development*. St. Louis: C. V. Mosby.

Klein, G. S. (1976), Freud's two theories of sexuality. In: Psychology Versus Metapsychology: Psychoanalytic Essays in Memory of George S. Klein, *ed.* M. Gill & P. Holzman. *Psychological Issues*, Vol. 9., No. 4, Monograph 36. New York: International Universities Press, pp. 14–70.

Kohut, H. (1971), *The Analysis of Self: A Systematic Approach to the Psychoanalytic Treatment of Narcissistic Personality Disorders*. New York: International Universities Press.

Lewis, M., & Horowitz, L. (1977), Intermodal personal schema in infancy: Perception within a common auditory–visual space. Paper presented at the meeting of the Eastern Psychological Association, April.

Lidz, T. (1973), *Origin and Treatment of Schizophrenic Disorders*. New York: Basic Books.

Lipsitt, L. (1966), Learning processes of newborns, *Merrill-Palmer Quart.*, 12:45–71.

Lourie, R. S. (1971), The first three years of life: An overview of a new frontier for psychiatry. *Amer. J. Psychiat.*, 127:1457–1463.

Lowery, L. G. (1940), Personality distortion and early institutional care. *Amer. J. Ortho.*, 10:546–551.

Mahler, M. S., Pine, F., & Bergman, A. (1975), *The Psychological Birth of the Human Infant*. New York: Basic Books.

Meltzoff, A., & Moore, K. (1977), Imitation of facial and manual gestures by human neonates. *Science*, 198:75–78.

Murphy, L. B. (1974), *The Individual Child*. DHEW Publication No. (OCD) 74-1032. Washington, DC: U.S. Government Printing Office.

———Moriarty, A. (1976), *Vulnerability, Coping and Growth*. New Haven, CT: Yale University Press.

Nemiah, J. C. (1977), *Alexithymia: Theories and Models*. Proceedings of the Eleventh European Conference on Psychosomatic Research. Basel, Switzerland: Karger.

Parens, H. (in press), Development of aggression. In: *The Course of Life*, Vol. 2, ed. S. Greenspan and G. Pollock, Madison, CT: International Universities Press.

Piaget, J. (1962), The stages of the intellectual development of the child. In: *Childhood Psychopathology*, eds. S. Harrison & J. McDermott. New York: International Universities Press, pp. 157–166.

———(1968), *Structuralism*. New York: Basic Books, 1970.

Poisson, S. S., (1968), *Structuralism*. New York: Basic Books, 1970.

———Hofheimer, J. A., Strauss, M. E., & Greenspan, S. I. (unpublished), Inter-observer Agreement and Reliability Assessments of the GLOS Measures of Caregiver Infant Interaction. National Institute of Mental Health, 1983.

———Lieberman, A. F., & Greenspan, S. I. (unpublished), *Training Manual for the Greenspan-Lieberman Observation System (GLOS)*, National Institute of Mental Health, 1981.

Porges, S. W. (1983a), Heart rate oscillations: An index of neural mediation. In: *Psychophysiological perspectives: Festschrift for Beatrice and John Lacey*, eds. M. G. H. Coles, J. R. Jennings, & J. A. Stern. Stroudsburg PA: Hutchinson & Ross.

———(1983b), Heart rate patterns in neonates: A potential diagnostic window to the brain. In: *Infants Born at Risk: Physiological and Perceptual Processes*, ed. T. Field & A. Sostek. New York: Grune & Stratton.

———Bohrer, R. E., Keren, G., Cheung, M., Franks, G. J., & Drasgow, F. (1981), The influence of methylphenidate on spontaneous autonomic activity and behavior in children diagnosed as hyperactive. *Psychophysiol.*, 18:42–48.

Provence, S. (1983), *Infants and Parents: Clinical Case Reports*, Clinical Infant Reports, No. 2. New York: International Universities Press.

———Naylor, A. (1983), *Working with Disadvantaged Parents and Their Children; Scientific and Practice Issues*. New Haven, CT: Yale University Press.

Rachford, B. K. (1905), *Neurotic Disorders of Childhood*. New York: E. B. Treat & Co.

Rheingold, H. (1966), The development of social behavior in the human infant. *Monogr. Soc. Res. Child Dev.*, 31:1–28.

Sander, L. (1962), Issues in early mother-child interaction. *J. Amer. Acad. Child Psychiat.*, 1:141–166.

Shapiro, R., & Zinner, J. (1975), Family organization and adolescent development. In: *Task and Organization*, ed. E. Miller. New York: John Wiley.

Shapiro, T., Sherman, M., Calamari, G., & Koch, D. (1987), Attachment in autism and other developmental disorders. *J. Amer. Acad. Child & Adol. Psychiat.*, 16/4:480–484.

Skinner, B. F. (1938), *The Behavior of Organisms: An Experimental Analysis*. New York: Appleton-Century-Crofts.

Sorce, J. F., & Emde, R. N., (1981), Mother's presence is not enough: The effect of emotional availability on infant exploration. *Development. Psychol.*, 17/6:737–745.

Spelke, E. & Owsley, C. (1979), Intermodal exploration and Knowledge in infancy. *Infant Behavior and Development*, 2:13–27.

Spitz, R. & Cobliner, W.G. (1965), *The First Year of Life*. New York: International Universities Press.

Sroufe, L. A. (1979), Socioemotional development. In: *Handbook of Infant Development*, ed. J. Osofsky. New York: John Wiley.

———Waters, E. (1977), Attachment as an organizational construct. *Child Develop.*, 48:1184–1199.

——— ———Matas, L. (1974), Contextual determinants of infant affective response. In: *The Origins of Fear*, eds. M. Lewis & L. Rosenblum. New York: John Wiley, pp. 49–72.

Stern, D. (1974a), Mother and infant at play: The dyadic interaction involving facial, vocal and gaze behaviors. In: *The Effect of the Infant on its Caregiver*, eds. M. Lewis & L. Rosenblum. New York: John Wiley.

———(1974b), The goal and structure of mother–infant play. *J. Amer. Acad. Child Psychiat.*, 13:402–421.

————(1977), *The First Relationship: Infant and Mother*. Cambridge, MA: Harvard University Press.

————(1985), *The Interpersonal World of the Child*. New York: Basic Books.

————(1988), Affect in the context of the infant's lived experience: Some considerations, *Internat. J. Psycho-Anal.*, 69/2:233–238.

Strachey, (1969), On mutative interpretation. *Internat. J. Psycho-Anal.*, 50:275–292.

Tennes, K., Emde, R., Kisley, A., & Metcalf, D. (1972), The stimulus barrier in early infancy: An exploration of some formulations of John Benjamin. In: *Psychoanalysis and Contemporary Science*, Vol. 1, eds, R. Hold & E. Peterfreund. New York: Macmillan, pp. 206–234.

Tomkins, S. (1963), *Affect, Imagery, Consciousness*, Vol. 1. New York: Springer.

Turquet, P. (1975), Threats to identity in the large group: A study in the phenomenology of the individual's experiences of changing membership status in a large group. In: *The Large Group: Dynamics and Therapy*, ed. L. Kreeger. London: Constable, pp. 87–158.

Werner, H., & Kaplan, B. (1963), *Symbol Formation*. New York: John Wiley.

————(1962), The stages of the intellectual development of the child. In: *Childhood Psychopathology*, eds., S. Harrison & J. McDermott. New York: International Universities Press.

Weil, A. (1970), The basic core. *The Psychoanalytic Study of the Child*, 25:442–460. New York: International Universities Press.

Winnicott, D. W. (1931), *Clinical Notes on Disorders of Childhood*. London: Heinemann.

Wynne, L., Matthysse, S., & Cromwell, R. (1978), *The Nature of Schizophrenia: New Approaches to Research and Treatment*. New York: John Wiley.

Name Index

361

Subject Index

Abstracted values, 253–255
Abstracting behavior, 310–311
Abstracting capacity, 34–35
  maturation and, 49
  visual-spatial capacities in, 76
Abused infants, fear in, 31
Acting out, 47–48
Affect. *See also* Emotions
  avoidance of, 283
  differentiation of, 25
  disturbances of, 72–75; clinical
    example of, 80–84; delay and,
    82–83; developmental pro-
    cesses leading to, 70, 75–80;
    hypotheses regarding, 68–72,
    75–80
  gestures, 39
  isolation of, 85–86, 108
  lability of, 232
  limitations on, 17
Affective states
  abstraction of, 177–179, 310–
    311, 315
  inability to differentiate, 271
Affective-thematic domain
  in character disorder, 284–285

compartmentalization of, 289–
  290
developmental levels and, 136–
  137; increasing range of at,
  150–156
engagement in, 233–234
identification of core, 154–155
range of, in children, 303
relationships among, 155
sending power of, 23–24
stability and, 139
transformation of, to higher
  states, 154
Affective-thematic experience, 6
  in attachment stage, 17–18
  at behavioral action pattern
    mode, 47–48
  in behavioral organization, ini-
    tiative, internalization stage,
    32–33
  categories of, 119–120
  in homeostasis development, 9–
    10
  integration of, 46–47
  maladaptive, 9–10
  methods of assessing, 92–93

363